VOCATIONAL EVALUATION
for
REHABILITATION SERVICES

PUBLICATION NO. 877

American Lecture Series

A Publication in
The Bannerstone Division of American Lectures
in Social and Rehabilitation Psychology

The American Lecture Series in Social and Rehabilitation Psychology offers books which are concerned with man's role in his milieu. Emphasis is placed on how this role can be made more effective in a time of social conflict and a deteriorating physical environment. The books are oriented toward descriptions of what future roles should be and are not concerned exclusively with the delineation and definition of contemporary behavior. Contributors are concerned to a considerable extent with prediction through the use of a functional view of man as opposed to a descriptive, anatomical point of view.

Books in this series are written mainly for the professional practitioner; however, academicians will find them of considerable value in both undergraduate and graduate courses in the helping services.

VOCATIONAL EVALUATION

FOR

REHABILITATION SERVICES

RICHARD E. HARDY, Ed.D.

Professor and Chairman
Department of Rehabilitation Counseling
Virginia Commonwealth University
Richmond, Virginia

JOHN G. CULL, Ph.D.

Professor and Director
Regional Counselor Training Program
Virginia Commonwealth University
Fishersville, Virginia

CHARLES C THOMAS · PUBLISHER
Springfield · Illinois · U.S.A.

Published and Distributed Throughout the World by

CHARLES C THOMAS • PUBLISHER

BANNERSTONE HOUSE

301-327 East Lawrence Avenue, Springfield, Illinois, U.S.A.

© *1973, by* CHARLES C THOMAS • PUBLISHER

ISBN 0-398-02724-2

Library of Congress Catalog Card Number: 72-92170

With THOMAS BOOKS *careful attention is given to all details of manufacturing and design. It is the Publisher's desire to present books that are satisfactory as to their physical qualities and artistic possibilities and appropriate for their particular use.* THOMAS BOOKS *will be true to those laws of quality that assure a good name and good will.*

Printed in the United States of America

N-1

This Book Is Dedicated To

Edward Newman, Ph.D.,
For His Services To
Handicapped Persons

The following books have appeared thus far in this Series:

VOCATIONAL REHABILITATION: PROFESSION AND PROCESS
John G. Cull and Richard E. Hardy

CONTEMPORARY FIELD WORK PRACTICES IN REHABILITATION
John G. Cull and Craig R. Colvin

SOCIAL AND REHABILITATION SERVICES FOR THE BLIND
Richard E. Hardy and John G. Cull

FUNDAMENTALS OF CRIMINAL BEHAVIOR AND CORRECTIONAL
SYSTEMS
John G. Cull and Richard E. Hardy

MEDICAL AND PSYCHOLOGICAL ASPECTS OF DISABILITY
A. Beatrix Cobb

DRUG DEPENDENCE AND REHABILITATION APPROACHES
Richard E. Hardy and John G. Cull

INTRODUCTION TO CORRECTIONAL REHABILITATION
Richard E. Hardy and John G. Cull

ADJUSTING TO WORK
John G. Cull and Richard E. Hardy

THE DECEIVED: DRUG ABUSE & ABUSERS
John G. Cull and Richard E. Hardy

GROUP COUNSELING AND THERAPY IN SPECIAL SETTINGS
Richard E. Hardy and John G. Cull

SPECIAL PROBLMES IN REHABILITATION
A. Beatrix Cobb

〉〉 CONTRIBUTORS

C. THOMAS ALLEN, M.S.: Research Specialist, Materials Development Center, Department of Rehabilitation and Manpower Services, University of Wisconsin—Stout. Formerly instructor of Psychology, University of Northern Iowa.

DAVID D. CLARK, Ed.D.: Independent practice of psychology; consultant, Delgado College Program for the Deaf; President and Founder, New Orleans Remedial Clinic; Licensed psychologist in the State of Louisiana. Formerly assistant professor of psychology, Texas Tech University and assistant professor of education and educational psychology, Louisiana State University in New Orleans.

CRAIG R. COLVIN, M.Ed.: Assistant Professor, Regional Counselor Training Program, Department of Rehabilitation Counseling, School of Community Services, Virginia Commonwealth University; Associate Editor of *Job Placement Division Digest*. He has held positions with the North Carolina Division of Vocational Rehabilitation as a counselor for the mentally retarded as well as holding a general caseload. Also, Mr. Colvin was the state coordinator acting as a liaison representative between Vocational Rehabilitation and the Department of Correction in North Carolina; he is co-author, *Contemporary Field Work Practices in Rehabilitation*. He has made several contributions to the professional literature.

ROBERT H. COUCH, A.B., M.A.T.: Assistant Professor, Division of Rehabilitation Services Education, Department of Vocational and Adult Education, School of Education, Auburn University, Auburn, Alabama: Coordinator of S.R.S. Region IV Evaluation Training Program and instructor, advisor and intern supervisor in undergaduate Rehabilitation Services Program. Past President, Vocational Evaluation and Work Adjustment Association, past President Alabama VEWAA unit, past Chairman, National Rehabilitation Association's Council of Division Presidents, member and past officer Region IV Council of Facility Specialist, President-Elect, Alabama Rehabilitation Association, Technical Consultant, Rehabilitation Services Administration. Formerly public school social science teacher, Montevallo, Alabama; Supervisor, Work Adjustment Center, Darden Rehabilitation Center, Gadsden, Alabama; Rehabilitation Counselor, Alabama Division of Vocational Rehabilitation. Contributor to the *Vocational Evaluation and Work Adjustment Bulletin* and co-author monograph entitled *The Work Oriented Facility,* published by the Rehabilitation Facilities Section, Florida Division of Rehabilitation, Florida State Department of Education. Student in and candidate for the Doctorate of Education degree with a major emphasis in Rehabilitation in Auburn University's Counselor Education Department.

STANLEY H. CROW: Project Director, Vocational Evaluation Project, Vocational Evaluation and Work Adjustment Association (VEWAA); member of the Board of Directors, National Rehabilitation Association 1969-72, and Houston Area Rehabilitation Association 1972; past President, VEWAA; member of *Ad Hoc* Committee to form VEWAA; formerly Chief, Department of Human Services, Goodwill Industries of Houston, Inc.; Branch Manager for Houston Goodwill's Sabine-Neches Division (in Beaumont, Texas); Director of Rehabilitation and evaluator at the Houston Goodwill.

JOHN G. CULL, Ph.D.: Director, Regional Counselor Training Program and Professor, Department of Rehabilitation, School of Community Services, Virginia Commonwealth University, Fishersville, Virginia; Adjunct Professor in Psychology and Education, School of General Studies, University of Virginia; Technical Consultant, Rehabilitation Services Administration, U. S. Department of Health, Education and Welfare; Vocational Consultant, Bureau of Hearings and Appeals, Social Security Administration; lecturer, Medical Department Affiliate Program, Woodrow Wilson Rehabilitation Center; Consulting Editor, *American Lecture Series in Social and Rehabilitation Psychology,* Charles C Thomas, Publisher. Formerly Rehabilitation Counselor, Texas Commission For The Blind and Texas Rehabilitation Commission; Director, Division of Research and Program Development, Virginia Department of Vocational Rehabilitation. The following are some of the books Dr. Cull has co-authored and co-edited: *Vocational Rehabilitation: Profession and Process, Contemporary Fieldwork Practices in Rehabilitation, Social and Rehabilitation Services For The Blind, Fundamentals of Criminal Behavior and Correctional Systems* and *Drug Dependence and Rehabilitation Approaches.* Dr. Cull also has contributed more than fifty publications to the professional literature in psychology and rehabilitation.

RICHARD E. HARDY, Ed.D.: Chairman, Department of Rehabilitation, School of Community Services, Virginia Commonwealth University, Richmond, Virginia; Technical Consultant, Rehabilitation Services Administration, U. S. Department of Health, Education and Welfare; Consulting Editor, *American Lecture Series in Social and Rehabilitation Psychology,* Charles C Thomas, Publisher; and Associate Editor, *Journal of Voluntary Action Research,* formerly Rehabilitation Counselor in Virginia; Chief Psychologist and Supervisor of Training, South Carolina Department of Vocational Rehabilitation and member South Carolina State Board of Examiners in Psychology; Rehabilitation Advisor, Rehabilitation Services Administration, U. S. Department of Health, Education and Welfare. The following are some of the books Dr. Hardy has co-authored and co-edited: *Social and Rehabilitation Services For The Blind, Vocational Rehabilitation: Profession and Process, The Unfit Majority, Fundamentals of Criminal Behavior and Correctional Systems* and *Drug Dependence and Rehabilitation Approaches.* Dr. Hardy has contributed more than fifty publications to the professional literature in psychology and rehabilitation.

PAUL R. HOFFMAN, Ed.D.: Chairman, Department of Rehabilitation and Manpower Services and Professor, School of Education, University of Wisconsin—Stout; Technical Assistant, Division of Rehabilitation Facilities, Rehabilitation Services Administration, Department of Health, Education, and Welfare; First President of the Vocational Evaluation and Work Adjustment Association; Developer of first graduate program in Work Evaluation and initiation of National Materials Development Center in Work Evaluation and Work Adjustment; Recipient of distinguish service award from the University of Arizona Alumni Association. Doctor Hoffman is the author of numerous articles and various publications including national and foreign professional journals.

BRUCE C. HUME: General Manager, Centre Industries, Sydney, Australia (eleven years), a viable manufacturing facility producing electronics and telecommunication equipment, employing 270 disabled and 600 able-bodied; consultant, Commonwealth Government of Australia, Department of Social Services, Sheltered Employment (Assistance) Act; Formerly Manager of Pope Electronics, television, radio and communication manufacturer; consultant to industry. Papers published include *Ergonomics in the Field of Rehabilitation, Employment of the Handicapped—Educating the Community,* and *Rehabilitation and Industrial Productivity.*

RICHARD D. JONES, Ph.D.: U.C.L.A., Assistant Professor at the University of Georgia. Work experience in state rehabilitation agencies. Consultant to state agencies and business and industry.

GORDON C. KRANTZ, M.S.: Assistant Director, Cooperative School-Rehabilitation Centers, Minnetonka and Director, Information System Project in Developmental Disabilities, Professional Data Systems, Inc., St. Paul, Minnesota. Formerly: rehabilitation counselor and district supervisor, Minnesota DVR; psychologist, Opportunity Workshop; psychologist, school rehabilitation project, Minneapolis Public Schools; research coordinator, Cooperative School-Rehabilitation Centers; founding editor, Vocational Evaluation and Work Adjustment Bulletin; President, Minnesota Rehabilitation Association. Mr. Krantz has contributed articles to the professional literature but more extensively to informal and mimeographed professional exchanges.

FRED McFARLANE: Ph.D. University of Georgia. Assistant Professor at San Diego State College. Graduate work in vocational evaluation at Stout State University. Work experience in state and private rehabilitation agencies.

ROBERT P. OVERS, Ph.D.: Research Coordinator, Curative Workshop of Milwaukee; Co-editor, *Milwaukee Media for Rehabilitation Research Reports*. Editor, *The Wisconsin Psychologist;* Editor, *Wisconsin Alcoholism Research Group Newsletter;* Editorial Board, *Vocational Guidance Quarterly*. Formerly, Research Director, Vocational Guidance and Rehabilitation Services, Cleveland; Counseling Psychologist, Veterans Administration Buffalo; part-time instructor, University of Buffalo, University of Wisconsin-Milwaukee, Marquette University. Author, *The Theory of Job Sample Tasks* and co-author, *Abstracts of Sociological Studies of Occupations*.

BERNARD ROSENBERG, M.A.: Director, Vocational and Industrial Rehabilitation, ICD Rehabilitation and Research Center, New York, New York; Technical Consultant, Rehabilitation Services Administration, Department of Health, Education, and Welfare; Vocational Consultant Expert, Social Security Administration, Bureau of Hearing and Appeals, Department of Health, Education, and Welfare; formerly instructor in Rehabilitation Counseling Program, New York University; past President, National Rehabilitation Counseling Association (Region II); past President, Metropolitan Chapter of National Rehabilitation Association; former member of Executive Council, Vocational Evaluation and Work Adjustment Association; formerly Rehabilitation and Placement Counselor, ICD Rehabilitation and Research Center, New York, New York. Mr. Rosenberg has written extensively in the professional literature on rehabilitation counseling, work evaluation and placement.

ARNOLD B. SAX, Ed.D.: Director, Materials Development Center, and Associate Professor, Department of Rehabilitation and Manpower Services, School of Education, University of Wisconsin—Stout; Associate Editor, *Vocational Evaluation and Work Adjustment Association Bulletin.* Formerly Work Evaluation Supervisor, Texas Institute for Rehabilitation and Research; Director, Sheltered Workshop, Houston Council for Retarded Children; School psychologist and counselor, Lamar Consolidated School System; and Teacher of Mentally Retarded, Houston School System. Dr. Sax has contributed numerous articles to the professional literature on Rehabilitation.

CHARLES SMOLKIN, M.Ed., A.G.S.: Chief of Vocational Rehabilitation Services, Department of Rehabilitation Medicine, Sinai Hospital of Baltimore, Inc.; and Vocational Expert, Bureau of Hearings and Appeals, Social Security Administration. Formerly Vocational Evaluator, Baltimore League for Crippled Children and Adults. President, Vocational Evaluation and Work Adjustment Association, 1972-73; Co-Editor, *New Directors in Vocational Rehabilitation: The Stroke Patient.* Mr. Smolkin has contributed several articles about the role of vocational evaluation in Rehabilitation Medicine.

JOHN K. STOUT, Ed.D.: Assistant Director, Rehabilitation Programs, University of Scranton, Scranton, Pennsylvania; Vocational Consultant, Bureau of Hearings and Appeals, Social Security Administration; Chairman, Ethics Committee, Vocational Evaluation and Work Adjustment Association. Formerly Vocational Diagnostic Counselor, Williamsport Technical Institute, Williamsport, Pennsylvania; Assistant Professor of Education, Rehabilitation Counseling Project, The Pennsylvania State University.

RICHARD R. WOLFE, Ph.D.: Chairman, Department of Social and Rehabilitation Service, School of Special Education and Rehabilitation, University of Northern Colorado; Project Director, Rehabilitation Counselor Training Program; and Member Regional In-Service Training Advisory Committee; and Consultant, Western Interstate Commission on Higher Education. Formerly, Rehabilitation Counselor, Pennsylvania State Office for the Blind; School Counselor in Pennsylvania Schools; and Secondary Teacher, Pennsylvania Schools. Co-Author and Editor, *Use of Support Personnel in Vocational Rehabilitation, and Issues Relating to Rehabilitation of Individuals with Behavioral Disorders.* Dr. Wolfe has contributed to the professional literature in rehabilitation.

〉〉 PREFACE

〰〰〰〰〰〰〰〰〰〰〰〰〰〰〰〰〰〰〰〰〰〰〰〰〰〰〰〰〰〰

THERE HAS long been concern about the real lack of practical information and materials for persons involved in the highly complicated process of work evaluation. Many outstanding individuals throughout the entire field of social and rehabilitation service have labored long and hard in order to develop various useful theories and practices in evaluation. The evaluation of an individual for work is of ultimate importance in meeting rehabilitation goals in that if he is unsuccessfully adjusted on the job, his rehabilitation is more than likely a definite failure.

There is a sizable body of literature in the field of vocational evaluation; yet, little material is available which has been compiled and developed for the ready use of the professional practitioner. The work presented here, we hope, will help the practitioner in further developing his ideas about important topical areas in work evaluation. The information which appears in this book is by no means complete, nor does the mastery of it assure an understanding of the rapidly changing requirements of work and evaluation for work.

The reader will note that in this book there is an intermixing of the terms *vocational evaluation* and *work evaluation*. In that these terms have not yet been given definitions which have been agreed upon by the community of work evaluators, the authors have chosen to use them interchangeably. It has been difficult to discern substantative differences between the terms. A real contribution would be the development of useful definitions which would be acceptable to the *field*.

Many of the concepts in evaluation are rather hazy and ill-defined. Another semantic problem raises its head in the term prevocational evaluation. Some persons have indicated that there is no such *animal* as prevocational evaluation. In this book the term *prevocational* concerns determining the adequacy of the individual in terms of his having accomplished the workmanship traits which are necessary for all jobs. These include activities of daily living skills, and also the type of relationships which the individual is able to develop with other workers and supervisors. This concept also includes some of the basic requirements for following instructions, for persistance on a job, for engaging in goal directed activity. The authors have taken the approach that a work adjustment program is one which helps train an individual in these areas or in other words prepares him as a worker by helping him acquire these worker skills. After the individual has completed a period of work adjustment and has mastered some of the basic skills required of workers, it is the position of the authors that he may then be given a vocational evaluation or work evaluation. Based then on the vocational or work evaluation, the evaluator prescribes the appropriate type of vocational training.

We wish to express special thanks to the contributors who tolerated our letters, calls, criticisms and at times suggestions which may or may not have been appropriate. Without them and their substantial interest, this book would not have been completed. With contributors to the professional literature of the caliber of the ones who gave their time and efforts to make this book possible, surely vocational evaluation will become a highly defined system which will be of great benefit to many persons in their search for meaningful work which can be performed with distinction.

RICHARD E. HARDY
JOHN G. CULL

⟩⟩ CONTENTS

		Page
Contributors		ix
Preface		xvii

Part One
OVERVIEW OF EVALUATION

Chapter

I.	WORK EVALUATION AN OVERVIEW	5
II.	THE ROLE OF EVALUATION IN THE REHABILITATION PROCESS	29
III.	THE COUNSELING IMPACT OF WORK EVALUATION	40

Part Two
VOCATIONAL EVALUATION AND PROFESSIONALISM

IV.	THE VOCATIONAL EVALUATION AND WORK ADJUSTMENT ASSOCIATION LOOKS TO THE FUTURE	65
V.	EVALUATING THE EVALUATOR	104
VI.	THE MATERIALS DEVELOPMENT CENTER: A NATIONAL RESOURCE FOR MATERIALS ON WORK EVALUATION AND ADJUSTMENT	124

Part Three
VOCATIONAL EVALUATION APPROACHES
AND PROCEDURES

VII.	THE WORK SAMPLE APPROACH TO VOCATIONAL EVALUATION	139
VIII.	THE MODAPTS APPROACH TO VOCATIONAL EVALUATION	167
IX.	THE WORK EVALUATION REPORT	177

Chapter   *Page*

  X. THE UTILIZATION OF THE DICTIONARY OF OCCUPATIONAL
       TITLES IN WORK EVALUATION 195

  XI. PREVOCATIONAL EVALUATION 242

 XII. SCIENTIFIC OBSERVATION IN WORK EVALUATION 255

Part Four

EVALUATIONS IN SPECIALTY AREAS

XIII. PURPOSE OF PSYCHOLOGICAL TESTING IN WORK EVALUATION 265

 XIV. PURPOSES AND APPROACHES OF EDUCATIONAL EVALUATION . 275

  XV. A MODEL FOR THE VOCATIONAL EVALUATION OF THE
        DISADVANTAGED 297

 XVI. THE REHABILITATION FACILITY'S ROLE IN EVALUATING THE
        WELFARE RECIPIENT 337

      Index 351

VOCATIONAL EVALUATION
for
REHABILITATION SERVICES

PART ONE

OVERVIEW OF EVALUATION

Work Evaluation an Overview

The Role of Evaluation in the Rehabilitation Process

The Counseling Impact of Working Evaluation

I

WORK EVALUATION AN OVERVIEW

Paul R. Hoffman

Definitions
Historical Background
Educational Qualifications for Work Evaluators
Methodologies of Work Evaluation
Factors Evaluated
Utilization of Work Evaluation
Responsibilities of Rehabilitation Counselor and Work Evaluator
Work Evaluation Today and Tomorrow
Summary
References

WORK EVALUATION has become a positive force in helping to assess the vocational strengths and weaknesses of the handicapped and disadvantaged and to develop a plan to assist them in obtaining a more meaningful and rewarding place in society. Although work evaluation has not proved to be a panacea that helps us towards adequate assessment and development of adequate plans in all cases where we previously failed, it has become an important technique that has helped us where before we were failing.

DEFINITIONS

There are a number of terms in this field which are ill-defined and, unfortunately, cause considerable confusion at this time. These are the terms of *prevocational evaluation, vocational evaluation, work evaluation* and *work adjustment.*

5

The term *prevocational evaluation* means different things to different people. To some professionals, it means the evaluation of such factors as activities of daily living, social development and basic educational abilities. These are characteristics which an individual must have before he can even consider preparing for a vocation or being evaluated for a vocation. The term *vocational rehabilitation* came into vogue in the fifties; however, then it was utilized more in relation to the evaluation of aptitudes, potentials and abilities, the type of evaluation we now refer to as work evaluation. The author's preference would be to limit the term *prevocational* evaluation to the former concept.

Vocational evaluation for some has been defined as evaluation for pertinent medical, psychological, vocational, education, cultural, social and environmental factors. For others, it has been defined as a more limited endeavor— that is, the evaluation of an individual's vocational strengths and weaknesses through the utilization of work, real or simulated. Work evaluation is never defined as the broad concept that was mentioned for vocational evaluation but as evaluation of vocational strengths and weaknesses of the handicapped and disadvantaged through the utilization of some specific methodologies, mainly the utilization of work, real or simulated.

Work adjustment, a treatment process utilizing work or aspects of work to modify behavior, is also at times defined as an evaluation process. It is not an evaluation process but is, as the words indicate, an adjustment or treatment process. While evaluation does take place during work adjustment, the objectives of the evaluation are different from that of the work evaluation process. In work evaluation, the objectives are to assess the vocational strengths and weaknesses as related to developing a vocational plan. In work adjustment, the objectives are to determine the success or failure of the adjustment plan and to determine when to terminate the work adjustment process. Prevocational, vocational and work evaluation are assessment processes, and work adjustment is a treatment process.

Confusion does exist in the field in relation to these terms, and there is a need for standardization. In this chapter, it will be necessary to use the terms *work evaluation* and *vocational evaluation* interchangeably. In relation to the author's own thoughts and reference to some sources, the term *work evaluation* is used. In reference to some other sources, the term *vocational evaluation* is used. The process being referred to is the assessment of vocational strengths and weaknesses through the utilization of work, real or simulated, for the purpose of developing a vocational plan of action.

HISTORICAL BACKGROUND

Work evaluation is not new, although it has been gathering considerable momentum in the last few years. Morton Bregman (1967), in a speech entitled *The Use and Misuse of Vocational Evaluation in the Counseling Process,* noted that in World War I, the Portvillez School in Belgium believed a disabled soldier could be helped to select an appropriate trade training program only by trying out in several trade classes. By this method of evaluation, the soldier could select a course in which he was interested and in which he had showed a potential. Mr. Bregman further noted the development of the scientific job analysis and the early work of Munsterberg, one of the pioneers in the field of psychological testing. When confronted with the problem of developing a test to select streetcar operators for the Boston Railroad Company, Munsterberg built a model streetcar on which he was able to try out prospective operators.

Psychometric testing became a force in this country during the 1900's. Of special importance to the field of work evaluation were job performance tests developed by the military during the Second World War. For example, the United States Air Force developed the two-hand coordination test as part of the Air Force Classification Test Battery and, to help select pilots, the complex coordinator test which required a person who has never flown a plane to operate a stick and rudder bar on an instrument on which he had to follow a pattern flashed before him.

There is a situational or simulated approach to testing in which the client is placed in an actual work situation. This technique has been the mainstay of work evaluation in the sheltered workshop movement, where it had developed to the greatest extent. Situational evaluation in a sheltered workshop mainly takes the form of placing a client on the production line in the workshop. The situational technique was utilized in a different setting in a planned, applied manner by the Office of Strategic Services during World War II, when they set up problem-solving situations in which groups of men were placed in actual conditions with resource materials available but not specified. The personnel in the groups were forced to solve a problem in a *live situation*.

In the mid thirties, the Institute for the Crippled and Disabled (ICD) in New York City instigated what was known as a Guidance Testing Class. This became the forerunner of some of the work undertaken by ICD. After passage of Public Law 565 in 1954, the Institute undertook a five-year project with the United Cerebral Palsy Association of New York City, the New York Division of Vocational Rehabilitation and the New York Employment Service to explore improved techniques of determining the potential of the cerebral palsied. The five-year project led to separate facilities adapted to the needs of the group. Next, the Institute for the Crippled and Disabled obtained a five-year Research and Demonstration (R & D) project from the Vocational Rehabilitation Administration and developed the TOWER System. TOWER is an acronym for the words, *Testing, Orientation and Work Evaluation in Rehabilitation.*

Another important facility in the history of the development of work samples is the Vocational Guidance and Rehabilitation Service of Cleveland, Ohio. During the years 1959-1964, they undertook research in obtaining and using job samples. Resulting from this project was the R & D report entitled *Obtaining and Using Actual Job Samples in a Work Evaluation Program,* which was under the direction of Robert Overs. This project also received support from the then Vocational Rehabilitation Administration.

A recent and valuable work was the research undertaken by the Jewish Employment and Vocational Service of Philadelphia in 1968, through a grant from the Manpower Administration.

This had led to important findings concerning the validity of the technique of work evaluation and the development of a series of work samples. The history of the development of this battery of work samples dates back to the thirties when the Jewish Employment and Vocational Service of Philadelphia began to search for a way to adequately assess Jewish immigrants to this country. A severe language barrier hampered assessment by the standard methods.

Until recent times, there has been a paucity of literature on work evaluation. One of the early articles, by Henry Redkey (1957), was entitled *The Function and Value of a Pre-Vocational Unit in a Rehabilitation Center*. Walter Neff (1966), wrote an article, *Problems of Work Evaluation*, that has become a classic in the field and is often quoted and referred to. Another major paper and first attempt at a theory was written by William Gellman (1968). This paper, *The Principles of Vocational Evaluation*, was presented at a workshop at Stout State University in 1967 and was published in 1968 in *Rehabilitation Literature*. Pertinent information to assist in organizing and operating a work evaluation program can be found in a 1966 publication of the Vocational Rehabilitation Administration (now Rehabilitation Services Administration) entitled *Guidelines for Organization and Operation of Vocational Evaluation Units: A Training Guide*. Literature in this area is on the increase in recent times. An annotated bibliography on work evaluation has been published and is kept up to date by the Materials Development Center of Stout State University.

Until recent times, the only training programs for those performing in the field of work evaluation were short-term institutes. The Institute for the Crippled and Disabled in New York City is well known for six-week programs on work evaluation, utilizing the TOWER system. Auburn University in Alabama was the first university to undertake regular short-term training for personnel in this field. The program in Sheltered Workshop Administration at the University of Wisconsin held some one-week training programs in work evaluation.

As the field of work evaluation developed, a body of knowledge accumulated, and the role of the evaluator was defined. It became apparent that short-term programs were not sufficient to train a *qualified work evaluator*. Through a pilot study funded by the Vocational Rehabilitation Administration, professional training at the graduate level for work evaluators was established. Stout State University, University of Arizona and Auburn University established graduate training programs for work evaluators in the order listed.

A national center for the collection, development and dissemination of materials on work evaluation and work adjustment has been established by the Research and Demonstration Division of the Social and Rehabilitation Services, Department of Health, Education and Welfare. This is the Materials Development Center of Stout State University, through which information and materials on work evaluation and work adjustment are made available to professional workers in the field of vocational rehabilitation.

In 1965 the American Association of Work Evaluators was founded in the state of Georgia. Soon the organization drew the interest of people from other states. In 1966, at the annual conference of the National Rehabilitation Association (NRA) in Denver, a group of interested persons gathered to discuss the development of an organization within the NRA framework for people in work evaluation. From that conference, an *ad hoc* committee was formed to investigate the development of a work evaluation division of NRA. From this committee, the Vocational Evaluation and Work Adjustment Association was formed, and it became an official division of the National Rehabilitation Association at the annual conference in New Orleans in 1968.

THEORY ON WORK EVALUATION

There is no single comprehensive theory for the field of work evaluation. The field has borrowed from a number of sources. It has borrowed from the field theorist psychologists who pose that the behavior of individuals cannot be understood until the individual's environment, his perception of that environment and the resulting interaction with the environment are understood.

Kurt Lewin stated this in his formula in which behavior is a function of the person plus his environment. Another psychologist, Henry Murray, emphasized both the needs within the individual and the pressures from his environment and the vectors resulting from these two interacting forces.

Donald Fiske (1960), indicated that the performance of any task is a complex function of the individual's capacity to carry out the task, the appropriateness of direction of his effort and the effort itself. Combining this and ideas from the field theorist, the author has stated in a paper presented first at a conference in Texas that performance is a function of an individual's capacities, his efforts and the appropriateness of his efforts plus the effect of his environment.

William Gellman (1967), notes that vocational evaluation is ahistorical—that is, it is concerned not with the past but with the present and with future prediction. The theory he sets forth denotes four correlates between the theoretical and the empirical aspects of vocational evaluation. The first correlate is that of the work sector, characterized by achievement-oriented behavior using acquired behavioral patterns and skills to obtain an economic objective. The second correlate is that of work personality, a characteristic pattern of work activity displayed by an individual in a work situation. The third correlate states that work personality is developmental and is acquired during growth. His fourth correlate states that each culture uses different types of work personalities as ego models for training, selecting and rewarding people who are or will become productive. He notes that vocational evaluation is a means of determining the stage and the type of work personality in an individual. It is impractical to review this entire article at this time, but it should be noted that Dr. Gellman goes on to discuss goals, processes, techniques and principals.

Gordon Krantz (1968), examined two models currently being utilized for the basis of work evaluation and finds them lacking. He notes that one model is based upon clinical psychology and is mainly concerned with such factors as defensive mechanisms, impulse control and gratification of needs. The second model he has labeled *Homespun-Eclectic Theory*. He notes that such factors as mechanical aptitude, grooming and relating to supervisors are the bases for the work evaluation programs. Mr. Krantz prefers to utilize a model based upon the theory of employability and suggests using the methodology of critical incident technique to observe the kind of employment problems currently experienced by the population for which the program is designed. Having defined these problems, the evaluator is then to describe them in terms of the client behavior. Description is in positive terms, such as seeking work with a specific minimum frequency, appropriate interview behavior, rate of production appropriate to the job setting or adequately traveling in the community. Assessment then consists of looking for the specific behaviors or lack of the specific behaviors.

Julian Nadolsky (1969), notes that both vocational evaluation and existential analysis are developments resulting directly from a dissatisfaction with traditional approaches that have been utilized to understand man's behavior. In both there is an attempt to obtain a more total self comprehension by the individual through somewhat unstructured and individually oriented programs and procedures. Existentialism may be "viewed as a period or epic of individual supremacy where the emphasis is upon analyzing the subject-object relationship and the endeavor is to understand the emerging or becoming of a total human being through such relationships." Vocational evaluation is defined as a "process which attempts to *assess* and *predict* work behavior primarily through a variety of subject-object assessment techniques and procedures." In Mr. Nadolsky's framework, existential philosophy is applicable to work evaluation technology.

Unfortunately, little, if any, research has been done in relation to theoretical factors. Rehabilitation facilities have developed their particular work evaluation programs for a variety of reasons, but theoretical reasons have not been one of them. Sheltered workshops have tended to make a virtue out of the so-called real work situations and have not attempted to go beyond these techniques. Rehabilitation centers without subcontracts or other forms of production have developed and defended work samples as offering a wide range of test situations and as giving the opportunity for developing tests in graded levels and other innovations. Neither type of facility has, for the most part, developed a work evaluation program on the basis of theoretical factors.

At this stage of development, work evaluation borrows heavily from other fields of endeavor for thoretical foundations and is eclectic in nature. The research undertaken by the Jewish Employment and Vocational Service of Philadelphia, mentioned earlier, has resulted in data supporting the work evaluation process, but further research and study are needed. Also needed is a careful examination of the objectives to be obtained when establishing work evaluation units, in order to decide on the methodology to use.

EDUCATIONAL QUALIFICATIONS FOR WORK EVALUATORS

Not too long ago, the common belief of personnel in rehabilitation facilities throughout the country was that a good evaluator was an individual who had worked in industry or business. Little concern was given to educational qualifications. When the pilot study for initiating the first graduate program in the field of work evaluation was undertaken, considerable opposition was met as to the need for high-level training programs. A few thought that a graduate program was needed, a few more felt that a program at the undergraduate level would be best, but the majority seemed to feel that if any training was needed, a short-term program would suffice. This feeling is not nearly as prevalent today, and it is now quite common to sample opinion that reflects favorably towards the need for a good training program for work evaluators. Rehabilitation facilities are discovering this need every day as they attempt to set up work evaluation departments and hire personnel. The individual being hired who lacks training for the job, discovers it fast. Every training program in existence today and every well-established work evaluation program receive many letters requesting all known information on work evaluation. These letters are efforts to obtain help in setting up a work evaluation program and are most often from individuals who are hired as developers and administrators of work evaluation departments but who lack the appropriate knowledge and skills.

A questionnaire study of the type of information that should be provided in training work evaluators was conducted in 1966 by Stout State University. Two hundred and fifty questionnaires were sent to rehabilitation facilities in the United States with work evaluation units. A total of 189 questionnaires, or 75.6 percent, were returned. The results indicated that information was needed, first of all, on procedures of work evaluation. Further, information was needed on work methods and job sampling, the vocational rehabilitation process, medical and psychosocial aspects of disability, report writing, counseling theory as it applies to working with individuals directly on the floor of the rehabilitation facility, principles of communication, occupational information and analysis, cost quality and contract procurement procedures, psychological testing, community resources, and information about the world of work.

At two short-term training workshops for work evaluators at Stout State University, job analysis was conducted by the attending work evaluators on themselves. The evaluators were from a variety of work evaluation programs and different parts of the country. Based on a sample of thirty-three, which is recognized as being grossly inadequate in number, it is noted that thirty-six separate factors were listed as knowledges and skills required in the field of work evaluation. Among the more often mentioned factors were accuracy; manual dexterity; knowledge of machines, tools and shop equipment; counseling and interviewing skills; supervisory skills, teaching and training skills; organizational ability; interpersonal relations skills; communication skills; research principles; methodology and statistics; job analysis; and manpower needs. Some of the less often quoted factors were such things as time-and-motion study, production management, personality theory, developmental psychology and learning theory.

Seventeen separate duties were identified by the thirty-three work evaluators. The items checked by more than half the evaluators in rank order from first to last were the following: report writing and record keeping; staffing and coordination; work sample administration, scoring and interpretation; behavioral assessment; training and teaching; work sample development; and psychometric testing. The other items listed, but by less than half the group in continuing rank order, were the following: counseling; supervision of clients; supervision of employees; behavior modification; group work; and case management or client programming. It is repeated that this study is not quoted as a valid study of the duties of work evaluators due to the limited sample and the bias of the sample, but it does point up some of the duties, knowledges and skills required as seen by practicing work evaluators.

Karl Egerman, in research undertaken while he was director of the Research and Training Center in Vocational Rehabilitation at Johnstown, Pennsylvania, reports on duties of evaluators. This study was also biased; the names of the persons sampled were obtained from the National Rehabilitation Association as best they could identify work evaluators in those days. This was not a true sampling of work evaluators throughout the country, and the sample was heavily influenced by personnel from the southeastern region of the United States, but the study does have considerable value. It indicated that work evaluators were engaging in the following: attending and participating in scheduled staff meetings; observing clients at work; helping clients adjust to the work environment; writing reports; administering work samples or other performance measures; developing recommendations for training and placement; teaching clients good work habits; interviewing people who knew the clients; interviewing clients' families; lecturing periodically on vocational evaluation procedures; and supervising the workshops in vocational evaluation and prevocational training.

In essence, the job of the work evaluator is complex and comprehensive. The day when a work evaluation unit can be set up by an untrained individual has passed or should have passed. When possible, it would be desirable, in obtaining administrators for work evaluation departments, to hire an individual specifically trained for his field—that is, someone who has a master's degree from one of the training programs in the field of work evaluation. Such personnel are in short supply, however, and will be for a considerable amount of time. In lieu of this, it is recommended that facilities turn to allied professional training to obtain administrators for their units. Allied fields would be rehabilitation counseling, psychology, industrial arts and occupational therapy. Each of these fields has certain limitations for personnel entering work evaluation, and it would be best for persons trained in one of these fields to have experience in work evaluation prior to being hired as administrators.

Pertaining to secondary personnel in work evaluation programs, people with master's degree would be desirable, but due to the shortage and upward mobility of people with master's degrees and the expense involved to hire them, it is necessary to turn to lesser trained persons. Rehabilitation facilities must then carefully select the type of people they will utilize in secondary positions. If separate departments are set up in the work evaluation units, such as mechanics and clerical, then personnel with educational backgrounds in these particular fields may be obtained, but it will be necessary to provide them with extensive in-service training on the many subleties that go into evaluation.

METHODOLOGIES OF WORK EVALUATION

Job Analysis

Walter Neff (1966), writing in the *Personnel and Guidance Journal,* as quoted earlier, listed job analysis as a methodology of work evaluation, along with psychometrics, work samples and situational testing.

Job analysis is a process of defining the significant worker traits and requirements, and the technical and environmental facts of a specific job. It is an important technique for the work evaluator to know. It can assist him to (a) identify job requirements and specific qualities required of workers for various jobs, (b) develop work samples and (c) do client evaluation. The job analysis formula of measuring what the worker does, how he does it, why he does it and the skill involved in doing it lends itself readily to evaluating the qualifications and abilities of a client placed on a job. However, it is rare that job analysis, when used, is used to evaluate a particular client. It is used more often as an adjunct technique to learn about the requirements of a job so as to help select clients who have the qualifications to succeed on the job or to lay the foundation for building a work sample. Once the traits required to do a job are known, it is posible to compare worker traits with the traits required by specific jobs. Perhaps this would be best referred to as *worker-trait comparison* or *job-man analysis.*

Psychometric Testing

Psychometric testing is of value to work evaluation. It is quick, relatively inexpensive and objective. The range of psychometric testing is broad. There are tests for measuring intelligence, interests, aptitudes, dexterities, academic abilities and personality. Where are tests pertaining to the field of clerical work, mechanical work, electronics, drafting, computer programming, business and many others. There are tests for people with high intelligence and much education and tests for persons with limited intelligence and poor education.

With proper use, psychometric tests have a place in work evaluation. Their use by work evaluation programs will depend upon the staffing pattern of a rehabilitation facility and the presence of psychologists and psychometrists. Tests have their servere limitations, and their very limitations are what led to the development of the work evaluation methodologies of work samples and situational work settings.

Work Samples

A work sample is a test that is an actual job or a simulated job. A work sample may be an actual job, administered and observed under standard conditions, or it may be a mock-up of one component of a job. It may be a job made up by the evaluator to resemble an actual job in industry or business and to measure traits important to successful employment. There are a number of advantages to the work sample method of evaluation. One of the major advantages is that it tends to look like work and often holds the interest of clients as opposed to the psychological test. The client can objectively see how well he is or is not performing, and the work sample test often holds more meaning for him because of this factor. The work sample offers the evaluatior the opportunity to observe actual work behavior, and an experienced evaluator can innovate work samples to meet the particular needs of a client. Language inadequacies, reading disabilities, speech impairments, educational deprivation and cultural differences are often less influential on work sample evaluation than evaluation through psychological tests. Work samples may be established in a large variety of areas in order to get a more comprehensive measure of client potential.

There are disadvantages to this method. It is expensive. The expense is that of the time and materials it takes to build, maintain and administer work samples and in the replacement of parts or supplies. Work samples are time-consuming on the part of the evaluator since most of them require the presence of an evaluator for timing and for observation of behavior. Work samples also have the disadvantage of requiring continual reconstruction and standardization.

The Situational Approach

Evaluating an individual who is placed on a job or jobs in the sheltered workshop has been referred to as the situational approach because it attempts to simulate actual working conditions. This approach has advantages. It offers work situations simulating work in which to conduct evaluations; wages are paid; work is performed with actual commodities destined for sale; foremen are present who set standards for quality and quantity of work; regular working hours are maintained; interpersonal relationship situations can be similar to those in business and industry; and in general, the overall situation more closely resembles that of industry and business than in a work sample facility. The author would point out, however, that the sheltered workshop is definitely not the same as industry or business for fairly obvious reasons.

There are limitations to this method of evaluation. Sheltered workshops are limited by the work contracts they have, and it is impossible to reproduce, within the confines of a workshop, the vast variety of types of employment or to measure for the many types of basic skills which go into different jobs. Another limitation is related to one of the advantages—the complexity of the situation of a worklike setting makes it difficult to separate the variables that are producing the effect.

Job Tryout

The utilization of work stations under actual work conditions is another technique of work evaluation. These may be work stations in institutions, rehabilitation facilities, schools or in business and industries.

Work stations within institutions, rehabilitation facilities or schools, such as in food services, laundry, maintenance, and buildings and grounds, may be utilized as an evaluative method. This method of evaluation also has certain advantages. It provides an opportunity to observe attitudes, motivation, initiative, ability to follow orders, work quality and quantity, and other factors pertinent to employment and vocational development, while still in the institution or other setting. The individual under observation may be observed under actual work conditions and can be placed in a role where he must meet standards and expectations close to that of normal workers. There are also limitations to this method of evaluation. Sometimes the situation is not a *real work situation* as too often in these settings, no wages or only token wages are paid. One of the major problems is obtaining cooperation of the regular work supervisors who at times do not wish this extra responsibility or who sometimes use such placements as a source of *cheap* help.

The other job tryout method is the use of work stations in business and industries. In these situations, wages are paid, usually by the business or industry offering the work station. In some situations a subsidy is given to the business or industry by the sponsoring program. The advantage here is similar to the above. The individual may be observed under actual work conditions. The major difficulty is obtaining the cooperation of employers, including not only the head of the business or industry or a department chief but also the immediate floor supervisor. Without the cooperation of the latter, the program will fail.

FACTORS EVALUATED

The process of work evaluation focuses upon two classifications of factors to be evaluated, *general employability factors* and *specific employability factors.*

General employability factors are those which an individual must possess in order to be generally employable. These include such factors as social development, grooming and hygiene, work personality, work habits, physical tolerance and performance rate. Examples of factors under work personality include relation to supervisors, relation to co-workers, frustration tolerance, and reaction to instructions and criticism. Work habits include such factors as attendance rate, punctuality, not leaving a work station inappropriately and safety consciousness. If these factors are acceptable, the individual is generally employable and may be evaluated for a specific vocational plan. If not, the individual will require either social development or referral to work adjustment for improvement of those factors found to be below the level of acceptability for general employment.

Specific employability factors include skills, aptitudes, dexterities, achievement, interests, intellectual level of functioning, personality factors and physical tolerance. These are factors pertinent to specific vocational development and employment. It will be noted that some of the factors are repeated from the list of those under general employability. There are personality factors such as *reaction to supervisors* which are related to general employability and other factors related to specific jobs. As examples, it would be undesirable to recommend sales work to someone who prefers to be alone with minimum interaction with people or a position beyond one's physical tolerance.

UTILIZATION OF WORK EVALUATION

As indicated in the preceding section, the technique of work evaluation can and should reveal more about a client than merely skills and things he can do. The technique of work evaluation can provide information as to aptitudes, dexterities, skills, intellectual level of functioning, interests, work habits and personality factors. The amount of information for the different categories will vary from client to client. For one client, considerable information as to personality factors will be obtained while for a second, very little. To the trained evaluator, however, work evaluation can produce a wealth of information.

The performance of a client on a work sample for business skills, handtool manipulative ability, power tools, assembly tools, and the like, will, of course, reveal information as to the client's skills, aptitudes and dexterities. Similar information can be obtained by observing him on various jobs in the sheltered workshop, but this kind of information comes best from work samples.

Intellectual level of functioning can be obtained by administration of intelligence tests and academic achievement tests (such as the Wide Range Achievement Test) and by careful observation of his behavior during the evaluation program. A client who can do a task from written instructions has a higher level of academic verbal ability than a client who requires that instructions be read, but the latter has a higher level of intellectual functioning than the client for whom the instructions must be demonstrated. Two clients may measure approximately the same on intelligence tests, but one may reveal a higher degree of functioning from the standpoint of learning ability. This can be observed in a work evaluation program in relation to the rate of learning exhibited on work samples. This factor can also be observed by the rate of learning exhibited on production tasks in a sheltered workshop. The way a client approaches a task can reveal the manner in which he tackles problems. In attempting to solve problems, an individual approach may be that of trial and error, concrete or abstract approach, and with plan and forethought or impulsivity.

The work evaluation program can also reveal information as to a client's interests, especially in a work sample department with a wide range of work evaluation tasks. One technique for measuring interest is to obtain the client's preferences and nonpreferences for the various tasks. A second procedure is to observe carefully his verbal and nonverbal reactions. Example of the latter would be his facial expressions with various tasks or his performing below the expected level on a particular task.

It is to be expected that some clients will dislike all of the tasks of the evaluation program. This may be due to a number of reasons. The variety of tasks may be too limited to present the client with an area he likes. This would be especially true in a sheltered workshop with only a limited number of contracts. The client may be unable to correlate some or all of the tasks with specific jobs. The clients may not be motivated towards working but may be seeking other gains, such as support by society.

Obtaining a client's reaction to the various tasks can revel information other than interests. It can reveal a discrepancy between interests and ability. For example, a client may indicate that the task or tasks which appeal to him most are those above his ability level. On the other hand, those tasks which appeal most to the client may be ones below his level of ability. The results of the work evaluation can, at such times, become a valuable tool in counseling and working with the client.

Work evaluation offers the opportunity to observe the client under a variety of conditions and over a period of time. As such, it offers an excellent opportunity for the observation and evaluation of his personality. How does he react to authority figures? to male authority figures as opposed to female? to his successes and failures? to older persons? to persons his age? to younger persons? to frustrating situations? to difficult tasks? to the unexpected? to pressures created by time limitations? Is he dependent or independent, or does he manifest a mixture of dependency and independency according to the situation? Is he aggressive, passive or passive-aggressive? Is he a loner or gregarious?

Work evaluation, especially in the sheltered workshop situation, lends itself to the observation of work habits. Does he report on time? Does he waste time during assignments? Is he dependable? responsible? Is he grooming appropriate? Does he take care of equipment?

Not every individual serviced by the vocational rehabilitation process requires work evaluation. A client with at least average intelligence, a grade school education and with some appropriate motivation can usually be evaluated faster and more economically by standard procedures. There are many clients, however, for whom work evaluation should be used as an adjunct to standard procedures or as the preferred methodology. Some guidelines for such clients are as follows: (a) low intelligence, (b) poor education, (c) cultural background different from that upon which most psychological tests are standardized, (d) subcultural backgrounds, such as youth gangs, that create negative attitudes to interfere with standard assessment, (f) immaturity, (g) lack of adequate work experiences, (h) history of many low-level jobs, (i) aspirations which exceed or are below ability level, (j) handicapping conditions that prevent adequate assessment by standard procedures and (k) presence of basic questions not answered by other procedures.

The work evaluation process may now be utilized to determine eligibility for rehabilitation service. Public Law 89-333 authorized rehabilitation counselors to utilize work evaluation to assist them in making the determination as to *reasonable expectation for success* required before rendering rehabilitation services. From the above description of the work evaluation process, the potential of work evaluation for aiding the counselor in this decision should be obvious. The chance to observe a client under the conditions of work evaluation and for an extended period of time will result in information about a client not available through medical examination and standard psychological testing. When should a counselor use work evaluation for assisting in this decision? He should use it when there is a questionable doubt in his mind from other assessment techniques (interview, review of history, medical examination and psychological examination) as to the decision of *reasonable expectation for success.*

RESPONSIBILITIES OF REHABILITATION COUNSELOR AND WORK EVALUATOR

The rehabilitation counselor has some definite responsibilities towards the work evaluation process. No counselor should send a client to a facility with a simple statement, "Please evaluate." The counselor should carefully state the specific questions he has in relation to the client. This will not prohibit the work evaluation department of a facility from evaluating beyond these questions, if such evaluation is called for and agreed upon by the counselor, but it will assist the work evaluation department in meeting the needs of the counselor. The counselor should also prepare the client for the process and not have him enter work evaluation with false conceptions and unanswered questions.

The counselor should provide the work evaluation program with information on the client. This will include pertinent information on medical and psychiatric data, psychological tests, family history, work record and educational attainment. Work evaluation is not a passive process that simply measures objective factors but takes on meaning dependent upon the background of the client. As indicated in the section, *Theory on Work Evaluation,* work evaluation is a historical and concerned with the future, but an evaluator with the knowledge that a client has a third grade education, was a common laborer all his life or once held a high-level job can render more effective evaluation and interpretations. Since he needs to know if the client has a history of psychiatric or other problems, the evaluator usually has to spend time interviewing the client if this information is not supplied by the counselor.

The counselor should become familiar with the work evaluation program he uses and visit as often as time and distance permit. Visitation to work evaluation programs will familiarize the counselor with the process, enable him to determine which program is best suited for a particular client and establish effective communication with personnel of the work evaluation programs.

The work evaluator also has definite responsibilities. If a client is referred for a specific purpose, the evaluator should contact the counselor before pursuing a different track, if that seems desirable, unless arrangements are made ahead of time. The evaluator should keep the counselor abreast of developments for clients in evaluation for long periods of time. He should write reports in clear and concise language without a lot of professional jargon and should do more than just report facts. A series of facts about a client, while they may cover the essential findings, need to be integrated to render effective interpretation. The work evaluation report should answer the specific questions asked by a counselor or indicate why the evaluator is unable to answer those questions.

The evaluator must remember that it is the counselor who is buying the services. At times, evaluators tend to act as if they were the ones mainly involved with the client and can do as they please. When effective communication is worked out between counselor and evaluator, there will be few problems.

WORK EVALUATION TODAY AND TOMORROW

In the recent past, utilization of the methodology of work evaluation was limited to rehabilitation centers, sheltered workshops and the clients served by these facilities. Today, work evaluation programs are found in these facilities, in institutions for the retarded, the mentally ill and the public offender, and in high schools with special education groups. The recent amendments to the Vocational Education Act earmarked 10 percent of the funds for the handicapped. Through this allocation, there will be further application of the methodologies of work evaluation serving the population covered by the act. Programs such as WIN (Work Incentive Program) submit their clients to work evaluation methodologies. The Manpower Development and Training Programs supported by the Department of Labor have begun either to refer clients to work evaluation units or use the technology themselves.

Work evaluation projects have been funded mainly by the Rehabilitation Services Administration of the U. S. Department of Health, Education and Welfare. They are not being supported by other federal agencies, such as the Department of Labor. It was the Department of Labor, through the Manpower Administration, that sponsored the Research and Demonstration project at the Jewish Employment and Vocational Service in Philadelphia.

Work evaluation has been utilized mainly with the handicapped and disadvantaged. This author sees the technology of work evaluation as having considerable relevance to those whom we do not consider disadvantaged or handicapped. There are large numbers of young people in our high schools and vocational schools who do not know what it is they want to pursue in life, and a comprehensive and well-developed work evaluation unit could offer much to help these young people make pertinent decisions. It is one thing to read about an occupation in a two-to-four-page pamphlet put out by professional vocational guidance organizations and another to do the job. Written information is cold and sterile, and it is difficult to visualize what it is really like to undertake a particular type of work. Through the realities of work samples, however, an individual may determine exactly what potentials he has at the moment, what potentials he can develop through instructions of graduated work samples, and he can also get an actual feeling for the work involved. Through work samples, the young person can learn not only of his current level of ability but of his potential and his interest. This combined with information from pamphlets and the counselor, could help him more readily select a suitable occupation in life.

SUMMARY

Work evaluation is a process of assessing vocational strengths and weaknesses through the utilization of work, real or simulated, for the purpose of developing the vocational plan of action. There is, unfortunately, considerable confusion in the field concerning terms pertaining to this process, and there is a need for standardization of terms.

Work evaluation is not a new process, although its development and utilization have accelerated in recent years. Theoretical principles have been borrowed from other disciplines, but in recent times theorists in the field have attempted to set down specific theoretical principles for work evaluation.

The process of work evaluation includes the techniques of psychometric tests, work samples, situational settings and job tryout. Job analysis is important as an adjunct technique to provide information for job-man matching and to assist in building work samples. Work evaluation focuses upon evaluation of general and specific employability factors and is used with persons for whom other standard assessment techniques have failed to generate a vocational plan of action. The process of work evaluation and the duties of the work evaluator have developed to the point of requiring professionally trained evaluators.

REFERENCES

Bregman, Morton H.: The use and misuse of vocational evaluation in the counseling process. *Some Recent Advances and Research in Vocational Evaluation.* Research and Training Center in Vocational Rehabilitation. Johnstown, University of Pittsburgh, 1967.

Egerman, Karl, and Gilbert, James L.: The work evaluator. *Journal of Rehabilitation, 35* (No. 3) : 12-14, May-June 1969.

Fiske, Donald W.: Problems in measuring capacity and performance. *Proceedings of the Iowa Conference on Pre-Vocational Activities, Conference at the University of Iowa.* Iowa City, University of Iowa, 1960.

Gellman, William: The principles of vocational evaluation. *Vocational Evaluation Curriculum Development Workshop.* Stout State University, April, 1967, and *Rehabilitation Literature, 19* (No. 4) : 98-103, April 1968.

Hoffman, Paul R.: Work Evaluation. A speech presented at the rehabilitation conference sponsored by the Texas Division of Vocational Rehabilitation, Houston, Texas, February 1969.

Institute for the Crippled and Disabled: *TOWER: Testing, Orientation and Work Evaluation in Rehabilitation.* New York, Institute for the Crippled and Disabled, 1967.

Jewish Employment and Vocational Service: *Work Samples: Signposts on the Road to Occupational Choice.* Final Report on Experimental and Demonstration Project, Contract No. 82-40-67-40, U. S. Department of Labor, Manpower Administration. Philadelphia, Jewish Employment and Vocational Service, 1968.

Krantz, Gordon: Theory Underlying Vocational Evaluation. Unpublished paper presented at Stout State University, 1968.

Lewin, Kurt: *A Dynamic Theory of Personality.* New York, McGraw-Hill Book Co., 1935.

Murray, Henry A.: *Explorations in Personality.* New York, Science Editions, Inc., 1962.

Nadolsky, Julian M.: The existential in vocational evaluation. *Journal of Rehabilitation, 35* (No. 3) : 22-24, May-June 1969.

Neff, Walter S.: Problems of work evaluation. *The Personnel and Guidance Journal, 44* (No. 7) : 682-688, March 1966.

Redkey, Henry: The function and value of a pre-vocational unit in a rehabilitation center. *American Journal Occupational Therapy, 11* (No. 1) : 20-24, January-February 1957.

Redkey, Henry, and White, Barbara: *The Pre-Vocational Unit in a Rehabilitation Center,* Washington, D. C., U. S. Department of Health, Education and Welfare, Office of Vocational Rehabilitation, 1956.

Vocational Guidance and Rehabilitation Services: *Final Report: Obtaining and Using Actual Job Samples in a Work Evaluation Program,* Research and Demonstration Project RD-412, Department of Health, Education and Welfare, Vocational Rehabilitation Administration. Cleveland, Vocational Guidance and Rehabilitation Services, 1959-1964.

Vocational Rehabilitation Administration: Guidelines for Organization and Operation of Vocational Evaluation Units: A Training Guide, Rehabilitation Service Series Number 67-50. Washington, U. S. Department of Health, Education and Welfare, 1966.

II

THE ROLE OF EVALUATION IN THE REHABILITATION PROCESS

STANLEY H. CROW

Facilities

The Elements of Evaluation

A Model for the Rehabilitation Process

Summary

References

THERE WAS A TIME when *rehabilitation* was merely a service which one expected to find in a large medical facility. When we thought of rehabilitation, we thought of such things as physical medicine, physical therapy, and braces. Today when we use the word *rehabilitation* we could be referring to the processes or the techniques in any one of many professions which are designed to enable an individual to become as independent as possible.

Hopefully, we have passed through a period in which rehabilitation had only one goal—*vocational* (i.e. to turn an individual who was not supporting himself into an individual who was totally self-reliant in the production of his income). Legislation was passed and appropriations approved on the basis of such phrases as *turning tax eaters into taxpayers;* people were placed on jobs because of such half-truths as *handicapped people make better workers than non-handicapped people. . .,* and we were told that rehabilitation was *good business* because it saved the taxpayer money. This demonic concept which assigned value only to those who could provide for their own maintenance, left many individuals who could have led more meaningful lives had they been offered the help available through government funded rehabilitation services, to a life of mere existence in back rooms and nursing homes.

Rehabilitation has been defined in many ways over its period of existence within the helping professions. It began as an adjunct to the medical profession, when doctors began to realize that merely saving lives and reducing and preventing suffering, was not enough. Obermann (1965) points to the *birth* of "rehabilitation as the specialty. . .known as physical medicine, which addresses itself to. . .insuring that the patient should reach as nearly full functional recovery as possible." The first rehabilitation personnel were specialists such as physical therapists, occupational therapists, and rehabilitation nurses. Because of its medical orientation, these *professionals,* who worked with the *patient* were allowed to work only under doctors' orders.

From the early concept, the idea of rehabilitation has grown into the concept of enabling a person to return to or to attain as much function and independence as possible. The field has developed specialists in many areas who work toward enabling handicapped and disadvantaged individuals through specialized assistance.

If one were to characterize the field of rehabilitation and point to the area of its strength, it would be that rehabilitation has been a discipline which deals with each client as a special individual with special needs. William Spencer (1972), Director of Texas Institute for Rehabilitation and Research, has defined the goal of rehabilitation as "providing the situations in which an individual can have self-determined options for living." If we are to take that as a goal for rehabilitation, then the system has, from time to time, broken down. Historically, it has been a system in which the professional has made the decisions for the client and, as such, has created a dependency relationship which might be characterized as the *cold beer and warm TV syndrome,* (in which the client says to the counselor, "I'll be at home. If there is anything you can do for me, just call me.") .

Olshansky (1969) states that every client, within the vocational rehabilitation process, "should be dealt with as *the de-cision maker*. He should decide whether: (1) he wants to be vocationally rehabilitated. . . (2) which of his problems he wants to deal with. . . (3) to which workshop (or facility) he should go . . . (4) once there, he should have the right to decide whether to terminate or to stay, and. . . (5) he should decide which of the supportive services (casework, counseling, or psychotherapy) he wants, if any." Evaluation might be seen as the tool which enables the individual to make those decisions.

The evaluation dynamic of the rehabilitation process is a tool used by most professionals in the field of rehabilitation, but which is seldom passed on to the client for his use. It is because of this that the rehabilitation of many individuals breaks down. If the goal is *self-direction* among the options for living, then the individual client must be enabled to evaluate both the options and his relationship to the options. One of the reasons professionals frequently give for their paternalistic approach to their clients is that *the client has no basis on which to make a decision*. Does that justify the professional's making the decision? Is it ethical to do other than seek to provide the client with those tools which will allow him to participate creatively in the direction of his future?

Historically, the evaluation program grew out of the testing situation. Normative tests were developed or adapted early within the rehabilitative process to determine which client would be eligible for which service and which was *not feasible for service*. These tests were based upon restricted data, usually gathered from the white middle class of the society who had the opportunity for a good education. These tests created what Holtzman (1971) calls "restrictive creditionals for job entry" which were "an efficient means of building a technological society. They did so by exact-ing a heavy toll on those members of society who failed to con-form to the majority." The rehabilitation professionals soon saw that they must have other criteria on which to base the decisions for rehabilitating their *less than normal* clients, and there grew up a number of techniques for doing this. The most basic of which was the counselor-client interview in which the experienced counselor was able to elicit data. This interview plus data from medical, psychological, and aptitude testing were the only *helpful clues* with which the counselor had to work. Evaluation sprang from the necessity to have more data on which to make decisions about the rehabilitation process than was available from either medical information or aptitude testing. Many of the first evaluations were simply on-the-job tryouts or a trial by way of a simulation of the tasks which the individual might perform. In addition, the more resourceful the counselor, the more data was obtained. Job tryouts, placement in sheltered workshops, the creation of work samples, the development of knowledge about work and it's requirements, were all tools which the counselor either developed or sought sources to provide.

FACILITIES

Because the counselor was not able to do all of the evaluation himself, but needed assistance, a number of facilities were established which sought to provide the type of data which the client and the counselor needed. In addition, many existing rehabilitation facilities began to develop these services. As federal legislation was made available to provide the funding for these services, more and more facilities and rehabilitation centers got into the act. At all too many facilities, however, evaluation became *observation under the microscope*. All too frequently, individual clients were placed in different settings without any clear context for their being there. They were *observed by the evaluators*. The observations, mixed with equal parts of the evaluator's bias, were then surreptitiously slipped to the counselor without the evaluator having ever discussed his recommendations with the client. It was no wonder that many clients resented that type of evaluation. Evaluation, which was created out of a frustration with *cutting scores* and *job requirements*, developed its own built in limiting factors. Clients frequently were offered training programs which the counselor decided they needed to take and were dropped as *unmotivated* if the clients did not take advantage of the opportunity even if it did not answer their needs or relate to their self-image.

Evaluation should never be a professionally operated sifting process which relegates, like different textures of sand, different individuals to different levels. Evaluation is only valid as a process when it *prescribes possibilities* for every individual. In order to do that, it must be taken out of the realm of the vocational evaluator and must be thought of as a dynamic, in which every individual in the rehabilitation process, especially the client, plays a part.

THE ELEMENTS OF EVALUATION

Perhaps the elements of evaluation seem too simple to consider. However, one school of practice leaves out a major portion of evaluation, and that omission does not allow the dynamic to take place. The three steps of evaluation might be called (1) data gathering, (2) hypothesis formulation, and (3) evaluative interpretation.

The first step, *data gathering*, is what is often described when evaluation programs are discussed. When evaluation programs first began, they were set up primarily to gather and develop information about the client. There have been many ways developed to gather data regarding an individual and to help that individial gather the data himself. These include: (1) casework interview, (2) questionnaires, (3) psychological testing, (4) dexterity testing, (5) academic achievement testing, (6) counselor interviewing, (7) work samples, (8) interest inventories, (9) job tryouts, (10) situational assessments, (11) medical examination, and (12) physical and occupational therapy examinations. During this limited period of time, the client, the counselor, and other professionals working with the client are seeking to gather as much data as possible.

There are many dangers inherent in data gathering. One is the feeling that decisions cannot be made until all the data are in. Both the professional and the client must remind themselves that decisions are *always* made on insufficient information. Evidence of this feeling about evaluation is shown when the report is a thick document with relatively little prognosis but much information. Good evaluation programs put little emphasis upon the data gathering. It is rather just the necessary first step upon which is built the second and third steps. A second danger associated with data gathering in an evaluation program appears when the final evaluative decision is made only on the basis of the data gathered, rather than upon both the data and the results of the hypothesis formulations.

The second step in evaluation, and the one most frequently left out, is *hypothesis formulation and testing.* Very soon after data begins to come in, some initial hypotheses are formed. As an example, a hypothesis, formulated in an early interview with a client, might lead a counselor to direct a client to a rehabilitation facility for further evaluation in areas which the counselor and the client wish to experiment or test hypotheses. Likewise, within a facility evaluation program, it is essential that hypotheses begin to be developed early in the program, and that these hypotheses be tested. For instance, early data may indicate interest in a particular area, such as welding, and psychological and medical data would not be contraindicative. A hypothesis would then be formed that welding might be an appropriate vocation for the individual. This hypothesis could then be tested in simulated job or an actual job tryout.

Continued data gathering, of course, goes hand in hand with hypothesis formulation and testing and often will change the initial hypothesis. However, early hypothesis and testing usually will spark the individual to do his best as he can see the reason why he is performing certain tasks.

The third, and final, step in the evaluation process, is the *evaluative interpretation* of the data gathered and the hypothesis formulated. In one sense, of course, the final decision is still only a hypothesis, but if hypotheses have been formed and tested during the evaluation period it will be a far sounder basis for moving ahead with a particular rehabilitative step. Utilizing all information, the best advice, his own personal emotions, preferences and perception of his abilities, the client must here be trusted to make the *evaluation.* If the rehabilitation team has done its job, the client will have the data, the tools, and his response to the experimentation to make an adequate decision. While there is obviously great anxiety which could be associated with this approach and which accompanies the counselor's feeling that the client may not make a "right" decision, Olshansky (1969) counters, "of course, one might ask embarrassing questions about the frequency of counselors' wrong or poor decisions."

The function of the rehabilitation professional is never to evaluate. His function is to teach his clientele the steps of the evaluation process. His intention, as he sets about working with individuals, should be to structure his program so that the client experiences evaluation. It should be a process whereby the client evaluates himself, and then his use of the exaluation process is critiqued. Evaluation is experimental, and practice in evaluation is one of the primary functions of a rehabilitation facility.

Evaluation personnel who see their function as *judge* provide a paternalistic function, but are not utilizing evaluation as a part of the rehabilitation process. Observation type evaluation may well lead an individual into the correct type of job area, but cannot be credited with helping the client to choose among the options available for his life.

A MODEL FOR THE REHABILITATION PROCESS

A systems analysis of the rehabilitation process would probably show *evaluation* somewhere on a chart, with arrows coming from medical evaluation and arrows pointing out again to a number of options, including day care services, training, placement, etc. A typical illustration might show a series of stair steps leading toward the final goal of *rehabilitated client*. Evaluation would be written on the tread of one of the many steps toward reaching that goal. Processes, however, and especially the rehabilitation process, cannot be broken down into static pictures. The rehabilitation process is a series of dynamics or interrelated functions, most of which are carried on tangentially, and which affect each other to a great degree. The chart on this page lays out what might be a graphic interpretation of this moving process.

Good rehabilitation should begin at the time of the onset of disability. Medical teams who understand the need for rehabilitation make their recommendations as to the best ways to return their patient to maximum participation in a life of self-directed

THE REHABILITATION PROCESS

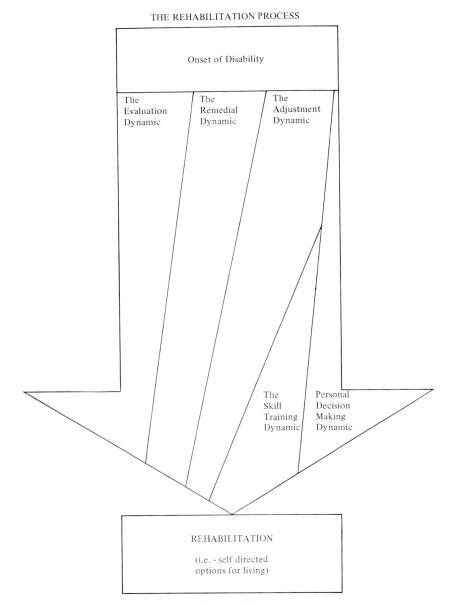

Figure II-1.

options. That is where evaluation begins. It is an evaluation by a medical team using the evaluation methodology. Remedies or practical plans are set in motion to relieve the problem which blocks the individual from achieving his full potential. Within the allied medical professions of occupational therapy and physical therapy, similar evaluations and remedial steps are taken quickly.

Most charitable hospitals employ social workers who evaluate other necessities such as the family situation, problems of financing for the individual and the family during the period of time in which the individual must recover. Their recommendations for the removal of those blocks are based upon their evaluation. When an individual is referred to a rehabilitation counselor, the process begins again with his evaluation and recommendations for moving past those problems which would keep his client from experiencing life at its best.

The adjustment process begins from the day that the client discovers that he has a disability, and continues throughout his rehabilitation process. He must adjust to his disability. He must adjust to his own new relationship to jobs, to activities in which he can no longer engage, to his physical relationships with other people, etc. Most rehabilitants must develop new skills. Even though they may return to their previous work, many must learn to utilize braces and wheelchairs. Those with mental problems may need to learn to function with tranquilizers, if they are going to return to any type of employment.

Personal decision making is the reflection of evaluation. It is the function of the rehabilitation process to teach the individual both to evaluate and to make decisions. In essence, it is the function of the rehabilitation process to enable a client to take responsibility for his life. The profesisonal in rehabilitation is out to break the dependency cycle. His function is to help his clientele to be able to *make it* without him.

If we were to look at the rehabilitation process, as ongoing and convergent dynamics, we might have a far more realistic view of evaluation. Ongoing evaluation is the key to successful rehabilitation.

SUMMARY

If evaluation is a dynamic of the rehabilitation process, then it does not hold that it is done by a *professional evaluator*. Every living person is constantly making evaluations of his and other peoples' situations. One evaluates a used car before he buys it, he evaluates his potential spouse before *popping the question,* he evaluates where he should go to work, where he should live, where he should shop, and he evaluates the decisions of many others with whom he comes in contact.

The ideal evaluation is done by the individual client with the help of staff members in the facility, of medical doctors, and of rehabilitation counselors. The role of the professional in evaluation is to enable the individual to make realistic decisions by imparting the use of evaluation to the client. That is easier said than done. Evaluation programs must begin the first day by offering choices among which the client must decide. The program must, on a daily basis, provide such opportunities through an increasingly harder series of choices.

If the client is not getting *evaluation training* in an evaluation program, then the counselor is not getting his money's worth, nor is the client justified for wasting his time. Rehabilitation facilities should specialize in teaching individuals, no matter how handicapped, to make responsible, independent decisions. That is to say, how to participate in self-determined options for living. Certainly, the options for one will not be the options for another. Programs which attempt to treat all handicapped or disadvantaged as a group are not providing rehabilitation. The benefit of rehabilitation is the fact that it is a discipline which is individually oriented.

Every individual is, or can be, an evaluator. He can decide about his life despite handicaps, limited abilities, or having been taught that he was not capable of decision making.

Steps of evaluation are simple. Most individuals can learn to gather data, form theories or hypotheses about that data, test their hypotheses, and finally make an evaluative decision regarding the data and their hypotheses experimentation. The professional must learn to allow the client to make his own decisions and to react positively to those decisions, even though the decisions may not be the same decision that the professional would have made were he making a paternalistic decision on behalf of the client.

REFERENCES

Holtzman, W. H.: The changing world of mental measurement and it's social significance. Presidential Address of Division V, presented at the Annual Meeting of the American Psychological Association, Miami Beach, Florida, Sept. 1970; printed in the *American Psychologist, 26* (6), June 1971.

Obermann, C. E.: *History of Vocational Rehabilitation in America,* Minneapolis, T. S. & Co., Inc., 1965.

Olshansky, S.: The client as decision maker, *VEWAA Bulletin, 2* (3), July-September, 1969.

Spencer, W.: unpublished remarks made at the Southwest Conference on the Rehabilitation of the Homebound, Houston, Texas, March 10, 1972.

III

THE COUNSELING IMPACT OF WORK EVALUATION

Richard D. Jones and Fred R. McFarlane

Philosophy of Work Evaluation

Evaluator Impact

Essential Characteristics of the Helper That Leads to Constructive
    Behavioral Change in the Clients

Ineffectiveness of Traditional Approaches

Effectiveness of the Nonprofessional

Systematic Training in Human Relations

Activity Counseling as a Catalyst for Effective Evaluation

References

SOME REHABILITATION PERSONNEL appear to believe that as work evaluators they have little or no therapeutic function in the treatment or rehabilitation process. These evaluators frequently have been told that they should leave the counseling to counselors, the teaching to teachers and the social working to the social workers. They have been taught to perceive their role as one of making assessments of the strengths and weaknesses of clients and then making a report to the counselor or social worker. They are taught to be objective, analytical, and precise. Indeed, if an evaluator is not all this, then how can he hope to be a professional?

PHILOSOPHY OF WORK EVALUATION

The philosophy of work evaluation evolved from a variety of settings and disciplines. Neff (1968) indicated that the industrialization of the United States and the need to predict vocational success led to the assessment of potential employees. The initial use of work evaluation was the assessment of abilities and skills and their relationship to existing industrial criteria. Dunn (1971) stated that *work evaluation* has as its objective the comprehensive description of a client's work behavior. This includes descriptions of needs and motivators as well as abilities. The scope of work evaluation has evolved into the identification of an individual's total work personality including vocational, social, and personal characteristics. Hoffman (1971) summarizes this philosophy by indicating that the evaluator must accomplish the following tasks: (1) observe behavior, (2) synthesize and analyze behavior, (3) interpret behavior, (4) vocationally diagnose, and (5) make recommendations.

Many authorities in the field see the function of the evaluator as primarily assessment. Take as an example the following commonly accepted definitions of work evaluation:

1. Process of assessing an individual's physical, mental and emotional abilities, limitations, tolerances, in order to predict his current and future employment potential and adjustment (Virginia Commonwealth University, 1966).
2. Process whereby an individual's attitudes, aptitudes, interests, abilities, capabilities, physical capabilities, and tolerance are evaluated by the utilization of standardized tests, job sampling, job trait, and other specialized techniques and procedures (Stout State University, 1967).
3. Assessment of vocational potential through the use of real or simulated work tasks (Rosenberg, 1967).
4. Specialized technology that utilizes aspects of work to evaluate the vocational strength and weakness of persons (Hoffman, 1969).
5. Assessment of client's strengths and weaknesses which utilizes work as the means, vehicle, or focal point of the evaluation (Roberts, 1970).

To accomplish these tasks, the evaluator must become involved with the client. He must be able to establish a meaningful relationship if he is to accomplish his goals. This relationship is the one thing that has received little emphasis in the area of work evaluation. It appears that the effects the evaluator has upon the evaluation and/or upon the client are not worthy of recognition. It is almost as if the counseling impact of work evaluation is of little, if any, importance.

EVALUATOR IMPACT

Assessment represents a needed and useful tool in the rehabilitation process. Yet, making assessments does not maximize the potency of the evaluator. The evaluator can become, and in many cases already is, a *helping person*. That is, a person who is able to provide a significant realtionship to a client where constructive change or gains may take place.

Gellman (1968) feels that the evaluation should be designed to "develop a treatment program." This implies that no treatment, or in counseling terms, no behavior change is attempted or occurs during the evaluation.

In the evaluation process does only evaluation occur? The evaluator has no therapeutic or counseling impact upon the client? If these things are true, it would seem to neutralize the research of Van der Veen (1965) and Jantzen and Anderson (1965). In his work with hospitalized schizophrenic patients, Van der Veen (1965) found that both patient and therapist influenced each other's behavior; while Jantzen and Anderson (1965) found that the patient's perception of his therapist greatly influenced his evaluations.

There are, however, some who have tried to recognize the therapeutic impact of the evaluator. At the Training Institute on Factors in Work Evaluation (Virginia Commonwealth University, 1966) it was recognized that evaluators often function in much the same role as counselors and that it was relatively impossible to separate evaluation and counseling into discrete categories.

Now if indeed it is difficult to separate counseling and evaluation, then does it not seem logical to assume that some *counseling* could and probably does occur during evaluation? Thus, it appears that the evaluation process and even the evaluator himself could have a significant influence on the client and that this influence subsequently affects the entire rehabilitation process. Jorgensen (1968) refers to this influence when he states that "the objective, authority-dominated relationship between an evaluator and the client minimizes interaction and mutual attractiveness." This minimization must, of course, affect the assessment and outcome of the evaluation process.

In another study concerning the impact that parents have on their children, Baldwin, Kalhoun, and Breese (1945) found that the parents who were warm and had a democratic attitude produced more emotionally secure and functional children than did parents with a cold, objective, authoritarian attitude.

There has been extensive research (Carkhuff and Berenson, 1967; Truax and Carkhuff, 1967) indicating that helping and human relationships may have constructive or destructive consequences. Any time a client is involved in any process, *something* of either a positive or negative nature may occur. How many times does anything occur to a client that is of a neutral nature? Even an activity such as a secretary gathering routine information leaves the client with some feelings or attitude toward the process, and indirectly toward rehabilitation. The secretary who is cold and routine in her manner will impart a different feeling from another secretary who is concerned and warm toward a client. If this is true for the activities and attitudes of a secretary, then it must be doubly so for the evaluator, who is, after all, more involved with clients than most secretaries.

The evaluator maintains a unique position within the rehabilitation structure. He is an authority figure but does not usually represent the threat to the client that a counselor may. It is for this very reason that what happens to the client in evaluation can be as impactful as that which happens in counseling. Because the evaluator is in a position of authority, he becomes what is referred to as a *significant other* in the rehabilitation process. The positive or negative impact of the evaluator is of extreme importance. The evaluator is not, as many have stated, only an objective observer, and those evaluators who try and function only in this capacity are selling themselves short.

Aspy's (1967) work with the differential effect of high and low functioning teachers upon student achievement points out

how the authority figure affects those under him. The study looked at the influence that the emotional climate of the classroom
had upon the cognitive growth of the students. The high or low
teacher was determined by three experienced raters using rating
scales of empathy, congruence, and positive regard. The results of
the study indicated that:

1. the procedure produced measures of a part of the classroom
   climate which related positively to student achievement.
2. higher conditions related positively to higher achievement.
3. lower conditions related to lower achievement.

Higher conditions seemed to enhance achievement while lower
conditions retarded it.

Another study on the effect of high and low level facilitative
functioning counselors upon counselors-in-training was done by
Carkhuff and Berenson (1967). They found that, in general, the
trainees of the high functioning counselor achieved a higher level
of functioning than did the trainees of the low functioning
counselor.

Flanders (1965) related warm teacher behavior to greater
work involvement and interest, increased creativity, greater self-
direction, more positive social-emotional adjustment and greater
group cohesiveness. Generalizing these findings to objective indexes of academic achievement, Christensen (1960) found teacher warmth to be related to vocabulary and arithmetic achievement of elementary school children.

From the evidence available (Eysenck, 1960; Levitt, 1957), it
is conclusive that counseling, therapy, evaluation, or for that
matter, almost any human interaction can be for the better or for
the worse. Just because a program has been set up to help clients,
it does not mean that the only outcome will be positive. If a program or person has the potential for helping, they also possess the
potential for being harmful. This aspect of the human atmosphere is a critical one for rehabilitation and evaluation.

It is the attitudes and feelings of the evaluator, rather than his
theoretical orientation, which are important. The procedures and
techniques that he uses are less important than his attitudes and
the way he relates to clients. It is also important to realize that

the client's perception of these attitudes and procedures is a crucial factor.

It is easily seen that the functioning level of the trainer or even the evaluator might have a significant effect upon the functioning level of the client. The scarcity of research in evaluation at this time has, however, neither proved nor disproved this contention. it does seem logical that the evaluator, and not the tests or procedures, is the most important element in work evaluation.

It is a very narrow concept of evaluation which, today, considers assessment to be the sole function of the evaluator. Increasingly, the evaluator is conceived of as an evaluator-counselor. The evaluator-counselor's function is expanding to include the treatment of individuals and groups within the work lab; treatment which leads hopefully, to improve performance as well as improved adjustment. Evaluation should not be designed to develop a treatment program but should be the beginning of the treatment program in itself. The counseling impact of work evaluation has been neglected in the past. The entire rehabilitation program has suffered because the evaluators were not used to their fullest professional potential.

The evaluation relationship is critical because it is the vehicle by which the evaluator-counselor becomes both model and agent for the client's change and gain. An effective relationship may become the modality through which clients may learn to function at higher levels in physical and emotional-interpersonal, as well as intellectual, spheres of functioning.

The purpose of a helping profession is to enhance personal development, promote psychological growth, and develop social maturity in clients.

ESSENTIAL CHARACTERISTICS OF THE HELPER THAT LEADS TO CONSTRUCTIVE BEHAVIORAL CHANGE IN THE CLIENTS

In spite of the multitude of theories and concepts available and the difficulties encountered in synthesizing the various approaches, it is evident that a certain amount of agreement is reached concerning which variables are considered helpful in producing constructive client change. Hobbs (1962), Strunk (1958), and Strupp (1960), eclectic theorists; psychoanalytically-oriented theorists such as Alexander (1948) and Schafer (1959); and client-centered theorists such as Jourard (1959), Rogers (1951, 1957) and Tyler (1961) stress the need to accurately and sensitively understand the client. They also feel that in addition to accurate and empathic understanding the communication of this deep understanding to the client is important. Truax and Carkhuff (1963) looked at many of the *schools* of psychotherapy and counseling and found that most stressed the importance of warmth and acceptance of the client by the helper and the genuineness of the relationship.

So far what has been described is a warm, understanding, empathic, accepting person who is able to relate in a meaningful way. This is the type of person that people seek out when they have a problem. Think for a moment about the type of person you like to talk to about any problems that you might have. It's a good bet that he will be high in dimensions that have already been discussed. Look around you and reflect on the helpers (evaluator-counselor, social workers, counselors, teachers, etc.) that you know. Now divide these people into two groups; ones you consider helpful and the others you consider less helpful. It should be clear that the people who establish helpful relationships have different characteristics from those people who establish relationships which are unhelpful.

Carl Rogers (1957) felt this way, when he tried to conceptualize and define the "necessary and sufficient condition of therapeutic personality change." This has been recognized as probably the first organized attempt to clearly define the conditions necessary to produce constructive client change. Included in these conditions are empathic understanding, unconditional positive regard (respect), genuineness, and the communication of these conditions. Rogers (1957) stated that if these conditions are present on a sustained basis, regardless of the situation or client, constructive change will occur. Each person is probably able to support Rogers and his conditions from their own experiences. Research support is also provided by Brammer and Shastrom (1964).

After Carl Rogers' initial work, many others have come forward to substantiate his findings. Representing the psychoanalytical viewpoint, Harper (1959) found that positive regard (respect), understanding and empathy were common elements of all forms of psychotherapy. Other researchers (Hobbs, 1962; Vance and Volsky, 1962) have emphasized the necessity of an open, honest relationship in which the client has an opportunity to understand and incorporate a plan of action. The value of the interpersonal relationship and the commonality of helpful elements are evident.

Empathy, respect, genuineness and *concreteness* are the conditions that have received the primary focus, but there are other conditions considered by many to be important for constructive change. Barrett and Lennard (1962), Dickerson (1965), Jourard (1964), and Martin (1967) have presented evidence supporting the value of the helper voluntarily revealing himself as a unique person to the client. Others have felt that openness and flexibility (Piaget, 1967), and confidence, spontaneity, and intensity (Barnard, 1967) are other dimensions important to positive client change. No one list or classification of helpful conditions will probably ever prove acceptable, but it seems that many of the differences between theories is mostly semantic.

It now seems possible to delineate certain conditions of the interpersonal process that training could focus on to produce more effective helpers including the evaluator-counselor.

An important thing to remember is that these conditions have not been generally taught in our professional training programs. Rogers (1965) indicated that these conditions are not constituted of technical knowledge or ideological sophistication. They are personal human qualities—something the helper experiences, not something he knows. The evaluator-counselor is expected to possess these personal human qualities to function in a helpful manner. The evaluator-counselor must encourage the client to relate on an open and honest basis. It is not the philosophy nor methods that affords the evaluator a medium for assessment. It is his presentation, his verbal and nonverbal modeling, that will facilitate the observable behavior. Rosenberg (1970) indicated that an evaluator should be:

an intelligent person who possesses a verbal and quantitive ability to think, reason, analyze, scrutinize, and solve problems with logic and perception. His interests should reveal a desire to work with people, but he should be scientific enough to consider and utilize the challenge of social behavior and individual differences. He should manifest an acceptance of self and the model aspects of his own behavior without *using* clients to satisfy his personal needs beyond the limits imposed by his professional role. He must have a tolerance for ambiguity and recognize the sources of frustration and be flexible enough to witness, understand and deal with all kinds of human behavior within his capacity. In addition, he must continually possess an intimate and up-to-date knowledge of occupations, local work conditions, employment opportunities, and future outlook of the labor market. A set of ethics and a sensitivity to people must be established to support the client's needs and goals, interpersonal relationships, client-evaluator relationships, and family relationships. Effective communication must be established with other professional disciplines to gain acceptance as a distinct profession (p. 31).

In addition to the above characteristics, Hiten (1970) added that the evaluator should:

possess character. He must posses those traits which make him agreeable and socially acceptable. He must possess those powers of leadership which will be accepted by his clients. He must be a living example of fairness. He must be obviously honest. He must deserve and have the confidence of his clients. He must know his standing with his clients at all times (p. 8).

The evaluator-counselor must possess basic knowledge about industry and the methodologies of work evaluation. Yet, as reflected in the above statements the most critical characteristics of a competent evaluator-counselor is his ability to relate to the client and other professionals.

In essence, the characteristics and human potential qualities which have been identified as integral components for constructive growth—empathy, respect, warmth, genuineness, and concreteness —are comparable to those characteristics expected of the counselor-evaluator. It is these human potential qualities that allow the evaluator-counselor to develop a relationship with the client directed toward constructive growth. Yet, the development of these qualities does not conform to the traditional training methods now employed.

INEFFECTIVENESS OF TRADITIONAL APPROACHES

There exists considerable evidence which suggests that traditional training approaches are not as effective as their advocates presume them to be (Truax, 1966). In fact, considerable evidence indicates that counseling and psychotherapy as typically practiced from a traditional orientation is not superior to an absence of treatment (Eysenck 1962; Levitt; 1957, 1963). In one research article, it was noted that about two-thirds of neurotic patients improve after traditional treatment regardless of the type of psychotherapy, but that the improvement rate is essentially the same for comparable patients who received no treatment at all (Frank, 1961).

Borendregt (1961) looked at a group of neurotic patients and compared them in terms of traditional psychotherapy, psychoanalysis, and no treatment. In the results no significant evidence was found that favored any of the three groups. In another large study, Brill and Beebe (1955) analyzed the results of treatment of war neurosis occuring during World War II. The general findings indicated that the nontreated group's improvement rate was slightly higher than the treated group's improvement rate.

It is not the purpose of this review of research to try and prove that all conventional approaches to helping are ineffective. There are many instances where traditionally-trained helpers have been shown to be effective (Baymurr and Patterson, 1960; Schlien, Mosak, and Driekurs, 1962) It is, however, logical to assume that in therapy as the research shows some clients are helped while some others are harmed. Eysenck (1961) and Levitt (1957, 1961) present evidence on the average ineffectiveness of therapists and counselors showing that the effects of an ineffective counselor nullifies the effect of an effective counselor. This supports the feeling of Traux and Carkhuff (1967) that counseling and psychotherapy can be for better or worse.

Another study showing the ineffective results of counseling were the ones conducted by Richardson (1960) and Goodstein and Crites (1961). These studies compared the effectiveness of traditional counseling with students to achieve academic improvement.

It seems that Eysenck (1960) and Levitt's (1957) data reach the conclusion that on the whole, traditional counseling and psychotherapy are no more effective than the absence of treatment.

EFFECTIVENESS OF THE NONPROFESSIONAL

One of the most important things to remember is that the core dimensions, which are the primary conditions of change in the helping relationship, are not the exclusive property of the professionally trained counselor or psychotherapist. As is evidenced from research (Carkhuff and Berenson, 1967) these therapeutic conditions are available from nonprofessionally trained helpers. In other words, a person need not be professionally trained in the traditional sense and does not have to bear the title of counselor or psychologist in order to be helpful to clients.

Some evidence from the traditional training approaches in academic settings show that on the dimensions related to constructive client gain or change, that the students deteriorate in function (Bergen and Soloman, 1963; Carkhuff, Piaget and Pierce, 1968). Other researchers (Bergen and Soloman, 1963) have found that the therapeutic effectiveness of graduate students in traditional training programs were negatively correlated with practicum grades and grade-point averages.

Carkhuff and Truax (1965) trained lay hospital personnel, primarily ward attendants as helpers. This represented an effort to determine the effectiveness of lay helpers as group counselors. In the treatment process the lay counselors were oriented only toward providing high levels of the core dimensions. Significant improvements were found on: (a) degree of psychological disturbance; (b) degree of constructive interpersonal and intrapersonal concern; and (c) degree of overall improvement over the past three months. The results demonstrate the effectiveness of lay group counseling after short-term training.

In his work with psychotic patients, Poser (1966) found that lay therapists achieved slightly better results than psychiatrists and psychiatric social workers in the provision of group therapy.

There are numerous other studies that illustrate similar results. It seems that the data shows (Truax, 1968) that the non-professional, not only can be effective in the area of interpersonal relationships, but even more so than the professional helper. There is now considerable evidence to support the contention that lay or nonprofessional persons can be trained to be effective in a helping relationship with other people (Broger, 1965; Truax and Carkhuff, 1965, 1967).

SYSTEMATIC TRAINING IN HUMAN RELATIONS

Carkhuff (1969) has made a strong case for the systematic training of professional and lay helpers in human relations and communications skills. His model of training has been applied widely to a large variety of populations in many clinical and non-clinical settings. He feels that a comprehensive program of training would consist of: (1) training in the interpersonal and other skills necessary to function effectively; (2) training in the methods of discerning and developing effective courses of action; and (3) training in the means and modalities necessary to implement the resultant programs.

It would be difficult to completely discuss the entire Systematic Human Relations Training Model. A review of the pertinent elements of this model are, however, important to both the evaluator-counselor and the evaluator-educator.

The basic concept of this facilitation training model[1] concerns the systematic development of the essential characteristics of the helper that leads to constructive behavioral change in clients. These essential characteristics or core dimensions are empathy, respect, concreteness, genuineness, self-disclosure, confrontation and immediacy.

Within a facilitation training program an environment which

---

[1]For a more detailed explanation of the Systematic Human Relations Training Model consult: Carkhuff, R.R.: *Helping and Human Relations, vol. I and II,* New York, Holt, Rinehart, and Winston, Inc., 1969.

is conducive to the development of these core dimensions must be established and maintained. Feedback on the present level of functioning and self-analysis are afforded each person. This self-analysis and helpful feedback promotes further exploration by each person of his own strengths and weaknesses. The goal of training is to have the person assume the responsibility of establishing a plan of action for improving his own level of helpfulness.

In order to improve this level of helpfulness it is important to become aware of the fundamental elements in a helpful relationship. These elements are (1) discrimination—the ability to listen accurately and identify the content and feeling of the verbal and nonverbal interaction between two persons; and (2) communication—the ability to convey a warm, accepting and genuine understanding of the discrimination, verbally and nonverbally, to the client. Of these two elements, both are of equal value, but one, discrimination must be present before effective communication can take place. A person can be an effective discriminator without necessarily being an effective communicator; but an effective communicator must be an effective discriminator. Many individuals understand what people, be they client, friend, or relative, say to them but are unable to put what they hear and/or feel into effective communication.

Discrimination ability is the key to becoming a fully functioning helpful person. Verbal and usually for that matter, nonverbal communication contain two messages; the first and usually easiest to recognize is the *content message*, the second and usually not so easily recognized is the *feeling message*. Look for a moment at the example below:

1. Client states: "Well, I've finished that work sample you gave me."

2. Client states: "Well, I finally finished that *damn* work sample you gave me."

It's easy to see that both statements contain basically the same content message, but the second statement reflects a different feeling on the part of the client. If the evaluator-counselor does not make an accurate discrimination or does not act on his discrimination, he might assign both of these clients an additional work sample without dealing with the hostility expressed. This would probably bias the outcome of the evaluation for the second client. This illustrates the importance of the discrimination process in evaluation.

A second definition of discrimination is the identification of what would be helpful for the counselor-evaluator to communication. It is this aspect where careful listening and accurate discrimination, is essential. For without accurate discrimination no effective communication can occur.

When training an individual to discriminate there is a necessity to emphasize reflective listening which requires no judgment, no moral assessment, and neutral understanding. It frees the client from being concerned about being judged and begins to build a base of understanding, respect, and warmth. The key to effective communication is acquiring the skill of effective listening. Effective listening can be interpreted as accurate discrimination or objective assessment. It is at this point where the evaluator possesses unique skills. The entire process of work evaluation has been designed as an assessment process which is the basis for helpful communication. The added dimension is the awareness by the evaluator-counselor for the two-fold meaning of all communication: (1) content and (2) feeling.

The second element fundamental to a helpful relationship is the process of communication. It is impossible to communicate effectively if there is an inability to discriminate. Yet, because an individual is an accurate discriminator does not automatically imply that he can communicate helpfully. View those individuals who are authority-oriented, manipulative, and opportunistic. These individuals are high accurate discriminators but utilize this ability for personal gain rather than mutual growth. Therefore, the role of helpful communication is to accurately discriminate the content and feeling of what was indicated, verbally and non-verbally, and respond with understanding, warmth, and genuineness.

This process of communication can be illustrated by the following diagram:

Communication ← Discrimination ← Evaluator-Counselor

The client sends a communication by both verbal interchange and nonverbal behavior. The receiver of this message is the evaluator-counselor. The evaluator-counselor discriminates the message and formulates an appropriate response. This response (message) is transmitted to the client and the process continues. The consequences of the evaluator-counselor's message dictates the consequence of the resultant interchange and begins to formulate the pattern of communication which will have a direct effect on outcome.

The following will provide an application of the communication diagram:

Client Message: "Well, I finally finished that *damn* work sample you gave me."

Evaluator-Counselor: receives the message

Discriminates: content—completion of the work sample

    feeling—anger and hostility

Communicates (choices); (1) "Why don't you wait at your table and I'll be over there in a moment."

    (2) You know the rules about cursing. What's wrong with you?"

    (3) "Something about that work sample really made you angry."

These three responses represent only a few of the possible ones available to the evaluator-counselor. There is no *right* statement to make. The *rightness* of any statement is determined by the discrimination of the client. If he feels that the evaluator-counselor understands and is trying to be helpful, then the statement becomes more *right* than when he feels that the evaluator-counselor does not understand him.

It is easy to see that the consequences of the three statements vary. The first statement may leave the client with a feeling that he is controlled by the evaluator-counselor and may result in decreased desire to continue the communication. The second response *attacks* the client and forces him to feel aggressive or defensive. The third response exhibits understanding and respect. It is these characteristics which are ingredients to building a relationship and fostering honesty and genuineness between the client and the evaluator-counselor.

Therefore, all three possible messages will have an impact on the relationship. It is the responsibility of the evaluator-counselor to model the type of impact that is desired. There is no one right or wrong way to respond to a client. Yet, every response elicits a behavior that affects the relationship. As can be valided by personal experience, negative stimuli (messages) generally receive negative responses. While positive stimuli (messages) generally receive positive responses.

The process of communication is a complex maze which is difficult to present in a didactic manner. All individuals are involved in communication and responses are usually based on unconscious discriminations. To train an individual in communication skills requires a conscious awareness of the interaction. Carkhuff (1971) indicates that helper (evaluator-counselor) understanding is the best means to helpee (client) understanding and helper action is the best means to helpee action. The helper provides the helpee with the experience of being understood and the experience of being with someone who acts upon his understanding. The helper also provides the helpee with a model to imitate just as the client imitates his parents: the helper is someone who understands and acts upon his understandings.

Therefore, helpful communication is composed of two basic elements: (1) accurate discrimination and (2) effective communication. If the evaluator-counselor is aware that in all interactions with clients, behavior change is shaped by the modeling of the evaluator-counselor and the client, then a concerted effort to communicate the core dimensions of understanding, warmth, respect, and genuineness can be exerted to allow the client to express and exhibit his true self.

ACTIVITY COUNCILING AS A CATALYST FOR EFFECTIVE EVALUATION

Activity counseling can be used as an effective medium for the evaluator-counselor. It combines the core dimensions of human potential qualities, communicative abilities, and work evaluation techniques into a meaningful activity which is more potent and effective than any single one of these elements.

The counseling impact of work evaluation does not necessitate the traditional concept of counseling which relies heavily on this verbal communication. Stranahan (1957) indicated that the use of activity counseling has served as the medium to bridge the gap between clients with a general distrust of authority and who lack acceptable verbal fluency. Activity counseling can be defined as:

> the use of any activity, such as a game or work, which is used as a medium through which helping relationships can be established, feelings can be expressed openly, and interaction can take place among the individuals involved (Blakeman, 1967).

When comparing this definition to work evaluation, there are explicit commonalities: (1) use of an activity to develop a relationship and (2) use of the activity to facilitate a *true picture* of the client. Activity counseling can be the vehicle through which work evaluation can develop a medium of mutual understanding and serve to build the base relationship between the evaluator-counselor and the client.

To place activity counseling in the context of work evaluation, consider the four approaches (activities) espoused by Neff (1968): (1) mental testing approach, (2) job analysis approach, (3) work sample approach, and (4) situational approach. The job tryout approach is also considered as an activity used in work evaluation. These five approaches form a basis for the activities employed in rehabilitation facilities. Hoffman (1968) indicated that an eclectic approach incorporating these activities afforded an opportunity for flexibility, integration, and more efficient services.

The use of these approaches in work evaluation can serve as

the vehicle to client growth. As discussed previously, the inter-action between the evaluator-counselor and the client is the critical variable in the evaluation process. When utilizing these ap-proaches, there seems to be three critical questions which must be answered: (1) does the client gain an understanding of his prob-lems, (2) can the client gain an understanding of his personal assets and limitations, and (3) what action can be initiated to enable the client to act on these understanding? Use of the com-mon approaches to work evaluation can serve as the activity which will enable the client to answer these questions and initi-ate constructive growth. The activity is of secondary concern when resolving these questions. The primary concern is the rela-tionship which develops between the evaluator-counselor and the client, through involvement in an activity. For it is through this relationship that meaningful client change will occur.

The following illustration will provide a realization of the use of these approaches in activity counseling.

Situation One: Administration of an interest test. The client may be apprehensive about completing the test. When the eval-uator-counselor administers the test he can:

(1) administer the test with no explanation except how to mark the responses;

(2) hand the test to the client with no feeling and a lack of expression; or

(3) acknowledge the client's apprehension, explain the ra-tionale of the test, and offer his assistance within the param-eters of the test.

The first and second alternatives may leave the client with the feeling of being an object. The third alternative attempts to ac-knowledge his feelings and concern while completing the evalua-tion.

This approach to evaluation is a realistic and ideal situation. For the evaluator-counselor has the opportunity to interact with the client on a verbal and performance basis. The necessity for client involvement in these tasks or activities is a precusor to ob-tain a realistic, honest, and open evaluation.

The therapeutic processes which apply to activity counseling are based on the involvement of the client in real problems. Ramsey (1964) indicated that through the use of a medium, such as work evaluation, activity counseling establishes a helping relationship where feelings can be expressed openly, interaction can take place, and where the client receives a feeling of satisfaction and well-being regardless of the success of the effort. It appears that since the same therapeutic processes apply, work evaluation is in effect, or at least should be, a form of activity counseling.

Shannon and Snortuni (1965) found that through such activities as work evaluation, group interaction provided a medium by which the client could test out their verbal insights learned from counseling. They concluded that client's involvement in a work activity done in a group setting seems to open the door for counseling. In a study dealing with disturbed children's attitudes and adjustment, Mustakas (1955) found that through activity counseling, disturbed children have adjusted their attitudes closer to the so-called *well-adjusted.*

It appears, however, that activity counseling also can have a generalizing effect. This effect has been found to exist by Lapidakins (1963) who stated that the use of occupational therapists and other activity staff in a residential treatment center for children has not only increased their effectiveness as professional staff members, but has also improved the total quality of therapeutic programming.

The core of activity counseling is the development of an atmosphere which is supportive, open, and realistic. One, in which the client feels free to express true feelings and function naturally in the setting. Without this, the data and observations compiled by the evaluator-counselor does not yield a true picture of the client.

An effective evaluator-counselor has the potential to become the most important element in the rehabilitation process. An effective evaluator-counselor, using activity counseling as a medium of work evaluation, should be able to establish a meaningful basis for constructive change in client behavior, attitude, and emotional maturity. Activity counseling brings together the core dimensions of Rogers, the discrimination and communication of Carkhuff, and the approaches of work evaluation defined by Neff into a meaningful and growth-producing relationship between the evaluator-counselor and the client.

REFERENCES

Alexander, F.: *Fundamentals of Psychoanalysis.* New York, W.A. Norton, 1948.

Aspy, D. and Hadock, W.: The effects of high and low functioning teachers upon student performance. Unpublished manuscript, University of Florida, 1967.

Baldwin, A. L., Kalhorn, J. I. and Breese, F. H.: Patterns of parent behavior. *Psychological Monograph, 268*(58):1-75, 1945.

Barnard, W. M.: Counselor spontaneity, confidence, and intensity. In R. R. Carkhuff (Ed.): *The Counselor's Contribution to Facilitative Processes.* Urbana, Parkinson, 1967, Ch. 11.

Barrett-Lennard, G. T.: Dimensions of the client's experience of his therapist associated with personality change. *Genetic Psychology Monograph, 76* (43), 1962.

Baymurr, F. B. and Patterson, C. H.: A comparison of three methods of assisting underachieving high school students. *Journal of Counseling Psychology, 7*:83-89, 1960.

Bergin, A. E. and Soloman, S.: Personality and performance correlates of empathic understanding in psychotherapy. Paper read at APA, Philadelphia, September, 1963.

Betz, B. J. and Whitehorn, J. C.: The relationship of the therapist to the outcome of therapy in schizophrenia. *Psychiatric Research Reports #5. Research Techniques in schizophrenia.* Washington, D.C. American Psychiatric Association, 1956, pp. 89-117.

Blakeman, J. D.: The effects of activity group counseling on the self-evaluation and classroom behavior of adolescent behavior problem boys. Unpublished doctoral dissertation, University of Georgia, 1967.

Brager, G.: The indigenous worker: A new approach to the social work technician. *Social Work, 10*(2): 33-40, 1965.

Brammer, C. M. and Shostrom, E. L.: *Therapeutic Psychology: Fundamentals of Counseling and Psychotherapy.* Englewood Cliffs, Prentice-Hall, 1964.

Brill, N. Q. and Beebe, G. N.: A follow-up study of war neuroses. *VA Medical Monograph,* Washington, D.C. Veteran's Administration, 1955.

Button, W. H., Kimberly, J. R., Lobow, B. K., and Kimberly, R. P.: *A Conceptual Framework for the Analysis of Work Behavior in Sheltered Workshops.* Ithaca,: Cornell Region II Rehabilitation Research Institute.

Carkhuff, R. R. and Berenson, B. C.: *Beyond Counseling and Therapy.* New York, Holt, Rinehart, and Winston, 1967.

Carkhuff, R. R., Piaget, G. and Pierce, R.: The development skills in interpersonal functioning. *Counselor Education and Supervision, 7:*102-106, 1968.

Carkhuff, R. R.: *Helping and Human Relations: A Primer for lay and Professional helpers,* vol. I and II, New York, Holt, Rinehart, and Winston, 1969.

Carkhuff, R. R.: Training as Necessary Precondition of education: The development and generalization of a systematic resource training model. *Journal of Research and Development in Education, 4*(2):3-16, 1971.

Christensen, C. M.: Relationships between pupil achievement, pupil affect-need, teacher warmth and teacher permissiveness. *Journal of Educational Psychology,* 1960, 51: 169-174, 1960.

Cowden, J. E. and Pacht, A. R.: Relationship of selected psychosocial variables to prognostic judgments. *Journal of Consulting and Clinical Psychology, 33*(27):254-256, 1969.

Dickinson, W. A.: Therapist self-disclosure as a variable in psychotherapeutic process and outcome. Doctoral dissertation, University of Kentucky, 1965.

Dunn, D. J.: Work adjustment, work evaluation, and employability. *Vocational Evaluation and Work Adjustment Bulletin, 4*(2):11-16, 1971.

Eysenck, H. J. (Ed.): *Behavior Therapy and the Neuroses.* New York, Pergamon Press, 1960.

Eysenck, H. J. (Ed.): *Behavior Therapy and Neuroses.* New York, Pergamon Press, 1961.

Eysenck, H. J. (Ed.): *Handbook of Abnormal Psychology,* Palo Alto,, Annual Reviews Inc., 1967.

Fiedler, F. E.: Quantative studies in the role of therapists feelings toward the patients. In Mowrer, O. H. (Ed.): *Psychotherapy: Theory and Research.* New York, Ronald Press, 1953, Ch. 12.

Flanders, N. A.: Teacher Influence, Pupil Attitudes and Achievement. Washington, *Cooperative Research Monograph,* No. 12, U.S. Department of Health, Education and Welfare, 1965.

Frank, J. D.: *Persuasion and Healing.* Baltimore, John Hopkins Press, 1961.

Gellman, W.: The principles of vocational evaluation. *Rehabilitation Literature, 29*(4):98-102, 1968.

Goodstein, L. D. and Crites, J. O.: Brief counseling with poor college risks. *Journal of Counseling Psychology, 8:*318-321, 1961.

Harper, L. A.: *Psychoanalysis and Psychotherapy.* Englewood Cliffs, Prentice Hall, 1959.

Heine, R. W.: A comparison of patient reports on psychotherapeutic experience with psychoanalytic, non-directive, and Adlerian therapists. Doctoral Dissertion, University of Chicago, 1950.

Hiten, H.: *Viewpoint on Vocational Evaluation.* Talladega, Department of Adult Blind and Deaf, 1970.

Hobbs, N.: Sources of gain in psychotherapy. *American Psychologist, 17:*8-12, 1962.

Hoffman, P. R.: *Work Evaluation.* Menomonie, Stout State University, Institute for Vocational Rehabilitation, 1968.

Hoffman, P. R.: Work evaluation: The child is growing up. Paper presented at the Georgia Rehabilitation Association Annual Conference, Atlanta, December 2, 1971.

Jantzen, A. and Anderson, H. C.: Patient evaluation of occupational therapy programs. *American Journal of Occupational Therapy, 19:*19-22, 1965.

Jaques, M. E.: Critical Counseling Behavior in Rehabilitation Settings. Iowa City, State University of Iowa, College of Education, 1959.

Jones, R. D.: Vocational evaluation as activity counseling. *Vocational Evaluation and Work Adjustment Bulletin, 4*(1):11-15, 1971.

Jorgensen, G. Q.: *Interpersonal Relationships: Factors in Job Placement.* Salt Lake City, University of Utah, Department of Educational Psychology, 1968.

Jourard, S.: I-thou realtionship versus manipulation in counseling & psychotherapy. *Journal of Individual Psychology, 13:*174, 1959.

Jourard, S.: *The Transparent Self.* New York, Van Nostrand, 1964.

Levitt, E. E.: The results of psychotherapy with children. *Journal of Consulting Psychology, 21:*189-196, 1957.

Lopidakins, J. E.: Activity therapy program: For emotionally disturbed children. *American Journal of Occupational Therapy, 17:*22-25, 1963.

McGowan, J. F. and Porter, T. L.: *An Introduction to Employment Service Counseling.* Missouri, University of Missouri, 1964.

Martin, J. C.: The communication of genuineness: Counselor self-disclosure. In R. R. Carkhuff (Ed.): *The Counselor's Contribution to Facilitative Processes.* Urbana, Parkinson, 1967, Ch. 3.

Mustakas, C. E.: The frequency and intensity of negative attitudes expressed in play therapy: A comparison of well-adjusted and disturbed young children. *Journal of Genetic Psychology, 86:*309-325, 1955.

Neff, W. S.: *Work and Human Behavior.* New York, Atherton Press, 1968.

Piaget, G.: Openness and flexibility. In R. R. Carkhuff (Ed.): *The Counselor's Contribution to Facilitative Processes.* Urbana, Parkinson, 1967.

Poser, E. G.: The effect of therapist training on group therapeutic outcome. *Journal of Consulting Psychology, 30*(4):283-389, 1966.

Ramsey, G. W.: Sociotherapeutic camping for the mentally ill. *Journal of Social Work, 9:*45-53, 1964.

Richardson, L. H.: Counseling and ambitious mediocre student. *Journal of Counseling Psychology, 7:*265-268, 1960.

Roberts, C. L.: Definitions, objectives, and goals in work evaluation. *Journal of Rehabilitation. 36*(1): 12-15, 1970.

Rogers, C. R.: *Client-Centered Therapy.* Cambridge, Riverside Press, 1951.

Rogers, C. R.: The necessary and sufficient conditions of therapeutic personality change. *Journal of Consulting Psychology, 22:*95-103, 1957.

Rogers, C. R.: The characteristics of a helping relationship, *Personnel and Guidance Journal, 37*:6-16, 1958.

Rogers, C. R.: The interpersonal realtionship: The core of guidance. In *Guidance: An Examination,* Harcourt, Brace and World, 1965.

Rosenberg, B.: *The Job Sample in Vocational Evaluation* (RD 561), Rehabilitation Services Administration, 1967.

Schafer, R.: Generative empathy in the treatment situation. *Psychoanalytic Quarterly, 28*:342, 1959.

Seeman, J.: Counselor judgments of therapeutic process and outcome. In Rogers, C. R. and Pymond, R. F. (Eds.): *Psychotherapy and Personality Change.* Chicago, University of Chicago Press, 1954, Chap. 7.

Shannon, P. D. and Snortuni, J. R.: An activity group's role in intensive psychotherapy. *American Journal of Occupational Therapy, 19*:344-347, 1965.

Spergel, P.: Vocational evaluation: Research on implications for maximizing human potential, *American Journal of Occupational Therapy, 19*:21-23.

Stout State University: *Vocational Evaluation Curriculum Development Workshop.* Memomonic, 1965.

Strupp, H. H.: Nature of psychotherapists' contribution to the treatment process. *Archives of General Psychiatry. 1960, 3*:219-231, 1960.

Strunk, O., Jr.: Empathy: A review of theory and research. *Psychology Newsletter, 9:* 57, 1958.

Truax, C. B. and Carkhuff, R. R.: The necessary stimulus complex in the therapeutic process: Toward a resolution of the tough- and tender-minded views of counseling and psychotherapy. Mimeograph, University of Kentucky, 1963.

Truax, C. B.: *Counseling and Psychotherapy: Process and Outcome.* Arkansas Rehabilitation Research and Training Center, University of Arkansas, 1966, p. 1.

Truax, C. B. and Carkhuff, R. R.: *Toward Effective Counseling and Psychotherapy: Training and Practice.* Chicago, Aldine, 1967.

Tyler, L. E.: *The Work of the Counselor* 2nd Ed. New York, Appleton-Century-Crafts, 1961.

Vance, F. L. and Volsky, T. C.: Counseling and Psychotherapy: Split personality of siamese twins? *American Psychologist, 17*:565-570, 1962.

Van der Veen, F.: Effects of the therapist and the patient on each other's therapeutic behavior. *Journal of Consulting Psychology, 1965, 29*:19-26, 1965.

Virginia Commonwealth University: *Proceedings of A Training Institute on Factors in Work Evaluation.* Richmond, Author, 1966.

PART TWO

VOCATIONAL EVALUATION
AND PROFESSIONALISM

The Vocational Evaluation and Work Adjustment Association Looks to the Future

Evaluating the Evaluator

The Materials Development Center: A National Resource for Materials on Work Evaluation and Adjustment

IV

THE VOCATIONAL EVALUATION AND WORK ADJUSTMENT ASSOCIATION LOOKS TO THE FUTURE

ROBERT H. COUCH

Introduction

The Development of Service Programs to Deal with Problems of
People

The Future

Enabling Legislation

The Future

Divergent Settings

The Future

Educational and Experiential Backgrounds of Practitioners

The Future

Available and Preferred Techniques

The Future

Training Programs

The Future

The Future

References

INTRODUCTION

THE VOCATIONAL EVALUATION and Work Adjustment Association (VEWAA) is a professional division of the National Rehabilitation Association. The expressed purpose of the association is to improve and advance the field of vocational evaluation and

65

work adjustment. The specific direction to be taken by the association in meeting these objectives has not yet been fully determined, and any prognostic glimpse into the future is mostly conjecture. Those now studying evaluation and adjustment services will, no doubt, be afforded an opportunity to fully participate in determining the course of the profession. Therefore, a student's prognostication regarding the future may well equal or surpass those offered by any contributor to this text. It may be helpful however, if the student examines the critical issues now facing the profession and explores the historical antecedents which continue to impinge upon the practices of vocational evaluation and work adjustment.

The major historical antecedents may be divided roughly and arbitrarily into six areas which have singly and by various interactions provided the thrust and direction of the field. These areas are: (1) program development via practical problem solving methods; (2) enabling legislation; (3) divergent settings; (4) varied educational and experiential backgrounds of practitioners; (5) available and preferred techniques; and (6) training and education programs. Each of these factors will be examined briefly in an effort to demonstrate their impact on the current state of the art and to illustrate their continuing influence upon the course of the profession.

THE DEVELOPMENT OF SERVICE PROGRAMS TO DEAL WITH PROBLEMS OF PEOPLE

The seeds of today's vocational evaluation and work adjustment service programs are many and diverse and may be found scattered throughout the history of numerous professions, within the changing values of society, and in the archives of any humanitarian, economic, religious or social movement. We consistently find various movements attacking a social problem in seemingly logical ways then discovering obstacles, in the form of new problems, which must be dealt with before the original objectives can be achieved. Evaluation and adjustment services apparently have emerged as a means to cope with and avoid such obstacles to originally conceived objectives. Thus, evaluation and adjustment services evolved as a method of assisting helping professionals to solve practical problems.

Many organized rehabilitative type programs began with the expressed purpose of providing vocational skills for the handicapped and thereby preparing their charges for employment and a better life. Those organizing such vocational training programs often were dismayed to find that skill training alone was not sufficient to prepare their students or clients to enter the labor market. In 1791, Henry Danette opened a school for the indigent blind in Liverpool, England. His objective was to train the blind vocationally so they might be ". . . comfortable in themselves and useful to the country." Danette's goals were sometimes obstructed by an extraneous variable which continues to plague social service programs. He explained that those ". . . long inured by habits of idleness and dissipation soon become disgusted with useful industry" (Obermann, 1965). Here, inadequate work habits were identified as obstacles to the training and employment objectives. Eventually, practitioners responded to such real problems by instigating various types of adjustment services. For instance, by 1799, London's school for the indigent blind had added the teaching of work habits to its list of goals (Obermann, 1965).

A similar problem solving approach can be seen in the early work of Samuel Howe at the first rehabilitation type workshop in this country. Begun in Boston as the New England Asylum for the Blind in 1829, the original objectives of education, vocational training, and subsequent competitive employment were often impeded by employer resistance to blind workers and a poor labor market in general. In facing these realistic problems, Howe developed the additional services necessary to achieve his original objective. He instigated a placement bureau to facilitate community placement and established a small industry or workshop which offered jobs to those not otherwise employed (Sink, 1970).

Although little progress has been made in conceptualizing the work adjustment process (Ross and Brandon, 1971), current development of adjustment services continues to reflect the search for answers to practical problems interfering with various program objectives. Evidence of this problem awareness may be seen at all levels and appears to focus on a variety of concerns. (Gellman (1961) has noted that improvements in physical and psychological rehabilitation resulted in an influx of clients who, though physically capable of working are not able to function in a job. Campbell and O'Toole (1970) suggested that traditional rehabilitation services were inadequate for the severely disabled who had been labeled unemployable and untrainable. Evaluators and rehabilitation counselors associated with the Gadsden (Alabama) Rehabilitation Center faced similar difficulties in 1960 with certain "problem clients" whose emotional difficulties prohibited successful entry into the labor market. This group observed that many of these *problem clients* responded favorably to a structured milieu during the brief span of the evaluation program and hypothesized that a longer range program with these clients in a similarly structured environment might provide a possible solution (Alabama School of Trades, The Rehabilitation Center, 1965). Sink, Couch, and Anderson (1968) suggested that parents of handicapped children and special interest groups involved at an intense emotional level often instigated the drive to create a rehabilitation facility. These groups were hopeful that services of a facility might offer a solution to their personally perceived problems.

As helping agencies have expanded to serve a wider client population, they too have faced problems not amenable to traditional techniques. Dunn and Hoffman (1971) editorialized that as rehabilitation services to the severely disabled, the mentally retarded, and disadvantaged have become available, a vast array of services designed essentially to develop basic employability have become necessary to attain the rehabilitation objective. Lovell (1970) reports a severe self-appraisal by the United States Training and Employment Service. This has led to new adjustment service type programs that have begun to respond to the needs of those whose potential for employment was neglected in previous screening processes. Davis (1970) discovered that new enrollees in Manpower programs were not equipped to be competitive in the world of work. Motivation and attitudes often were found to be the opposite of employer demands and Manpower staffs initially were hard pressed to ameliorate such problems.

In each of these examples from both antiquity and the present, adjustment services appeared to offer one possible solution to the problems impeding attainment of the habilitation goal. The response to these problems via adjustment service programs likewise has taken different forms. Gellman (1961) reports that the first vocational adjustment shop dates back to 1951 at Chicago's Jewish Vocational Service Center, where work experience and counseling were used to develop appropriate work behavior and attitudes. This format was followed and expanded in developing service programs in other rehabilitation facilities. Manpower introduced their Human Resources Development concept in 1966, and committed themselves to assist all who wanted to work regardless of employment barriers. This concept called for services such as counseling, training, orientation to the world of work, and other techniques necessary for improving employability of the disadvantaged. The Work Incentive (WIN) and Concentrated Employment (CEP) Programs are examples of this concept in action (Lovell, 1970).

Vocational Evaluation emerged in a similar manner. Dissatisfaction with available techniques for assessment and prediction was rampant and legislation was encouraging even more services to a wider, more severely handicapped client population. These developments coupled with a sincere desire on the part of the rehabilitation worker to better serve those with whom he worked, prompted both agencies and individual practitioners to push for better assessment and treatment services. Utilization of the problems solving process to meet these challenges can be seen clearly in the development of the TOWER (Testing, Orientation, and Work Evaluation in Rehabilitation) work samples. Rosenberg (1969) traces the history of the Institute for Crippled and Disabled's (I.C.D.) experience in selecting training areas for handicapped clients. Initially, clients toured the facility and simply selected a training area following their tour. Instructors then provided a trial training period and if the area proved unsuitable, the client moved to another training area. This tryout procedure was not unlike one utilized at the Pontvillez School in Belgium during World War I (Bregman, 1970). At I.C.D., this procedure proved too time-consuming, so the search for better assessment techniques continued. At about the same time, the Institute was experiencing difficulties with a group of clients exhibiting neuro-muscular conditions. Response to these needs led to the development of a special program utilizing handicrafts in exposing clients to tools used in many types of occupations. Meeting some success in this endeavor, the Institute launched, in 1936, another special program called the Guidance Class, which employed samples of occupations drawn from the trades training areas within the facility. Continued development of these work samples led to their publication as the TOWER SYSTEM in 1958 (Rosenberg, 1969).

The limitations of psychometric tests in assessing the handicapped and disadvantaged have been discussed at length (Goldman, 1970; Doppelt and Bennett, 1970; Neff, 1970). Neff (1966) summarizes the limitations by concluding that "psychometric tests become entirely inappropriate when our problem is to appraise the work potential of an ex-mental patient with long-term hospitalization, a borderline mental retardate with no work history or a socially and culturally disadvantaged school dropout." Other techniques proved equally disappointing. Nadolsky (1971) notes that rehabilitation personnel recognized the inherent limitations of traditional vocational assessment methodology several decades ago, and began gradually to incorporate more realism into vocational assessment techniques. This practical, realistic approach developed into today's vocational evaluation programs within facilities. The approach has become a major and essential diagnostic process in rehabilitation.

Evidence abounds which demonstrates the continuing efforts to seek better solutions to the problems of assessment. Social and Rehabilitation Services (SRS) and the Manpower Administration have provided the impetus for further development through various research, development, demonstration and training grants. Manpower has supported construction of *The Nonreading Aptitude Test Battery* (NATB) intended to measure occupational aptitudes of the disadvantages. They also supported the development of the Philadelphia Jewish Employment and Vocational Service Work Sample System for clients not adequately assessed by other means (Lovell, 1970). S.R.S. supported the development of the TOWER SYSTEM, various other research and demonstration projects and continues to provide training opportunities for evaluation and adjustment personnel.

THE FUTURE

There is no reason to believe that this type responsiveness will be curtailed in the future of evaluation and adjustment services and within the profession. In fact, even more responsiveness is indicated. With cultural changes, objectives may well change. Regardless of the agreed-upon objectives, we may rest assured that there will be obstacles impeding the attainment of our objectives. Whether in the form of a single obstacle facing the practitioner and an individual client or on a universal level of nations attacking vast social problems, we may continue to anticipate the influence of realistic practical problems upon the field of vocational evaluation and work adjustment. The course of the profession will be guided by the choice of solutions to such problems.

VEWAA then, must address itself to the practical problems facing man and society, as well as those of its membership. Gellman (1970) suggests that in the future, vocational evaluation and adjustment services will be used for most disemployed persons. Hoffman (1969b) concurs by relating that there are large numbers of young people who are neither disadvantaged nor handicapped in high school and vocational schools who truly do not know what they want to pursue in life. One group of professionals (Pruitt, 1970d) predicts that services will be made available to those already employed. These individuals include the working poor and their problem may call for assistance in finding avenues to upgrade themselves vocationally and otherwise.

The employment objective, long accepted as a value in rehabilitation and Manpower programs is now being questioned (Pruitt and Longfellow, 1970). It has been predicted that only half the population will be required to produce the necessary goods and services for this country in the future. In this light, evaluation and adjustment services may well change to concentrate on avocational pursuits. Rosenberg (1969) believes the evaluation process has potential application in the avocational realm.

Those who choose not to work, are unable to work, retiring from work, or who are not needed for work may be assisted in finding personally meaningful activities in life.

VEWAA members are already directly or indirectly involved with today's major social problems of crime, drug abuse, pollution, urban decay, war, and health. Inmates, addicts, the war-wounded, the physically and mentally disabled and human products of disintegrating environments may be found in today's rehabilitation and Manpower programs. More intensified efforts to better assist these individuals must be made and really workable solutions to their problems must be found. It is conceivable that the evaluation and adjustment process might one day be generalized and applied to the rehabilitation of environments.

Within the association, real and practical problems exist and must be faced. The current membership is composed largely of rehabilitation based personnel, yet there are growing numbers in Manpower, corrections, and schools whose work is primarily of an evaluative and adjusting nature. Therefore, the association must broaden its base of membership (Nadolsky, 1971a). Members continue to suffer from the lack of understanding of the evaluation and adjustment process by authority figures, related professions, and governmental bodies. Too often, the practitioner is perceived simply as a technician who gives routine tests. The association must demonstrate that the primary work of our profession is clinical in nature. These clinical judgments are sensitive and critical and must be made on a par with those of others in the allied health field (Smith, 1969).

In summary, the association must be responsive to the problems of those it serves. The individuals receiving help, the membership, and society must be afforded an avenue of feedback into our system that is capable of and permitted to change the system (Walker, 1970; Couch, 1971).

ENABLING LEGISLATION

Legislation relating to the handicapped and disadvantaged not only represents a form of problem solving, but reflects the changing values of society. So heavy is the impact of legislation upon the field of vocational evaluation and work adjustment that the uninformed might surmise that the Congress had actually legislated a profession. History shows us however, that legislation is generally a response to the demands of society and to the practical problems faced by that society. From earliest colonial days, we find that the colonists somewhat reluctantly looked after their own disadvantaged and handicapped with poor laws similar to those found in England. Communities were careful however, to protect themselves from nonproductive outsiders who might possibly become dependent burdens on a community's resources. Local laws with such explicit titles as "for the prevention of vagabonds and for the prevention of poor persons," left the distitute and disabled with only the alternative of begging as a means of livelihood (Obermann, 1965). In the intervening years, religious, social and economic forces altered society's attitude toward the handicapped, the disadvantaged, and the individual. The industrial revolution, education for the masses, war, and an increasing concern for individual rights each pressed hard to reshape our society's values (Nadolsky, 1971; Glanz, 1964). Gradually, religious, private, and governmental organizations took action reflecting these changing values.

Prior to World War I, assistance to the country's war veterans was limited to various pension plans. In 1918, the Soldier Rehabilitation Act was passed. This act provided a program of vocational rehabilitation for disabled World War I veterans. In 1920, a similar bill was passed providing vocational rehabilitation for disabled civilians and President Woodrow Wilson signed Public Law 236 on June 2, 1920. Initially limited to vocational training for the physically disabled, the initial program represented only a temporary congressional commitment. Public Law 113, the Vocational Rehabilitation Act Amendments of 1943, led to profound changes in the program. The mentally ill and mentally retarded were no longer excluded from services and physical restoration was permitted for the first time. The rehabilitation worker could indeed provide *any* service necessary to render a handicapped individual fit to engage in remunerative employment. One innovation growing from the freedom permitted by the law was the multidiscipline clinic. Initiated in Connecticut during World War II, these rehabilitation clinics were staffed by physicians, psychologists, rehabilitation workers, educators and employment service personnel. These professionals cooperatively interviewed and evaluated the disabled person. Following the evaluation, an attempt was made to place these disabled clients directly into appropriate war production jobs (Obermann, 1965).

Nineteen fifty-four marked another legislative breakthrough with particular relevance for evaluation and adjustment services. The Medical Facilities Survey and Construction Act (Hill-Burton) authorized the construction of comprehensive rehabilitation facilities. This act carried the stipulation that facilities constructed under the act must include vocational evaluation services. The Vocational Rehabilitation Act Amendments of 1954 (Public Law 565) included several provisions with far-reaching implications for evaluation and adjustment services. In addition to an overall increase in the federal-state program, the 1954 amendments provided financial assistance for expanding and remodeling buildings to make them suitable for facilities and workshops. Special project grants encouraged states to experiment with innovative approaches to rehabilitation. Many of these focused on evaluation and adjustment services (Newman, 1970). Support was also given for the establishment of various educational and training programs which would prepare professionals to work with the handicapped. Many evaluators, counselors, and related rehabilitation personnel continue to receive training through this provision. The 1965 amendments provided further expansion. Initial construction of rehabilitation facilities was permitted, and extended evaluation services were initiated (Hardy and Cull, 1969).

The nation's concern for the poor in the decade of the sixties resulted in a proliferation of programs designed to attack the problems of those in poverty. Such programs were mainly an outgrowth of the Economic Opportunity Act of 1964. Many of these programs continue today. Some of the most notable of these are currently under the auspices of the Manpower Administration within the Department of Labor. In refining these programs, Manpower has adopted evaluation and adjustment services in new and innovative ways (Lovell, 1970 and Davis, 1970). Rehabilitation, too, has addressed itself to the problems of the poor. Section 15 of the Vocational Rehabilitation Amendments of 1968, provides for vocational evaluation and adjustment services for the disadvantaged. Full implementation and support of this section could possibly catapult evaluation and adjustment services into the major service activity of vocational rehabilitation. This cogent possibility merits special consideration in light of the prediction that medicare and medicaid may supplant many physical restoration services previously provided by vocational rehabilitation.

THE FUTURE

These are only representative of the various federal legislative acts which have affected the growth and development of evaluation and adjustment services. State legislation, generally accommodating implementation of federal acts, has also provided impetus. Welfare reform may have an even greater impact upon the field. Should the proposed Family Assistance Plan (FAP) become a reality, all incapacitated FAP applicants would be referred to vocational rehabilitation for evaluation of their incapacity. Periodic reevaluation would also be necessary for this group (Newman, 1970). Implementation of this or other similar plans would, no doubt, involve professional evaluators in evaluation services similar to those now provided many disabled Social Security applicants. The size and scope of such a plan, however, may entail an entire revamping and revision of evaluation programs and processes.

The association must remain flexible to meet the interminable changes demanded by current and future legislation designed to serve unprecedented numbers in an ever widening, more troubled population. New systems to effectively serve these people must be devised cooperatively on a multiagency, multidiscipline level. Such a system would probably include various sequential levels or phases of screening, evaluation, and adjustment services (Little, 1970; Pruitt, 1970; and Couch, 1970).

VEWAA will join other related organizations that monitor and inform lawmaking bodies in an effort to assure that an equitable portion of the nation's resources are allotted to the solution of human problems. The association will seek a wider funding base for its services and will assume a responsibility for sponsoring legislation that may offer better solutions in serving people.

DIVERGENT SETTINGS

A rehabilitation facility takes various physical and functional forms and may be found in a host of diverse settings. The very definition of a rehabilitation facility permits this diversity. A rehabilitation facility, as defined by the Social and Rehabilitation Services Administration, is "operated for the primary purpose of assisting in the rehabilitation of handicapped individuals."

The definition is further qualified by the statement that such a facility: . . . provides one or more of the following:

> (1) testing, fitting, or training in the use of prosthetic devices, (2) prevocational or conditioning therapy, (3) physical or occupational therapy, (4) adjustment training, (5) evaluation or control of special disabilities or through which is provided an integrated program of medical, psychological and vocational evaluation and services under competent professional supervision; provided, that the major portion of such evaluation and services are prescribed by or are under the formal supervision of persons licensed to practice medicine or surgery in the state (H.E.W., R.S.A., 1967).

If this official definition does not elucidate the meaning of a rehabilitation facility, perhaps it illustrates the multidimensional objectives of rehabilitation facility services. Even more variegation can be seen in the settings where rehabilitation facilities are found. Rehabilitation units can be seen in public schools and in mental hospitals; in institutions for the retarded and on college campuses; in state tubercular hospitals and behind the bars of city, state, and federal prisons. Comprehensive centers, sheltered workshops, and activity centers are natural additions to the list. Manpower programs offering evaluation and adjustment services may also be seen in such diverse settings as employment security offices, Job Corps Centers, J.E.V.S. units, and at WIN, CEP, AND M.D.T.A. sites (Jewish Education and Vocational Services, Work Incentive Now, Concentrated Employment Programs, Manpower Development Training Act). Each of these settings in both Manpower and rehabilitation programs have their own special merits and limitations.

Consequently, evaluation and adjustment service programs may be goverened to a large extent by what a particular setting may permit or prohibit. The facility emphasizing *real work* as the central client activity may ignore the work sample evaluation approach. Likewise, a freestanding evaluation unit or a unit confined to a hospital setting may forfeit the potential of the real work situation as an evaluative tool. One can also imagine the reluctance of some prison wardens to the employment of the outside job tryout technique in the early assessment phases.

Burk (1971) has suggested that all professional practice in rehabilitation is determined more by social and political institutions and the administrative practices by which these institutions operate than by objectively derived concepts and testable procedures and theories. The influence the setting has on the practice of evaluation and adjustment is a prime example of Burk's indictment. Nadolsky (1970) and Barad (1971) concur, noting that the orientation of the particular facility is highly influential upon service programs.

THE FUTURE

The association takes pride in the divergent settings where evaluation and adjustment services are rendered. VEWAA members can boast correctly that they are in fact where the action is. This is, of course, insufficient justification to permit the setting itself to dictate the type, quality, and quantity of services that may be available to its service recipients. The association would not want to deny evaluation and adjustment services as a practical solution to problems faced by various institutions, agencies, or facilities, nor would it want to limit the setting where such services could be rendered. The guiding principle should be that each individual receiving services should be able to receive the same quality services, regardless of the setting. Such services should be rendered upon consideration of individual client needs and based upon tested scientific principles and standards of practice. Professional practice in this manner should be unobstructed by institutional settings and administrative or agency policies.

This question points to a major task of the association in the area of standards of practice. The issue is a delicate one within the association. Hardy and Cull (1969) have emphasized the need for adequate standards. Stout (1969) has delineated the difficulty of establishing standards, and Walker (1970) has pointed out the many possible pitfalls of standards. No one opposes high quality services for those with whom we work, but there is little agreement on any suitable measurement device by which such quality could be gauged.

The Policy and Performance Council of the Rehabilitation Services Administration (R.S.A.), the Commission on Accreditation of Rehabilitation Facilities (C.A.R.F.), Goodwill Industries, and others have published broad standards which include evaluation and adjustment services. The Council of State Administrators of Vocational Rehabilitation made up of state directors of rehabilitation agencies have resolved firmly that state agencies will soon utilize only those facilities meeting accreditation standards.

The association must act to ascertain and offer standards of practice. Not standards that are merely self-protecting nor measured necessarily by academic degrees. Rather, standards devised by practitioners who know the field and standards that can assure at least minimal quality of service for those who are served. In cooperation with C.A.R.F., VEWAA has undertaken a revision of the C.A.R.F. standards supplement at the practitioner level via local VEWAA Forums throughout the country. This may well lead to a viable consensus regarding standards of practice (Couch, 1971, 1972). The association's code of ethics (VEWAA, 1971) also contains certain guides relating to standards within the field.

Once the standards of practice are defined and accepted, the influence of the setting upon the field may diminish. The association may eventually subdivide its service components into subsystems that could function separately when linked to the total system. These need not be housed under one roof. In this eventuality, settings incompatible with the total system standards could provide an identifiable subsystem service that would both satisfy the settings requirements and assure quality services. In any event, the association's task is evident. Standards of practice based upon tested procedures and concepts must be developed. Practice in any setting will be based upon these standards of practice rather than upon extraneous circumstances which may be found within a particular setting.

EDUCATIONAL AND EXPERIENTIAL BACKGROUNDS OF PRACTITIONERS

Turning now to the individual who is responsible for rendering evaluation and adjustment services, one finds an even greater divergence than noted in the facility settings. It is no difficult task to find former clients, teachers, craftsmen, counselors, occupational therapists, and retired military men working alongside a master's degree evaluator. Newman, (1970) recalls that much of the early development of formalized and structured evaluation procedures was done in the field of occupational therapy. Nadolsky (1971) explains that dissatisfaction with psychometrics ushered in a new era of assessment primarily through the application of occupational therapy techniques within veterans' hospitals and other medical settings. Walker (1970) reveals however, that occupational therapists generally failed to move into and follow up with the potential offered by vocational evaluation.

When none of the existing professions stepped forward to claim the roles of vocational evaluator or adjustment specialist within facilities, facility administrators and agency personnel searched a variety of areas in their attempt to secure practitioners to fill their need. Their solutions differed considerably. Many agreed with Bregman (1969), who posited that basic education in one of the relevant disciplines was of primary importance. He suggested that specific training in evaluation and adjustment procedures should be added to this foundation in a particular discipline. Following this line of thinking, many employed various skilled craftsmen, vocational specialists, and industrial arts majors. Viewing evaluation and adjustment from perhaps another vantage point, some employers reasoned that those with such educational backgrounds as psychology, sociology, counseling, or education might be well-versed in assessment and adjustment procedures. No doubt, other criteria account for the heterogeneity found in today's practitioners. Sankovsky (1969) studied patterns of vocational evaluation services in 170 rehabilitation facilities and found that 75 percent of the evaluators held either a bachelor's or master's degree. Educational backgrounds of these evaluators were divided primarily among rehabilitation counseling, psychology, teaching, and industrial arts. Occupational therapy and sociology were the next most frequently listed educational backgrounds. Egerman and Gilbert (1969) reported that 88 percent of a responding sample of 293 evaluator members of The National Rehabilitation Association (N.R.A.) held at least a bachelor's degree and only 4 percent indicated no post-high school education. The undergraduate backgrounds of two-thirds of their respondents included: industrial arts (18 percent), psychology (17 percent), sociology or social science (15 percent), primary or secondary education (12 percent), and occupational therapy (6 percent). Graduate areas of emphasis were primarily rehabilitation counseling, psychology, occupational therapy, and education.

This pattern is seemingly consistent. Sankovsky (1971) found that 87 percent of the 159 VEWAA members sampled, held at least a bachelor's degree. Major undergraduate backgrounds reported were psychology (21 percent), industrial arts (20 percent), sociology or social science (16 percent), and occupational therapy (6 percent). Considerable variety was noted among the remainder of the sample with educational backgrounds ranging from philosophy to physics. Recognizing this divergence, the Rehabilitation Services Administration (H.E.W., R.S.A., 1967) standards for facilities and sheltered workshops make broad allowance for work evaluators (vocational evaluators). Among the alternatives reported for evaluators in the published recommended practices, one finds: (1) a master's degree in an appropriate field plus a year's experience in rehabilitation or other suitable experience; (2) an undergraduate degree with appropriate experience in such areas as education, industrial arts, occupational therapy, rehabilitation, psychology, social science, or manual arts therapy; (3) other combinations of experience and training in conjunction with completion of specialized rehabilitation-related courses. No mention is made of the adjustment specialist in the R.S.A. standards. Standards for vocational evaluators published by the Commission on Accreditation of Rehabilitation Facilities (C.A.R.F.) are similarly broad.

Current hiring practices in the field reflect full utilization of the breadth permitted by such published standards. Consequently, upon entry into the field, the only common ground shared by the vast majority of these divergent practitioners is a mutual lack of training in and knowledge of vocational evaluation and adjustment training procedures, processes, and techniques (Sink, 1969). In approaching his new position, the novice evaluator or adjustment specialist often is besieged with feelings of inadequacy and is overwhelmed with the complexity of his task. Seeking homeostasis and a modicum of anxiety reduction, he inevitably reaches back into his own frame of reference of experiences and training for assistance in his encounter with the client. Activities chosen in this manner may be either reinforced or extinguished in a variety of ways. Those activities which are reinforced become the accepted method for rendering evaluation and/or adjustment training in the practitioner's particular setting. In this light, it is not surprising that such variety exists in our practices. One is inclined to agree with Barad (1971) who concludes that we cannot really speak of the evaluation process nor the evaluator "as if these were unitary homogeneous entities." Thus, it is quite evident that the educational and experiential backgrounds of practicing vocational evaluators and work adjustment specialists have played a major role in charting the course of the field.

THE FUTURE

In the area of personnel, standards again will be an issue within the association. The profession must take the lead in delineating the competencies required of the evaluator and adjustment specialist. Once these competencies have been defined carefully then the association must work closely with training institutions and accrediting agencies. Curriculums must be relevant to the needs of the field and published standards must reflect the competencies deemed appropriate by the profession. If the traditional approach is followed, the next logical step would be the establishment of some type of licensing, registration, certification or degree requirements.

Hopefully, VEWAA will find more innovative means to assure the desired competency of those who may practice in the field. Walker (1970) suggests that in viewing other tottering professional systems, VEWAA may be able to escape irrelevance. The association therefore must explore other alternatives thoroughly. Rosenberg (1970) has suggested a three-level specialist in diversification as one such alternative. Calling his specialist a vocation-ologist, Rosenberg would permit a variety of backgrounds and educational levels entry into the field, but professional status could be attained only by demonstrating competence and skill in the particular areas of avowed competence. Walker (1970) stresses that evaluating the quality of service output should be the first concern. Then, based on the findings of such an evaluation, the type personnel needed to produce quality outcomes could be ascertained. Participants at the *Think Tank* Workshop at Stout University (Hoffman, 1969) agreed that the work evaluation process is a complex one requiring professional training on the part of the evaluator. Attractive as these alternatives are, the basic questions remain unanswered. What tested body of knowledge constitutes the field? How best can one gain the necessary competencies? How can the association best measure those competencies to assure quality services to service recipients? Perhaps there are no correct answers to these questions and a combination of answers will be required. By observing current practices within the field, the complexity of the task may be seen and various possible combinations may be discerned.

Both manpower and rehabilitation agencies are experimenting with aides and both appear to accept the career ladder concept that will allow the aide eventually to achieve professional status. Some junior colleges are offering associate of arts degrees in related fields. College graduates holding a baccalaureate degree with undergraduate majors in rehabilitation now are beginning to seek their entry levels in the field and wonder where they fit into the scheme of things. Those completing graduate degrees in the field may question the necessity of advanced training when they view other practitioners functioning in the same capacity with little or no training. Those with many years of hard-earned experience on the firing line may skeptically view the relevance of degree programs when they encounter graduates who may exhibit little knowledge of industry, tools, machines, and the world of work.

The frame of reference of each of these groups merit consideration in formulating any combination of personnel standards. The association must provide a forum and serve as a catalyst in seeking answers to the standards question. When this issue is settled, there will be a diminished divergence in the backgrounds of future professionals within the field. Hopefully, greater homogeneity will not block a fresh flow of ideas into the practice nor build protective walls against feedback from clients and input from other disciplines. The association certainly must promote research to build a body of knowledge within the field, but its members will continue unabashedly to borrow tested procedures and proven techniques from other fields of endeavor. The evaluator and adjustment specialist envisioned today for tomorrow is indeed a superman whose knowledge and skill must far surpass that of those who are practicing today, for as Rosenberg (1969) has predicted, the future of the profession depends on the ingenuity and creativity of those who practice the art of evaluation and work adjustment.

AVAILABLE AND PREFERRED TECHNIQUES

Hoffman (1969) notes the theoretical work of Fiske, Gellman, Krantz, and Nadolsky, but concludes that there is no single comprehensive theory of work evaluation. Pointing to the lack of research in the field, Hoffman explains that the field has borrowed extensively from other fields of endeavor for theoretical foundations. It appears that practitioners in the field of vocational evaluation and work adjustment have concentrated their efforts on processes and techniques.

Technique cults have emerged and their members may be found clustering around one of the major evaluation procedures. In advocating what Neff (1966) terms the situational approach, Anderson (1968) expounds that ". . . if evaluation is to be professionally sound it must contain exposure to real work." Even though granting that much work evaluation or simulated tasks can take on a *Mickey Mouse* appearance, Walker (1968) adeptly delineates the value and versatility of the simulated task. Others further point out the merits of the job sample approach (Rosenberg, 1969; Pruitt, 1970a; Kuhlman, 1971; and Overs, 1968). Goldman and Doppelt and Bennett (1970) defend the much maligned psychological test as a technique for assessing the handicapped and disadvantaged. Hadwin (1966) extols the virtue of the job tryout approach and others have pointed out the advantages of the job analysis. In many instances, those promoting the use of their favorite technique carefully point out the limitations inherent in the procedures advocated by others.

Neff (1966) carefully classified four major approaches to evaluation and has pointed out objectively the serious limitations of each. Thomas (1971) discerns a tendency of practitioners and educators to more or less accept the work sample as a *second coming* and cautions against dogmatically extolling the virtues of one technique over another. Friedman (1968) suggests we put to rest such arguments over preferred techniques and agrees with Gellman (1968) that "there are no absolutes in the selection of assessment techniques."

These statements are encouraging. A study of VEWAA members by Nadolsky (1971b) does reveal some commonalities among evaluators with respect to their acceptance of and degree of use of evaluative techniques and procedures. Threads of the past remain however, and preference for a particular technique continues to influence the daily practice of the evaluator and subsequently influences the field.

Access to a technique or procedure also has affected the practice of evaluation and adjustment services. Linked with the training issue, many practitioners are denied the use of certain techniques. Most Psychometric instruments are limited for use by those with certain levels of academic training in psychology. For many years, purchase and use of the TOWER System was contingent upon specified training in its use at I.C.D. in New York. The Employment Service has been reluctant in some states to permit training in and access to the General Aptitude Test Battery (G.A.T.B.) by any but their own personnel. Permission to purchase and utilize the J.E.V.S. work sample system is currently limited to a relatively esoteric group. For these various practical, valid, or arbitrary reasons, the fact remains that access to certain techniques has had its effect upon practices within the field.

THE FUTURE

Stout (1969) points out that many of the tools, techniques, and procedures currently used in vocational evaluation are completely unvalidated. Both Sax (1971) and Spergel (1970) are impatient to get beyond armchair philosophy, theory, and position papers. Sax advocates getting down to the more practical problems of how you do the job and to the development of materials, procedures, and acutal hardware relevant to the field. Spergel suggests application of the scientific method in testing our methodologies. The association therefore must turn a critical eye upon each technique and tool by applying the ultimate yardstick of predictive validity and applicability. Research then, is another major task of the association. Greater efforts must be generated to test not only the efficacy of our current techniques, but for the development of new and more relevant procedures as well. Test publishers should be made aware of the special needs of the field and pushed to respond to these needs. Private enterprise should be welcomed to develop appropriate tools, hardware and software for use in evaluation and adjustment services. Various governmental agencies must be made more cognizant of the developmental needs of the profession and additional resources solicited from them.

Current activity in the field indicates a growing awareness of these many needs and portends a brighter future. An expanding list of new ideas, refinements of established procedures and some promising research starts are now evident. Usdane (1967) reports that the work oriented facility is on the threshold of discovery in new innovative relations with industry. Pruitt (1970c) has suggested a functional-level classification system. Clemons (1970) discusses the increasingly popular mobile evaluation unit. Industrial engineers are offering their expertise for use in improving facilities' services (Hovater, Denholm, and Smith, 1969; Oswald and Parker, 1971). Anderson, *et.al.,* (1971) explore the possibility of the systems approach toward facility evaluation and adjustment services. Hume (1971) discusses the utilization of the Australian-developed Modular Arranged Predetermined Time Standards (MODAPTS). Private enterprise has developed the Singer/Graflex System as an innovative approach to evaluation screening. This system focuses upon the vocational exploration facet of evaluation (Gannaway and Caldwell, 1971). The JEVS work sample system is another recent innovation. Utilization of media in rehabilitation services has been discussed by Sankovsky and Knight (1971). Considerable progress has been made in computer technology for guidance purposes (H.E.W., Office of Education, 1969) and its relevance for evaluation has been explored (Benton, 1971). A materials development center has been developed at Stout State University and the Alabama State Rehabilitation Agency has established a comprehensive rehabilitation media service at Auburn University. Both Stout and Auburn Universities have published a book of readings (Sankovsky, et.al., 1970; Pruitt, 1970b). Hiten (1970) has offered *Viewpoints on Evaluation* and Baker and Sawyer (1971) have completed a manual relating to adjustment services. This first text in the field of vocational evaluation is another milestone and explores the application of many techniques and procedures.

Existing techniques are being examined and refined. Button, et.al. (1969), provided new, tested methodology in the critical area of observing behavior within facility settings. Barad (1970) reiterates the necessity for creativity on the part of the evaluator in utilizing improvised tasks to meet special client needs. Hardy (1970) stresses the use of background information. Couch and Brabham (1970) have discussed the evaluation staff conference and both Coffee (1970b) and Smolkin (1971) have suggested refinements in evaluation reporting. Stout State's Materials Development Center is engaged in field testing of a series of work samples and offer improved procedures for organizing and administering such samples (Sax, 1971).

Researchers too, are beginning to report some promising research starts relative to the effectiveness of vocational evaluation programs. Spergel (1970a) discusses early research done in conjunction with the development of the JEVS work sample system. This research suggested that the disadvantaged evaluated by this assessment method found vocational objectives better suited to their needs, demonstrated a better likelihood of completing counseling, and had a better chance of obtaining and holding initial job referrals. They were found also to adjust better to training programs. Button and Hogan (1971) report on some of the research at Cornell University's Rehabilitation Research Institute. Their data indicates ". . . that the ability to participate in and in part control one's social contacts is critical to the rehabilitation process." They have developed means to characterize and measure this ability which has been shown to discriminate between individuals who are successfully rehabilitated and those whose rehabilitation prospects are poor. Handelsman and Wurtz (1971) studied the validity of work sample evaluations with twenty-six community workshop clients. A follow-up of these clients after termination indicated that predictions based upon work samples was significantly related to employment outcomes. Tseng and his colleagues at the West Virginia Rehabilitation Research and Training Institute also have presented evidence relative to the predictive validity of some evaluative techniques. Recognizing the desperate need for research efforts in the field, VEWAA itself has made a gesture of support for research. A *mini-research* program was begun in 1971, offering token grants to practitioners and students in the field. Spergel (1970) has reviewed other research in the field and points out the limitations and design difficulties in some of these early efforts.

Limited and small in comparison with the need, these efforts have provided a promising direction by which the techniques and procedures utilized by practitioners can be improved. Marshalling the forces and necessary support to fulfill the research needs in the field represents another challenge to the association. Adhering to Gellman's 1971 principle that there are no absolutes in the selection of assessment techniques, the future evaluator will not base his practice upon the availability of or preference for a particular technique or tool. Rather, he will be versed in and equipped with a potpourri of reliable, valid procedures, techniques, and tools from which he can select to meet a client's needs at a particular point in time.

TRAINING PROGRAMS

A slowly-emerging factor destined to exert a major influence in the future may be found in the various educational and training programs for evaluators and adjustment personnel. Baker (1969) notes that until recent years, practitioners were forced to resort to the trial and error method of developing philosophically and technically sound programs of evaluation and adjustment. With the advent of institutional programs designed to provide training for evaluation and adjustment personnel, a new trend toward a common set of competencies may be discernable. To date, however, on-the-job or apprenticeship-type training remains the predominant method by which individuals are prepared to work in the field. The multiplicity of influences described earlier may account partially for the vast difference in the orientations of practitioners trained by the apprenticeship method.

The earliest training programs were held in rehabilitation facilities and represented an organized approach to the on-the-job approach to training. The most notable of these is the short-term training program offered at the Institute for Crippled and Disabled (I.C.D.) in New York. Beginning in 1956, the program focused on the use of the TOWER System. The program continues today and more than 350 individuals from this and other countries have completed the TOWER program at I.C.D. (Rosenberg, 1969). The impact of this program can be seen in many evaluation units throughout the country where the TOWER unit serves as the model. In the early sixties, a limited number of newly-employed evaluators from six southeastern states participated in an O.V.R. (now Rehabilitation Services Administration) supported short-course in evaluation at the Darden Rehabilitation Center in Glasden, Alabama. Under the direction of Mrs. Betty Vinson, the Gadsden short-course also emphasized a practical "hands on" apprenticeship approach (Sink, 1971).

Auburn University in Alabama, was the first university to offer regular, short-term training for personnel in the field (Hoffman, 1970). Beginning with a regional pilot institute in 1966, the Auburn program began offering academic credit to participants from the southeastern (R.S.A. Region IV) states in 1967. Stout State University, Menomonie, Wisconsin, became the first university to offer a graduate degree in the field. The first class graduated from this program in 1967 (Church, 1970). The University of Arizona began admitting students to its graduate degree program in evaluation and work adjustment in 1968. Auburn University's first graduate student with a major emphasis in vocational evaluation received a master's degree in 1969. The staffs of these institutions have also been active in sponsoring and attending workshops, seminars, and conferences relating to rehabilitation and consequently have exposed many to the concepts, issues, and techniques of vocational evaluation and work adjustment.

Other university and facility training programs emphasize rehabilitation administration, workshop management and supervision and counseling. These too, have addressed themselves to the subject of evaluation and adjustment services and often conduct workshops devoted to these services. The three Rehabilitation Research and Training Centers for Vocational Rehabilitation have given considerable attention to evaluation and adjustment. Each center is university based and affiliated with a state vocational rehabilitation center. Located at the University of Arkansas, the University of Pittsburg, and at the University of West Virginia, these centers are developing procedures relevant to the field and provide training in their use.

The influence of these educational programs will no doubt grow as current programs expand and additional training programs are added to meet the tremendous manpower needs projected for the future. The association has maintained close ties with these university programs and E. B. Whitten (1968), executive director of N.R.A., suggested that this cooperation between practitioners and university personnel was further enhanced by the formation of VEWAA. Whitten also expresses hope that this cooperation will continue.

Training of Manpower personnel in evaluation and adjustment techniques began also with the traditional on the job training. Manpower moved to add out-service training programs, primarily in counseling, then developed a combination of these. In this evolution of concepts for training personnel, the Manpower Administration has adopted a policy of encouraging the employment of the disadvantaged for preprofessional entry level jobs, establishing career ladders, and promoting the use of the New Careers concept. In addition to their staff development along these lines, there is considerable evidence of commitment to upgrading all Manpower staff (Fantaci, 1970). In conjunction with the Manpower contracted development of the Jewish Employment and Vocational Service (JEVS) work sample system, Manpower also supports the training of Manpower personnel in the use of this system at the Philadelphia facility.

THE FUTURE

There is little dissent relative to the future demands for increased evaluation and adjustment services and for personnel trained to provide these services. At the third annual Conference of the American Association of Work Evaluators (now VEWAA) Gordon Haygood (1967) pointed out the forthcoming increased demand for facility services precipitated by sociological changes. At the National Conference on Vocational Evaluation and Work Adjustment Services in Manpower, Social Welfare, and Rehabilitation Programs (Pacinelli, 1970) numerous governmental agency officials spelled out their agencies' need for increased services. Deputy Commissioner of the S.R.S. Community Services Administration Joseph Hunt explained that comprehensive evaluation services are needed for a great many welfare clients. Ralph Church charted the increasing demand for facility services by contrasting the 2,500 vocational rehabilitation clients served by facilities in 1955, with the more than 132,000 served in 1969. Manpower's

Fantaci said that to meet his agency's personnel requirements all available training resources must be utilized. R.S.A.'s Commissioner Newman reported that a study on vocational rehabilitation and federal manpower policy revealed that among the many cooperative activities of the public program the key element was the provision of evaluation services. Newman offered that the whole Manpower and human social services needed the resources of vocational rehabilitation in the area of evaluation. Such demands have set the stage for an ever-increasing shortage of evaluation and adjustment personnel (Smith, 1969) and led Sink (1971a) to project that current facilities should consider two or three shifts each day if additional staff could be found.

Fulfilling current and future training needs of its members is a primary goal of the association. At its annual meeting in 1970, the association unanimously endorsed a resolution encouraging S.R.S. and R.S.A. support of existing training programs in the field and advocated additional training activities for evaluation and adjustment personnel (Couch, 1971). A study of the VEWAA membership (Sankovsky, 1971) revealed that a need for more training at all levels was the largest area of concern expressed by the members. The Social and Rehabilitation Service has been informed of the association's concern for expanded training opportunities, but more, much more must be accomplished in the area if qualified evaluation and adjustment personnel are to meet the anticipated demands of the future.

Other agencies must be encouraged to support training in the field. Manpower, education, corrections, mental health, and welfare as well as rehabilitation demand evaluation and adjustment services and draw upon the limited trained manpower within the field. They too, should share in the responsibility for training these individuals. A limited but promising start in this direction is being made in some agencies. Public institutions also have a responsibility for training evaluation and adjustment personnel. Smith (1969) summarizes well the task of the association with his statement that Congress must be brought to realize not only the value of vocational evaluation and work adjustment services, but the tremendous shortages of trained manpower in the field.

In addition to efforts along these lines and the aforementioned intentions of the association in the area of standards and curriculum involvement, the association itself must accept responsibility for training its membership. The beginning efforts of state VEWAA units in encouraging and conducting in-service training programs for its members is commendable. On the local level, VEWAA forums represent another admirable effort in self-training. It is at these firing line levels where experienced evaluation and adjustment personnel meet periodically to share common problems and seek realistic practical solutions that will advance the field. These efforts should be expanded rapidly in the future.

Finally, continued training for increased competency within the field rests ultimately with the VEWAA member. VEWAA is essentially each individual member dedicated to his own professional growth. He is determined in these early years to contribute substantially to his profession. He will master the available body of knowledge through training, but he will also demand more appropriate tools, proven techniques, and validated procedures. In facing the overwhelming problems offered by those with whom he works, he will seek and supply answers to the many unanswered questions. This individual growth and these individual contributions will no doubt govern the direction and acceptance of our profession. Therefore, the truly professional VEWAA member will train himself to be all that he can become (Couch, 1970).

The Association and the Future will, in varying degrees, continue to be influenced by the major factors outlined here. In meeting the many unresolved issues leading to full professional status, these same factors must be nurtured, surmounted, organized and even contended with. The future of the association rests largely upon its success in resolving the critical issues it now faces and in coalescing these forces for more effectively meeting the needs of the people it serves.

This is no mean task for there are those who seriously question the need for our existence and our pursuit of professional status. Jones (1971) has charged that ". . . in their haste to become professionals, vocational evaluators may be forcing themselves into meaningless pursuits." Kranz (1968) poses a relevant question of the moral sanction to evaluate another person. Burk (1971) asks, "Is there a body of knowledge that can be identified as distinctive to the field of rehabilitation?" Stout (1969) reminds us that there is no consensus on definitions within the field and cautions against attempts to build professional standards upon present ill-defined and unvalidated competencies. Sankovsky (1971) ponders if an association can be functioning adequately when 40 percent of its members report no formal training in the area of evaluation and adjustment. Walker (1970) recalls that in the not too distant past, evaluation services were located in buildings which were the first to go in urban renewal programs and noted that such programs were often staffed by those whose employability, at times, seemed only a step ahead of their clients. He suggests also that the field has been at the bottom of a lengthy and sophisticated pecking order. Ross (1971) sums up the current dilemma with the admission that it would be rather indefensible to state that the field is a bona fide profession.

Such charges may be discouraging to the current membership and to those who may be considering a career in the field. Admittedly, the association has no rigid qualifications for membership. There are no uniform standards, no degree requirements, no certification, nor are there patches on our sleeves. Equally disturbing is the absence of common objectives, terminology and a clearly identifiable, tested body of knowledge indigenous to the field. Undoubtedly, the association now would encounter difficulty in measuring up to most published criteria for professional status (Couch, 1971a).

These unresolved issues delineate the many current and continuing tasks of the association. The immediate future will be occupied by these concerns, for as Barton (1971) has observed, VEWAA is a profession in the making. The association must encourage concentrated research efforts to bridge the gap between current practices and a proven body of knowledge. Simultaneously, VEWAA will promote increased training and educational opportunities at all levels. The association will arrive at a consensus regarding objectives, terminology, and standards of practice. Appropriate legislation will be supported and new more sophisticated tools will be found. Sensitivity and responsiveness to the practical problems of those we serve will hopefully continue to be characteristic of the association. Broadening the base of the membership to actually include all those whose primary function is in the realm of vocational evaluation and work adjustment is another immediate task of the association.

Through the morass of issues, problems, and charges facing the profession, a gleam of hope can be seen in the strides that have been made in the relatively short span of VEWAA's existence. The growing emphasis on and interest in vocational evaluation and adjustment services by a multitude of agencies and institutions attests to its attractiveness as a process with which to deal with problems of people. This emphasis is evident in the increasing research activities and in the fact that relevant professional articles have quadrupled within the past five years. The *Journal of Rehabilitation* has devoted two entire issues to the subject and at least five books have been devoted to the subject within a three-year period. The association's own *Bulletin* has doubled its size and compares favorably with similar publications. The association has a code of ethics and has involved the membership in its cautious but persistant pursuit of standards. State units and local VEWAA Forums are organizing around the country. These are reporting meaningful training and mutual problem solving activities. Three universities offer graduate work in the field and others will no doubt be added in the foreseeable future. State agencies are giving increasing emphasis to in-service training for evaluation and adjustment personnel as these professionals are being added to merit system titles. The association takes pride in its embryonic research program and boasts that the membership has doubled.

These small gains do not negate the association's responsibility to take the major steps necessary to resolve the current issues and attain its goals. These goals are not necessarily professional standing, status, or prestige, but rather to better fulfill our responsibilities to those with whom we work. Toward this end, each member bears a responsibility to improve his success ratio, to find more reliable and valid techniques, and to identify and master those skills deemed appropriate to the task. Once sufficient steps are taken in this direction, the question of professional status is of little consequence.

To those in despair regarding the current state of the profession, many points which precipitate their dissatisfaction must be yielded. The youth of the association however, must be considered and patience should serve as an admixture to the hopefully productive discontent voiced by many. Viewed from a historical perspective, the association's problems are not unlike those experienced by other professions in their youth. Hicks (1955) records that medical schools in this country before the Civil War were a "social disgrace." These early medical training institutions existed primarily for profit and their graduates were a liability to society. As late as 1870, the head of one of the nation's best medical schools explained that written examinations were out of the question because a majority of the students were unable to write well enough.

When the American Psychological Association was in its seventh year, Ladd (1899) described psychology as ". . . nothing but the descriptive and explanatory study of the *souls* of men." He noted one of the problem areas within the psychology profession as ". . . the limited and faulty qualifications of psychologist." Commenting further on psychology as a science, Ladd observed that psychology was somewhat insecure in its professional role alongside the more established sciences. The Vocational Guidance Association, forerunner of today's American Personnel and Guidance Association, devoted its first *Bulletin* issue to psychological testing. In that issue, Procter (1921) complained that "Half-baked psychologists who claim to be able to chart minutely the aptitudes of people so they can be properly labeled and pigeonholed, have greatly hindered the movement." By 1923, the Vocational Guidance Association discussed issues similar to those now facing VEWAA. Arthur Payne (1923) complained of too much philosophizing and theorizing and posited that ". . . we must change from the philosophical 'I believe' to the scientific 'I know.' " Payne delineated their association's tasks as ". . . elucidating certain principles, defining certain terms, and defining and limiting our scope of responsibility and activity."

In the early years of these professional associations, there was concern over terminology, professional competencies, training objectives and even follow-up and outcomes. In this perspective, VEWAA's current status may be seen as paralleling that of other professional associations at a similar point in time (Couch, 1971a). The status of VEWAA in the distant future cannot readily be envisioned. Indeed, there may not exist an association or there may be no need for such an association. What then does the future hold and upon what does it actually depend? Rosenberg (1969) says the future depends upon the creativity and ingenuity of the evaluator. Walker (1970) says VEWAA can adopt a system of feedback which can insure that the field is capable of effectively responding to those it serves. Barton (1970) sees a movement toward our becoming vocational development specialists. Spergel (1970) says the limits are boundless. Neff (1970) believes the next step is to further extend our services into industry. Usdane (1972) sees district rehabilitation offices as rehabilitation facilities capable of providing the initial evaluation phases. Hoffman (1970) sees extension of service to students in vocational and public schools, Nadolsky (1971a) expands this further to all helping agency clients and Rosenberg (1969) takes a step into the avocational realm. Sankovsky (1970) predicts that future development depends upon justifying the movement's existence and Gellman (1971) sees a continuation of the humanistic approach. Sink (1971b) appropriately views the future as constant change. Regardless of what the distant future may hold, the immediate future offers well-defined challenges demanding the association's attention. While the association takes pride in the progress to date, there is much that remains to be accomplished. Hopefully, at some future date, one may look back on these early years and find that the Vocational Evaluation and Work Adjustment Association did find and take the necessary steps leading to a sound philosophy, a viable practice, and a contributing profession (Couch, 1971a) .

THE FUTURE

In the introduction to this chapter, the observation was made that students now studying vocational evaluation and work adjustment could possibly predict the future of the movement at least as well as others who might offer prognostications. The availability of opportunity for involvement in molding and guiding the association was also expressed. Further, the prediction was made that future evaluation and adjustment personnel would be better informed, more highly skilled, and better equipped than the practitioners of today. In this vein, the author would like to invite the thoughtful reader to complete the writing of this chapter with his own predictions regarding the future. Space has been provided for predictions herein. You may also want to inform the association of your predictions. These may be needed for future plans.

REFERENCES

Alabama School of Trades - The Rehabilitation Center: *A Method for Evaluating and Adjusting the Emotionally Handicapped Client and Older Disabled Worker for Competitive Employment,* Final report of H.E.W., R.S.A. Project 976d, Gadsden, Alabama, 1965, pp. 1-3.

Anderson, Alan: Real Work, *Vocational Evaluation and Work Adjustment Bulletin, 1*(2):2-5, 1968.

Anderson, Joel; Baker, Richard; Couch, Robert; and Sawyer, Horace: *Toward A Systems Approach to Evaluation and Adjustment Services.* Paper presented at the Vocational Evaluation and Work Adjustment Association, National Rehabilitation Association Annual Conference, Chicago, Illinois, 1971.

Baker, Richard J., and Sawyer, Horace W.: *Adjustment Services and Rehabilitation: Emphasis on Human Change, Rehabilitation Services Education.* Auburn Auburn University, 1971.

Baker, Richard J.: Vocational Evaluation and Work Adjustment Training Programs. *Vocational Evaluation and Work Adjustment Bulletin, 2*(2): 12-14, 1969.

Barad, Cary B.: A Survey of Vocational Evaluation Practices in Maryland and the District of Columbia. *Vocational Evaluation and work Adjustment Bulletin, 4*(2):6-10, 1971.

Barad, Cary B.: Improvised Tasks. *Vocational Evaluation and Work Adjustment Bulletin, 3*(3):15-17, 1970.

Barton, Everett H., Jr.: Topical Review. *Vocational Evaluation and Work Adjustment Bulletin, 4*(2):33-37, 1971.

Barton, Everett H., Jr.: Vocational Evaluation and Work Adjustment: Vocational Development Companions. *Journal of Rehabilitation, 36*(1): 35-37, 1970.

Benton, Richard G.: Neoteric Pothers in Vocational Evaluation and Work Adjustment: Do Not Fold, Bend, or Spindle. Paper presented at the International Association of Rehabilitation Facilities Annual Conference, Las Vegas, Nevada, May 11, 1971.

Bregman, Morton: Organization and Administration of the Vocational Rehabilitation Center Work Evaluation Program. In Pruitt, Walter, and Pacinelli, Ralph (Eds.), *Work Evaluation in Rehabilitation.* Washington, Association of Rehabilitation Centers, 1969, pp. 71-75.

Burk, Richard D.: The Science of Rehabilitation—Does It Exist? *Journal of Rehabilitation, 37*(2):2, 1971.

Button, William H. and Hogan, Gail: An empirical perspective. *Journal of Rehabilitation, 37*(4):16-19, 1971.

Button, William H.; Kimberly, John R.; Lubow, Bart K.; Kimberly, Robert P.: A Conceptual Framework for the Analysis of Work Behavior in Sheltered Workshops. *Studies in Behavior and Rehabilitation,* No. 1, Region II Rehabilitation Research Institute, Ithaca, Cornell University, 1969.

Campbell, John L. and O'Toole, Richard: *Work Adjustment: A Dynamic Rehabilitation Process.* Cleveland, Vocational Guidance and Rehabilitation Services, 1970, p. 1.

Church, Ralph: Staff Recruitment, Training, and Development Associated With the Delivery of Vocational Evaluation and Work Adjustment Services. In Pacinelli, Ralph (Ed.): *Vocational Evaluation and Work Adjustment Services in Manpower, Social Welfare, and Rehabilitation Services,* Washington, International Association of Rehabilitation Facilities, 1970, pp. 121-126.

Clemons, Roger W.: A Mobile Work Laboratory II. *Vocational Evaluation and Work Adjustment Bulletin, 3*(1):11-13, 1970.

Coffee, D.: Report Writing in Vocational Evaluation. In Pruitt, Walter (Ed.): *Readings in Work Evaluation I,* Materials Development Center. Menomie, Stout State University, 1970.

Couch, Robert H.: Group Report. In Pacinelli, Ralph (Ed.): *Vocational Evaluation and Work Adjustment Services in Manpower, Social Welfare, and Rehabilitation Programs,* Washington, International Association of Rehabilitation Facilities, 1970, pp. 149-152.

Couch, Robert H.: The Involvement of VEWAA in Training Standards and Research. *Vocational Evaluation and Work Adjustment Bulletin, 4*(2) 26-28, 1971.

Couch, Robert H.: President's Message. *Vocational Evaluation and Work Adjustment Bulletin, 3*(3):2, 1970.

Couch, Robert H.: Vocational Evaluation and Work Adjustment — A Profession? *Vocational Evaluation and Work Adjustment Bulletin, 4*(3):3-5, 1971A.

Couch, Robert H.: VEWAA Progresses. *Journal of Rehabilitation, 38*(1):37, 1972.

Couch, Robert H. and Brabham, Robert E.: The Evaluation Staff Conference. *Vocational Evaluation and Work Adjustment Bulletin, 3*(3):12-15, 1970.

Davis, Jessie: Research and Demonstration Projects and Innovative Approaches Pertaining to Vocational Evaluation and Work Adjustment Services in Manpower Programs. In Pacinelli, Ralph N. (Ed.): *Vocational Evaluation and Work Adjustment Services in Manpower, Social Welfare, and Rehabilitation Programs,* Washington, International Association of Rehabilitation Facilities and University of Pittsburg. Research and Training Center in Vocational Rehabilitation, 1970, p. 61.

Doppelt, Jerome E. and Bennett, George K.: Testing Job Applicants From Disadvantaged Groups. In Sankovsky, Ray; Arthur, Gary; Mann, Joe (Eds.): *Vocational Evaluation and Work Adjustment: A Book of Readings,* Alabama Rehabilitation Media Service. Auburn, Auburn University, 1970, pp. 40-45.

Dunn, Dennis and Hoffman, Paul R.: The Practice of Work Adjustment. *Journal of Rehabilitation, 37*(4):2, 1971.

Egerman, Karl and Gilbert, James L.: The Work Evaluator. *Journal of Rehabilitation, 35*(3):12-14, 1969.

Fantaci, Anthony: The Manpower Administration. In Pacinelli, Ralph (Ed.): *Vocational Evaluation and Work Adjustment Services in Manpower, Social Welfare, and Rehabilitation,* Washington, International Association of Rehabilitation Facilities, 1970, pp. 105-113.

Friedman, Simon B.: The Middle of the Road. *Vocational Evaluation and Work Adjustment Bulletin, 1*(3):3-5, 1968.

Gannaway, Thomas W. and Caldwell, T. J.: The Singer/Graflex Vocational Evaluation System. In Sax, Arnold (Ed.): *Innovations in Vocational Evaluation and Work Adjustment Bulletin, 4*(3):41-42, 1971.

Gellman, William: Principles Guiding Vocational Evaluation Practice. In Pacinelli, Ralph (Ed.): *Research Utilization in Rehabilitation Facilities,*

Washington, International Association of Rehabilitation Facilities, 1971, pp. 135-140.

Gellman, William: The Principles of Vocational Evaluation. *Rehabilitation Literature, 29*(4):98-102, 1968.

Gellman, William: Research and Demonstration Projects Pertaining to Vocational Evaluation and Work Adjustment Services in Rehabilitation Programs. In Pacinelli, Ralph N. (Ed.): *Vocational Evaluation and Work Adjustment Services in Manpower, Social Welfare, and Rehabilitation Programs.* Washington, International Association of Rehabilitation Facilities and the University of Pittsburg Rehabilitation Research and Training Center, 1970, pp. 98-99.

Gellman, William: The Vocational Adjustment Shop. *Personnel and Guidance Journal, 39*:630-633, April, 1961.

Glanz, Edward C.: *Foundations and Principles of Guidance,* Boston, Allyn and Bacon, Inc., 1964, pp. 24-31.

Goldman, Leo: Testing the Handicapped. In Sankovsky, Ray; Arthur, Gary; Mann, Joe (Eds.): *Vocational Evaluation and Work Adjustment: A Book of Readings,* Alabama Rehabilitation Media Service. Auburn, Auburn University, 1970, pp. 36-39.

Hadwin, T. C. Jr.: On the Job Evaluation. In *Regional Pilot Institute on Work Evaluation.* Auburn, Auburn University, 1966, pp. 59-62.

Handelsman, Robert D. and Wurtz, Robert E.: The Validity of Pre-Vocational Evaluation Predictions in a Community Workshop, *The Journal of Applied Rehabilitation Counseling, 2*(1):16-21, 1971.

Hardy, Richard E.: Use of Background Information. *Vocational Evaluation and Work Adjustment Bulletin, 3*(1):3-4, 1970.

Hardy, Richard E. and Cull, John G.: Standards in Evaluation. *Vocational Evaluation and Work Adjustment Bulletin, 2*(1):11-13, 1969.

Haygood, Gordon B.: Sociological Changes that Will Affect Rehabilitation Centers and Sheltered Workshops. Paper presented at the Third Annual Conference of the American Association of Work Evaluators, Atlanta, Georgia, May 15, 1967.

Hicks, John D.: *The American Nation.* Cambridge, Houghton-Mifflin Company, The Riverside Press, 1955, p. 93.

Hiten, Hollis: *Viewpoints on Evaluation,* Special Technical Facility. Talledega, Alabama Institute for Deaf and Blind, 1970.

Hoffman, Paul R.: An Overview of Work Evaluation. *Journal of Rehabilitation, 36*(1):16-18, 1970.

Hoffman, Paul R. (Ed.): *"Think Tank" Workshop on Work Evaluation.* Stout State University, 1969a, pp. 131-132.

Hoffman, Paul R.: Work Evaluation: An Overview. In Pruitt, Walter, and Pacinelli, Ralph (Eds.) *Work Evaluation in Rehabilitation.* Washington, Association of Rehabilitation Center, 1969b, pp. 1-18.

Hovater, A. K., Denholm, D. H. and Smith, L. A.: Industrial Engineering in Vocational Evaluation. *Rehabilitation Literature, 30*(11):322-323, 1969.

Hume, Bruce C.: Assessment and Objective Measurement of Work Capacity of the Severely Physically Disabled, Based on Predetermined Time Standards. In Pacinelli, Ralph (Ed.): *Research Utilization in Rehabilitation Facilities,* Washington, International Association of Rehabilitation Facilities, 1971, pp. 161-175.

Jones, Richard D.: Vocational Evaluation as Activity Counseling. *Vocational Evaluation and Work Adjustment Bulletin, 4*(1):13-15, 1971, pp. 13-15.

Krantz, Gordon C.: Basic Issues. *Vocational Evaluation and Work Adjustment Bulletin, 1*(4):18, 1968.

Kuhlman, Harold: The Jewish Employment and Vocational Service Work Sample Battery. In Sax, Arnold, Innovations in Vocational Evaluation and Work Adjustment. *Vocational Evaluation and Work Adjustment Bulletin, 4*(k):25-27, 1971.

Ladd, G. T.: *On Certain Hinderances to the Progress of Psychology in America, The Psychological Review, 7*:121-131, 1899.

Little, Neal D.: Group Report. In Pacineeli, Ralph (Ed.): *Voctional Evaluation and Work Adjustment Services in Manpower, Social Welfare and Rehabilitation Programs,* Washington, International Association of Rehabilitation Facilities, 1970, pp. 143-147.

Lovell, Malcolm R.: Vocational Evaluation and Work Adjustment Services in Manpower Programs. In Pacinelli, Ralph N. (Ed.): *Vocational Evaluation and Work Adjustment Services in Manpower, Social Welfare and Rehabilitation Programs.* Washington, International Association of Rehabilitation Facilities and University of Pittsburgh Research and Training Center in Vocational Rehabilitation, 1970, p. 19.

Nadolsky, Julian M.: *Development of a Model for Vocational Evaluation of the Disadvantaged,* Interim Report of H.E.W., S.R.S. Research Grant No. 12-P-551-40/4-01, Auburn, Auburn University, 1971, p. 51.

Nadolsky, Julian M.: Evaluation's Relation to Adjustment. *Vocational Evaluation and Work Adjustment Bulletin, 2*(2):2-6, 1970.

Nadolsky, Julian M.: Patterns of Consistency Among Vocational Evaluators. *Vocational Evaluation and Work Adjustment Bulletin, 4*(4):13-25, 1971B.

Nadolsky, Julian M.: VEWAA's Future: Responsive or Limited. *Vocational Evaluation and Work Adjusment Bulletin, 4*(3):31-32, 1971A.

Neff, Walter S.: Problems of Work Evaluation. *Personnel and Guidance Journal, XLIV*(7):682-688, March, 1966.

Neff, Walter S.: Vocational Assessment - Theory and Models. *Journal of Rehabilitation, 36*(1):27-29, 1970.

Newman, Edward: Human Evaluation: The Necessary Ingredient. In Pacinelli (Ed.): *Vocational Evaluation and Work Adjustment Services in Manpower, Social Welfare and Rehabilitation Programs,* Washington, International Association of Rehabilitation Facilities, pp. 39-46.

Obermann, C. Esco: *A History of Vocational Rehabilitation in America,* Minneapolis, T. S. Denison and Company, Inc., 1965, pp. 68-86.

Oswald, Jesse H. and Parker, Murl W.: Vocational Rehabilitation Viewed by an Industrial Engineer. *Journal of Rehabilitation,* 37(2):17-19, 1971.

Overs, Ropert P.: Job Sample Theory. In Longfellow, Richard: Topical Review, *Vocational Evaluation and Work Adjustment Bulletin,* 1(4):16, 1968.

Payne, A.: Problems in Vocational Guidance. *Vocational Guidance Association Bulletin,* 2(3):61-63, 1923.

Proctor, W. M.: Mental Tests in Vocational Guidance. *Vocational Guidance Association Bulletin,* 1(1):2-4, 1921.

Pruitt, Walter: Basic Assumptions Underlying Work Sample Theory. *Journal of Rehabilitation,* 36(1):24-26, 1970A.

Pruitt, Walter A.: Functional-Level Classification System. *Vocational Evaluation and Work Adjustment Bulletin,* 3(1):5-7, 1970C.

Pruitt, Walter: Group Report. In Pacinelli, Ralph (Ed.): *Vocational Evaluation and Work Adjustment Services in Manpower, Social Welfare, and Rehabilitation Program, International Association of Rehabilitation Facilities.* Washington, 1970d, pp. 139-142.

Pruitt, Walter A. (Ed.): *Readings in Work Evaluation I,* Materials Development Center, Stout State University, Menomonie, 1970B.

Pruitt, Walter A. and Longfellow, Richard E.: Work Evaluation: The Medium and the Message. *Journal of Rehabilitation,* 36(1):8-9, Jan.-Feb., 1970.

Rosenberg, Bernard: Development of the TOWER System. *Vocational Evaluation and Work Adjustment Bulletin,* 2(3):9-11, 1969.

Rosenberg, Bernard: Organization and Administration of Work Evaluation Programs. In Pruitt, Walter and Pacinelli, Ralph (Eds.): *Work Evaluation in Rehabilitation,* Washington, Association of Rehabilitation Centers, 1969, pp. 95-99.

Rosenberg, Bernard: The Professional in Vocational Evaluation. *Journal of Rehabilitation,* 36(1):30-32, 1970.

Ross, Donald R.: Conceptual Model of a Professional Evaluator. In Pacinelli, Ralph (Ed.): *Research Utilization in Rehabilitation Facilities.* Washington, International Association of Rehabilitation Facilities, 1971, pp. 176-180.

Ross, Donald R. and Brandon, Thomas L.: In Pursuit of Work Adjustment. *Journal of Rehabilitation,* 37(4):6-8, 1971.

Sankovsky, Ray and Knight, Mel: Can Media Improve Rehabilitation Services? *Journal of Rehabilitation,* 37(2):8-9,1971.

Sankovsky, Ray: Characteristics of the VEWAA Membership: 1971. *Vocational Evaluation and Work Adjustment Bulletin,* 4(2):17-26, 1971.

Sankovsky, Raymond: Patterns of Services in Vocational Evaluation. In

Pruitt and Pacinelli (Eds.): *Work Evaluation in Rehabilitation,* Washington, Association of Rehabilitation Centers, 1969, pp. 31-59.

Sankovsky, Ray: Toward a Common Understanding of Vocational Evaluation. *Journal of Rehabilitation, 36*(1):10-12, 1970.

Sankovsky, Ray; Arthur, Gary; and Mann, Joe (Eds.): *Vocational Evaluation and Work Adjustment: A Book of Readings,* Alabama Rehabilitation Media Service, Auburn, Auburn University, 1970.

Sax, Arnold: The Development of Materials for Vocational Evaluation and Work Adjustment. *Vocational Evaluation and Work Adjustment Bulletin, 4*(2):29-30, 1971.

Sax, Arnold: Materials Development Center: A National Resource for Materials on Work Evaluation and Work Adjustment. In Pacinelli, Ralph N. (Ed.): *Research Utilization in Rehabilitation Facilities,* Washington, International Association of Rehabilitation Facilities, 1971, pp. 303-307.

Sink, Jack M.: Change — The Need for Vocational Evaluation. In Pacinelli, Ralph: *Research Utilization in Rehabilitation Facilities,* Washington, International Association of Rehabilitation Facilities, 1971B, pp. 181-185.

Sink, Jack M.: The Development of a Rehabilitation Center on the Campus of Auburn University to Include an Integrated Program of Services, Research, and Education. Unpublished doctoral dissertation, Auburn, Auburn University, 1970.

Sink, Jack M.: Doing Can Be Teaching. *Vocational Evaluation and Work Adjustment Bulletin, 4*(4):4-6, 1971.

Sink, Jack M.: Evaluation — A Reason for Concern. In Pruitt, Walter and Pacinelli, Ralph (Eds.): *Work Evaluation in Rehabilitation,* Washington, Association of Rehabilitation Centers, 1969, pp. 61-69.

Sink, Jack M.: The Future. Paper presented at Auburn, Auburn University, 1971A.

Sink, Jack M.; Couch, Robert H.; and Anderson, Joel L.: *The Work Oriented Rehabilitation Facility,* Florida State Department of Education, Division of Vocational Rehabilitation, Tallahassee, 1968, p. 1.

Smith, David W.: Closing the Manpower Gap in Vocational Evaluation. In Pruitt, Walter and Pacinelli, Ralph (Eds.): *Work Evaluation in Rehabilitation,* Washington Association of Rehabilitation Centers, 1969, pp. 101-108.

Smolkin, Charles: Smolkin Report Writing Format. Materials Development Center. Menomonie, Stout State University, 1971.

V

EVALUATING THE EVALUATOR

JOHN K. STOUT

Introduction
Problems Evaluating the Evaluator
The Future
References

INTRODUCTION

T HE PURPOSE OF THIS CHAPTER is to focus on some general
guidelines and yardsticks by which the performance and
competence of the evaluator could be gauged and to provide a
general discussion of the individual, his background, and the
work he does. Writing on this general topic seemed easy at the
beginning since we nearly always evaluate others. I evaluate
graduate students in rehabilitation counseling; evaluators evaluate their clients; and supervisors evaluate their evaluators. However, as work began, and the more I thought about it, the more
difficult writing the chapter became. It seems nearly impossible to
reliably and validly evaluate any professional in the behavioral
sciences. We do not have any basis to adequately evaluate the rehabilitation counselor, the psychologist, the physician, the speech
therapist, or the vocational evaluator.

This chapter will focus on some of the issues and problems in
evaluating the professional person and look at some suggestions

I wish to express my appreciation to Dr. Donald L. Angell, colleague in the Rehabilitation Programs at the University of Scranton, for his many significant comments on the content of the chapter.

specifically within the field of vocational evaluation which may help to better evaluate the evaluator in the future. The individual evaluator working in a specific setting will be less in focus than the profession and its body of knowledge.

I believe that attempting to develop specific guidelines for evaluating the evaluator is currently an impossible task, but I want to detail the problems I encountered in reaching this conclusion. The problems seem to fall into three categories: the body of knowledge in the field of vocational evaluation; the criteria problem; and the profession of vocational evaluation.

To avoid possible confusion throughout the chapter, I have used the terms vocational evaluation and vocational evaluator synonomously with the terms work evaluation and work evaluator even though I feel there are distinctions between the two, both in process and in actual job (Stout, 1969). Also, I have attempted to eliminate specific documentation as much as possible and have used references only where I felt it essential or useful for further reading.

PROBLEMS IN EVALUATING THE EVALUATOR

The Body of Knowledge in the Field

Adequate evaluation of the activity and behavior of the professional is directly related to the evaluation of his profession and its body of philosophical, theoretical, and practical knowledge. There is simply no way to measure adequately except by comparing behavior with some stable, dependable foundation of knowledge. This, then, becomes our first evaluation problem since in the behavioral sciences we rest on largely unvalidated theories, tools, and techniques.

In the physical sciences, however, evaluation of both the student and the professional appears easier than in the behavioral sciences. By virtue of a longer scientific history and because of the nature of the data and objects of study, theories are more testable and relationships between variables are more functional. Certain operations or procedures, if correctly applied, produce specified outcomes with astonishing reproducibility. We can call this *if-then* stability; that is, if this is done, then that occurs. With this the case, evaluation is a matter of assessing the person's knowledge and his correct implementation of procedure, since the outcome is predictable. Not only are the data and objects of study more constant and/or predictable, but usually the process of study or evaluation interferes less with the nature of the subject being studied than is so often the case in the behavioral sciences. And a final crucial point should also be noted. In the physical sciences, the reliability and calibration of evaluation instruments are significantly more precise than in the behavioral sciences where we rely on interviews, observation, rating scales, work samples, psychological tests, and so forth.

I am suggesting that evaluation of the professional in the behavioral sciences can never be very meaningful, valid, or scientific until the behavioral sciences produce a body of reasonably well validated knowledge involving functional relationships between variables and processes. Borrowing from the field of psychology, Watson (1963) stated that the development of schools of psychology and psychotherapy does not indicate considerable knowledge, but rather deficits in knowledge. In vocational evaluation we are in this precise position with respect to our present knowledge, tools, and techniques. As long as there remain so many partial theories and models, tools, techniques, and individual biases from which the practitioner may choose, evaluation of the professional will depend largely on the subjective biases of the one doing the evaluation, the correspondence of the evaluee's operations with the theoretical orientation of the evaluator or on the philosophy and goals of the organization for which he works.

The Criterion Problems

The question of a validated body of knowledge leads us directly into the criterion problem. Indeed, no discussion on evaluating performance or competency can legitimately ignore the problems of criteria. This issue haunts us in research, in selection, and in evaluation in psychology, rehabilitation, counseling, business, the military, and in grading graduate students in rehabilitation counseling programs as well as in the specific area of evaluating the evaluator. It is the heart of evaluation, both of clients in the field of vocational evaluation and in attempting to answer questions involving the performance and competency of the vocational evaluator.

I want to look at the criterion problem in evaluating the professional in two ways. First are the problems involving process variables; that is, the selection, implementation, and interaction of specific models, tools, and techniques to produce desired outcomes. Is it possible to evaluate the evaluator as I previously discussed in relation to the physical scientist; that is, by his knowledge of the vocational evaluation process and by his correct application of procedures to bring about predictable outcomes? It does appear possible to evaluate an evaluator on his knowledge of components of the vocational evaluation process. Nadolsky (1971), for example, has provided a structural model of vocational evaluation suggesting that at least ten components can be identified. Unfortunately, as he himself points out, this level of model development leaves much to be desired in considering the specific nature and functions of variables within the process, their interrelationships, and the specific movement of clients through such a process. So while the evaluator may indeed be evaluated on the basis of his knowledge of procedures, tools, and techniques, we cannot evaluate him on the correctness of these procedures. Said somewhat differently, we can assess whether the evaluator knows about techniques such as psychological testing, work samples, and so forth, but the relationships between these variables and the process itself remain largely speculative. We have little basis to say that the evaluator is asking the correct questions, using the appropriate method of evaluation, or processing and synthesizing data adequately. Consequently, evaluating the evaluator is not possible on the basis of a grasp and application of scientifically validated knowledge, but rather on idiosyncratic and largely unspecified variables. This is probably the state of the art of evaluating any professional in the behavioral sciences and it is certainly true in the vocational evaluation profession. Largely, vocational evaluation appears to be a trial and error process, often rationalized as a sequential process. The client's performance is assessed through subjective, internal processes of the vocational evaluator or on the pooled subjective processes of several vocational evaluators in staff conferences. In the behavioral sciences, we have an uncanny proclivity for pooling ignorance and arriving at truth!

A second potential criterion in evaluating the professional is concerned with outcome—the results he produces. Hefferin and Katz (1971a and 1971b) discuss five approaches in evaluating rehabilitation programs. They include: tabulation and analysis of statistical data (e.g., services rendered, clients served, etc.), clinical or medical approaches (e.g. assessing improvement of physical or psychophysical symptomatology), the sociocultural approach (e.g., assessing appropriate social behavior and adjustment), the psychological approach (e.g. assessing intrapsychic mechanisms and personality adjustment), and the vocational or work approach (e.g. assessing appropriate vocational behavior and adjustment). Such specification seems to be the simple part of the evaluation problem. Developing reasonably well controlled research designs and reliable and valid instruments to measure such process and outcome variables constitute the problem and are limiting factors in not really knowing how successful are our rehabilitation programs.

Several of the evaluation approaches or general criteria suggested by Hefferin and Katz, especially the statistical and work criteria, have been employed by various agencies with simplified naivete. Evaluation of the program may be based on the number of clients served, the number and types of services rendered, dollars spent, or the number of clients trained or placed. Not only do both public and private agencies use these criteria to evaluate programs, they also are used to evaluate the professional working in the programs.

What are the problems with these types of criteria? I believe the statistical and vocational approaches are static and represent an all-or-none logic. Success or failure in training or placement, while a deceptively simple dichotomous variable, simply does not tell the whole truth about the work of the professional or the difficulties he encounters. In addition, it often ignores contingency variables which are either unknown or uncontrolled. For example, in placing the disabled person, labor market conditions and unemployment rates may be of more significance in success than all the rehabilitation or evaluation procedures employed. Also, various agencies may place greater value on different outcome variables. A similar profession and professional, then, is evaluated on different outcome variables depending upon the philosophy and goals of the agency for which he works.

The criterion problem remains with us, then, essentially unresolved. Neither the evaluation of process nor of outcome varibles, as presently defined are totally satisfactory in evaluating the evaluator: the former because of deficits in knowledge and the absence of functional models; the latter because of wide differences in valued outcome variables, its all-or-none basis and its present inability to deal with contingency variables. Quite possibly these rather simple unitary outcome criteria will have to be replaced by more elaborate multidimensional criteria before any degree of satisfaction is attained in evaluation.

The Profession of Vocational Evaluation

It is a short jump from deficits in knowledge in the field and serious criterion problems in the behavioral sciences to the present confusion in the field of vocational evaluation. In practice, in hiring, and in training, limited knowledge, criterion problems, and diversity of opinion pose serious problems for the field of vocational evaluation. These problems seem to manifest themselves in the profession in two ways: its ubiquity, on the one hand, and its ambiquity, on the other. There was a time, and not so long ago, when vocational evaluation (pre-vocational evaluation in those days) was generally unheard of except as small units often hidden in large closets of some hospitals dealing with very severely physically disabled persons and in small sheltered workshops serving the mentally handicapped. This is no longer the case. Today, vocational evaluation is gaining momentum and is provided mandates in federal and state legislation. As a practice it is found in numerous agencies, facilities, and institutions dealing with psychiatric, mentally retarded, physically and visually disabled, public welfare, disadvantaged, public offender, and special education clients. Briefly put, the process is being seen as applicable to many different target populations, in many different settings, and with many different interpretations of the process, methodologies, and goals.

But while gaining momentum and acceptance in the rehabilitation process, vocational evaluation remains clouded with ambiguity. We do not even have agreement on what the name of the field is to be—vocational evaluation or work evaluation. This was evident in the January-February, 1970 isue of the *Journal of Rehabilitation* which was devoted to evaluation. While the title on the cover was work evaluation, probably reflecting the personal preference of the editors, vocational evaluation, work evaluation, and vocational assessment were the terms used variously throughout the thirteen featured articles. Also, the field of vocational evaluation was variously defined and described by each of the authors, all of whom represent leaders in the field. While many would see the work situation involving work samples and job-tryouts as the core of evaluation, many would view these as simply one small aspect of the entire vocational evaluation process, which in turn is viewed as a part of the total rehabilitation evaluation process (Roberts, 1970). The importance of these issues is that how one describes and feels about these aspects determines to a considerable extent the nature of facility operations and procedures, as well as the emphasis given to various types of training of the evaluator—in-service, out-service, or graduate level training.

The practitioner in evaluation poses more difficulties. He still remains a rather unspecified and variable entity as reflected in the studies by Egerman and Gilbert (1969) and Sankovsky (1971) on the characteristics of the evaluator. The latter study provides some interesting insights into the characteristics of members of the Vocational Evaluation and Work Adjustment Association (VEWAA) who call themselves evaluators. It can be seen that few have a formal educational background specifically in evaluation, however it is defined, and that what formal education has been obtained in evaluation has been only of several weeks or months duration. While 87 percent of the evaluators listed a bachelor's degree, with the largest group being in industrial arts, few held bachelor's degrees in psychology, and the remainder scattered themselves through virtually every college curriculum imaginable, from physics to religion. Also, it is interesting to note that this group felt most competent in dealing with work samples and performance tests (some of the least well validated of our tools) and least competent in working with psychological tests (perhaps still the best validated of our tools).

Interestingly, it is becoming a very common practice today to downgrade or even to eliminate the use of psychological tests with many types of clients. Vocational evaluation, as well as numerous school systems, have perhaps overreacted to difficulties in psychological testing. The defects and problems in psychological testing lie not entirely with the tests, but also with the user and the use to which tests are put. A psychological test is only a sample of behavior which has some demonstrated relationship with other variables. Now the demonstrated relationship may not always be as great as we might desire, but we at least know approximately what it is. Psychological testing as used with the disadvantaged, has received special criticism because tests require reading and the use of abstract symbols and the disadvantaged usually do poorly in these areas. This may be true, but if we are trying to predict the attainment of a criterion involving reading and abstract symbols, then the information gained from certain types of psychological tests is quite important and very meaningful. Perhaps either too much or the wrong things have been asked from psychological tests and when the answers were not there, testing as a concept has been prematurely thrown out. I am not saying that psychological testing is always appropriate, but I am saying that testing is not always as inappropriate or as meaningless as some would have us believe. The effective use of psychological tests should be a part of the evaluator's armamentarium and this competence is not gained in five or ten weeks of in-service training!

It would be interesting to speculate what the characteristics are of practicing evaluators throughout the country who do not belong to VEWAA. It might be hypothesized that this group has even less formal educational background, less background in evaluation, less specialized short-term training in evaluation, work for less sophisticated evaluation facilities, or work in quite different types of evaluation facilities. A recent study by Barad (1971) indicates some support of most of these hypotheses.

Thinking about evaluating the evaluator makes one think about the employment criteria of various agencies in hiring evaluators since virtually any background appears to qualify a person to be an evaluator. This suggests that minimal formal skills and training are needed to be an evaluator, or that the facilities have exceptionally good in-service training programs, or that the profession is really a trade where on-the-job training is the true criterion for entrance, or that there really is not a great amount of skill or training needed to be an evaluator. But, then, are these not the logical results of knowledge deficits and criteria problems?

Conclusions

Thus far, I have attempted to discuss some of the major problems precluding the effective evaluation of the professional, especially the vocational evaluator. These pages have presented a highly critical view of the field. I am not suggesting, however, that this is the best we can offer. First of all, let us place things in proper perspective. The fascinating thing about the previous pages is that *rehabilitation counseling* or *psychotherapy* could have been substituted for vocational evaluation and the ideas would remain valid. This is to say that all professions in the behavioral sciences struggle with these same issues and with varying degrees of success. Psychotherapy has a history of three-quarters of a century and is only somewhat better off than the field of vocational evaluation; so too, with rehabilitation counseling with its half-century history. Both fields still regularly employ more unvalidated knowledge, tools, and techniques than validated data. Still, the conceptualization of the rehabilitation counselor (i.e., counselor or coordinator) haunts the field as does a question as to what activities constitute counseling and psychotherapy. Still in both fields there are serious questions concerning a valid conceptualization of process and outcome variables, and the issues of certification, required knowledge, ethical conduct, and work experience are lively issues in the rehabilitation counseling profession (Carnes, 1971).

Is the field of vocational evaluation unique? I think not. In fact, the field may be in a better position than its close colleague, rehabilitation counseling. There is probably a greater diversity of opinion within rehabilitation counseling as to what constitutes a rehabilitation counselor and his major role. Similar conceptual problems in vocational evaluation do not seem as diverse, nor are they grasped as tenaciously as in rehabilitation counseling. The rehabilitation counselor is more closely tied to state-federal vocational rehabilitation agencies as primary employers. This so often dictates the types of activities the counselor does, how he does them, and how he is evaluated (e.g., the outcome criterion of closure). The evaluator, while dealing to a great extent with public agency clients, is not necessarily tied to civil service classifications specifying his job and specific process or outcome variables. Rehabilitation counseling's long history has served to tie the field to the past and to models that worked with the physically disabled but which may be highly questionable for working with clients today, for example, the disadvantaged. Vocational evaluation is gaining acceptance and momentum, at least partially, on the intuitive basis of having something specific to offer to these types of clients where historical processes have failed. The profession of rehabilitation counseling and its professional associations also are tied to the past because of the personalities long identified as the leadership in the field. The evaluation field is much less dominated by such figures; in fact, the evaluation field is composed of a relatively young group of professionals who are hopefully more open to change, development, and the dynamism which a profession desperately needs. Its newness is an asset; that is, it is an asset to begin without being tied to the past in practices, in wornout models, in past leaders and philosophy, and in inappropriate outcomes variables gauging the success of the profession and the professional.

While we have both youth and newness working for us, we cannot excuse our deficiencies on that basis. Further development of the profession seems to be contingent upon developing a body of philosophical, theoretical, and practical knowledge.

THE FUTURE

Developing a Body of Knowledge

A considerable amount of space was devoted in the first part of this chapter to a discussion of the question of knowledge in the field of vocational evaluation, how deficits in validated knowledge present problems in evaluating an evaluator, and how a profession is obligated to develop a validated body of knowledge as one of its bases of operation. While the field of evaluation continues to gain acceptance and momentum, it is doing so largely on the basis of the face validity of our knowledge, tools, and techniques (i.e., they look good and seem appropriate) and through the default of other more historically accepted professions and processes which have failed to meet the current challenges. This failure on the part of other professions has created a vacuum in effective service delivery and the field of vocational evaluation has rushed in—hence its ubiquity. But as a profession develops, we must attempt to establish more than the face validity of what we are doing. Spergel (1970) rather succinctly states the challenge we are facing:

> The time has long past when those involved in the discipline of work evaluation can perpetuate the rationalization of being a young profession. This only serves to mask difficulties rather than deal directly with problems that must be solved. The age of armchair philosophy must now be supplanted by the application of the scientific methods.

So, if we do accept this challenge and commit ourselves to research and experimentation, what type are we going to do and how are we going to do it? Spergel (1970) feels the area of vocational evaluation lends itself rather nicely to reasonably well designed experimentation. I believe, however, that the typical type of outcome research which preoccupied the counseling field for so many years (is counseling effective?) and presently occupies many of the researchers in vocational evaluation may not be the only, or the most desirable, direction to proceed. This type of research ignores too many significant variables, both of the process type (the complex interaction of the personal variables of rehabilitation personnel, the client, and methods of vocational evaluation) and the contingency type (level of employment and varying outcome goals of different facilities, for example). Outcome studies are so often static, all-or-none in nature, and add little to our knowledge of specific variables and their interaction which contribute to overall success and failure. While this type of research should continue to add substance to the profession and its body of knowledge, our field, in its research infancy, should also strive to profit from research in other fields.

The trend in research in the field of counseling, for example, went through several stages. When the effectiveness of counseling was first seriously questioned, researchers began with the question, Is counseling effective? Although years of research of this type has never produced definitive answers, the profession decided that counseling was indeed effective, even with its rather unspecified techniques. Stemming from these efforts, however, came another thrust in counseling research and researchers began to ask the question, Are different counseling approaches more successful or more efficient than others? This issue is still hotly discussed, and with minimal research evidence different theorists enthusiastically carry the banner of their own personal counseling model. A few researchers in counseling today are asking questions such as, What counseling approaches and techniques, used by what type of person, are most effective with what types of clients?

The trend might be interpreted as follows: we must first attempt to justify our social and professional usefulness; then we try to say that our method is better than yours; and finally, we come to the interesting conclusion that they may all work to some degree, but we attempt to specify their role and effectiveness with greater precision. While the final question is the much more sophisticated in terms of research design, processes, and goals, it is also the most basic in terms of describing a body of knowledge. Once the components of a system or model are identified or described as in Nadolsky's (1971b) monograph, then the relationships between the components, the development of a more exact process, and specified outcomes should start to be described.

Research in the field of vocational evaluation is presently asking the first question, Are we effective? We will never know if that is the only level of question we ask. We should move to the second and third levels of question. These allow us to look more closely at our methods, our clients, and most importantly, at the evaluator as a personal variable in the process. With these types of questions, we might be able to develop functional models of vocational evaluation specifying what method (s) , used by what type of person, is most successful, with which clients, and under what circumstances. Barad (1971) is right on target when he says:

> . . .at some point in the development of our profession, we will be obligated to initiate large scale inter-agency factorial experiments designed to determine the differential utility of the various appraisal methodologies, the significance of the evaluator differences in educational level, experiential background, and theoretical orientation; the impact of the client's disability classification; and the effect of such *prognosis variables* as client socioeconomic status.

That point in the development of our profession is now!

With these types of research questions and designs we may find that the evaluator as a personal variable in the evaluation process is the discriminant variable as opposed to the method of evaluation. Sankovsky (1970) in a slightly different way alludes to this aspect:

> There is some evidence that vocational evaluators differ with respect to the amount of information needed, the type of information needed, and the amount of time needed in order to establish potential vocational objectives. What relationships exist between these factors and the personality, creativeness, or risk-taking propensities of vocational evaluators still remains unanswered.

We do know some things about the potency of interpersonal relationships and the placebo effect from research in counseling and psychotherapy. The methods of vocational evaluation, from psychological testing to job analysis and work samples, can be graded on the degree of relatedness to the criterion of work behavior and job performance. This closeness-to-criterion is often cited as a major reason for using work samples (Pruitt, 1970). These methods may be placed on another dimension, however. Specifically, each of these methods can be graded on the closeness of interpersonal relations between the client and his evaluator or another actual worker. It can be seen, then, that there is minimal interpersonal contact between the client and the evaluator in most standardized psychological testing situations, but increasing interpersonal relationship in the administration of work samples and a similar closeness between the client and actual workers in job tryouts. Perhaps the closeness of interpersonal contact, and the interaction of personality variables of the evaluator and the client, is a crucial variable affecting outcome. This situation would be somewhat analogous to the interpersonal contact involving operant conditioning studies with mentally retarded in sheltered workshops. Because of the interaction between the technique (operant conditioning) and the interpersonal relationships (giving the reward or attention), perhaps conclusions of the efficacy of operant conditioning techniques are more complex than they appeared initially (Zimmerman, Stuckey, Garlick, and Miller, 1969).

The purpose of this discussion of research is important I think for several reasons. To develop a profession, we must accumulate a body of knowledge and to do this, we must ask the correct questions in our research efforts. As the validated knowledge accumulates, we have a more realistic basis for choice between methods and vocational evaluation can become less an art and more a science. This certainly would aid in evaluating the evaluator as well as providing some basis for the selection and training of personnel for the field.

But the research activities suggested here are not enough to justify the existence of a profession. The development of a theoretical underpinning is also necessary (Gellman, 1968). Indeed, we might argue that both philosophical and theoretical underpinnings are crucial in directing the course of a profession. They form the basis for asking the correct research questions. Virtually all the present research in vocational evaluation is asking the question, Are we effective? While previously criticized on other grounds, this question can be further criticized on the ground of being totally atheroetical.

Nadolsky (1971b) provides an excellent discussion of the difference between structural and functional models in science. In essence, the structural model organizes and describes different variables; for example, the components of the vocational evaluation process. This is observation and classification, a necessary operation in model building. It tells us what exists. Functional models attempt to account for relationships and interactions between variables. For example, the course a client might take through the evaluation process; that is, because of the nature of this client, he need only be involved in these specific components of the process since they will provide the information needed. We have few, of any, functional models in vocational evaluation that would allow us to make a statement such as this. We cannot on any *a priori* basis, predict except within very, very broad limits, what the usefulness of a specific method of evaluation will be until after we use it. This reflects the lack of the *if-then* stability previously mentioned.

It is important to note that functional models do not automatically spring forth from descriptive research and structural models. Functional models showing relationships and interactions between variables and processes grow out of research which focuses on these aspects. Nadolsky's (1971a) finding that there is an interaction between the evaluator's educational level and evaluation techniques is an example. In other words, statements of theories and principles in the field of vocational evaluation provide the basis for asking the types of research questions from which functional models are derived. Further research validates, refines, and creates new functional models which form the basis not only for additional research, but also for practices in the field. So, as uncomfortable as it may be to theorize and develop principles for vocational evaluation, it seems necessary to the growth of a profession and its body of knowledge. We are starting to theorize with respect to the vocational evaluation process and with some of our tools and techniques. For example, within Pruitt's (1970) discussion of the assumptions underlying the theory of work samples are potentially testable hypotheses which, if re-searched, could certainly answer some of the criticisms directed at this evaluation method (Thomas, 1971). When these are sub-jected to research, we are beginning to get out of the armchair philosophy era and into the scientific era.

Curiously, though, in vocational evaluation we neither theo-rize about, nor do we discuss much, the theory and knowledge related to one of the major outcomes of our efforts in vocational evaluation—work. In fact, we seem to take work for granted even though there is a fairly rich body of knowledge concerning work, career development, interests and work values, job satisfaction and motivation. While this is not the place for a lengthy discus-sion of these issues, perhaps the point can be made by briefly looking at the concepts of motivation, work values, and job satis-faction. Vocational evaluators, as well as rehabilitation and guid-ance counselors, neglect an important variable in vocational coun-seling. Each of these professions are assessing an individual and his potential for work. Each use some combination of ability, ap-titude, interest, and personality observations or measures to de-termine whether a person is qualified for a specific educational or training program or a specific type of work. It is interesting, how-ever, that the factors related to the choice of and entrance into an occupation are different from the factors which motivate a person to perform on the job, create morale, and produce either job satis-faction or dissatisfaction (Zytowski, 1970). We use aptitude as-sessment to indicate the level of functioning; interests to assess where this level of functioning may be directed; and personality measures in largely unspecified ways since this is the least known variable in occupational choice. But this is where each of these professions stop. We either ignore or do not see that these apti-tudes, interests, and personality factors may not be the same fac-tors that cause a worker to be motivated to stay working or to be satisfied with his work. We are only doing part of our job. We must concern ourselves not only with job entry, but also later motivation to stay on the job and the worker's potential for satis-faction from it. It is essential, then, to continue to theorize about the process of and variables in vocational evaluation, but as a professional we cannot afford to ignore the body of knowledge developed in other areas which are obviously related to our activities.

A profession should not only have a reasonably well validated body of knowledge with theoretical underpinnings, but it also must have a philosophical base. Now this notion of a philosophical base will really scare some people. We have moved from practice to research to theory and now to philosophy! But why is this important? Implicit in psychological theories are assumptions about the nature of man, reality, and his role in the universe. The only aspect of man, at the philosophical level, that we as a profession have thus far discussed is man's relation to work. And, we have essentially only one statement of this aspect. In syllogistic form it is stated as follows: work is a basic reality of present society; man is a part of society; therefore, man should work. While I previously stated that as a relatively young profession we were not so tied to the past, this is one area where we definitely are. Vocational evaluation has unquestioningly and without reservations adopted the philosophy of the state-federal vocational rehabilitation program which idolizes work and gauges its success on the basis of the number of people placed annually in the labor force. There are enough factors in the present work world which should cause us to reflect more deeply on the goals we have so readily accepted. Again this is not the place for a lengthy discussion of the world of work, but out of a larger number, the following factors make me question our activities and goals for many of our clients: the changing nature of work, technological changes and automation, less unskilled and semiskilled jobs with more jobs requiring advanced education and technical training, job openings in the lowest paying and lowest status areas that no one want, less workers being needed to support our society at higher levels, the real possibility of re-defining the level of a full employment economy (e.g. the possibility that we are really running out of enough jobs for everyone!) , changing concepts of work and leisure and the four day work week, and increasing job dissatisfaction because of increasing job fractionalization and specialization. Many writers have been warning us of the potential problems involving these factors in the work world. Samler (1968) is, perhaps, one of the best original references for rehabilitation personnel.

What all of this means is that we have accepted the fact that everyone should work and possibly we have accepted this philosophy prematurely. Or, perhaps, we are the profession to challenge some of the long standing myths about work. We tie work to dignity and self-respect, with self-realization and identity, with independence and success. We look with pride and a feeling of professional satisfaction at the mentally retarded client who is working in a sheltered workshop separating nuts and bolts and earning $15.00 a week where one year ago he was only basket weaving, finger painting, singing and dancing, and taking trips to the zoo in his special education class.

Many of our clients enter into and remain in the labor force in the most menial, lowest paying, and lowest status jobs since these clients are often the most marginally talented and skilled. These are also the types of jobs that are almost always available since no one else wants them and most are devoid of any potential for either providing intrinsic or extrinsic satisfaction. We are asking much of many of our clients. I knew an evaluator who once remarked that regardless of what his agency did, sixty percent of their clients got janitorial jobs. The simple fact of not having enough jobs for everyone who wants them develops some interesting philosophical questions concerning who should and should not work. Are the handicapped the ones who will be singled out and perhaps paid for not working? Should they be? If not the handicapped, then who?

There are some of the issues that we must discuss if we consider ourselves an emerging profession—questioning not only our tools, techniques, body of knowledge, and competence, but also the societal goals and philosophical base on which we are going to stand in our culture.

Conclusions

I started the chapter attempting to develop guidelines for gauging the activity and performance of the evaluator. Whether or not this has in any way been accomplished is questionable. The field of vocational evaluation has numerous serious problems: some because of its relative newness; many because it shares similar characteristics with other behavior science disciplines.

It seems to me that the development of a body of knowledge is crucial to the development of a profession; to fulfilling its societal mandate; and for ultimately evaluating and certifying its own members. This is a difficult task, but we have begun. But not only do we need knowledge of the differential effectiveness of our processes, tools, and techniques, we also need the richness and depth of theory and a philosophy of man and his role in the universe to aid us and provide us direction.

REFERENCES

Barad, C. B.: A survey of vocational evaluation practices in Maryland and the District of Columbia. *Vocational Evaluation and Work Adjustment Bulletin, 4*(2):6-10, 1971.

Carnes, G.D.: The certification of rehabilitation counselors. *Rehabilitation Counseling Bulletin, 15:*72-79, 1971.

Egerman, K. and Gilbert, J. L.: The work evaluator. *Journal of Rehabilitation, 35*(3):12-14, 1969.

Gellman, W.: The principles of vocational evaluation. *Rehabilitation Literature, 29:*98-102, 1968.

Hefferin, E. A. and Katz, A. H.: Issues and orientations in the evaluation of rehabilitation programs: a review article; part I. *Rehabilitation Literature, 32:*66-74, 95, 1971.

Hefferin, E. A. and Katz, A. H.: Issues and orientations in the evaluation of rehabilitation programs: a review article; part II. *Rehabilitation Literature, 32:*98-107, 113, 1971.

Herzberg, F., Mausner, B., and Snyderman, B.: *The Motivation to Work.* New York, Wiley, 1959.

Nadolsky, J. M.: Patterns of consistency among vocational evaluators. *Vocational Evaluation and Work Adjustment Bulletin, 4*(4), 13-25, 1971.

Nadolsky, J. M.: *Development of a model for vocational evaluation of the disadvantaged.* Auburn, Auburn University. Duplicating Service, 1971.

Pruitt, W. A.: Basic assumptions underlying work sample theory. *Journal of Rehabilitation, 36*(1):24-26, 1970.

Roberts, C. L.: Definitions, objectives, and goals in work evaluation. *Journal of Rehabilitation, 36*(1):12-15, 1970.

Samler, J.: The counselor in our time. *Rehabilitation Counseling Bulletin (Special Issue), 11* (3-5P), 1968.

Sankovsky, R.: Toward a common understanding of vocational evaluation. *Journal of Rehabilitation, 36*(1):10-12, 1970.

Sankovsky, R.: Characteristics of the VEWAA membership: 1971. *Vocational Evaluation and Work Adjustment Bulletin, 4*(2):17-26, 1971.

Spergel, P.: Vocational evaluation: Research and implications for maximizing human potential. *Journal of Rehabilitation, 36*(1):21-24, 1970.

Stout, J. K.: Certifying the evaluator. *Vocational Evaluation and Work Adjustment Bulletin, 2*(4):4-6, 1969.

Thomas, K. R.: The omnipotence of work samples: a closer look. *Vocational Evaluation and Work Adjustment Bulletin, 4*(4):10-12, 1971.

Walker, R. A.: A future for vocational evaluation. *Journal of Rehabilitation, 36*(1):38-39, 1970.

Watson, R. I.: *The Clinical Method in Psychology.* (Science Editions) New York, Wiley, 1963.

Zimmerman, J., Stuckey, T. E., Garlick, B. J., and Miller, M.: Effects of token reinforcement on productivity in multiply handicapped clients in a sheltered workshop. *Rehabilitation Literature, 30*:34-41, 1969.

Zytowski, D. G.: The concept of work values. *Vocational Guidance Quarterly, 18*:176-186, 1970.

VI

THE MATERIALS DEVELOPMENT CENTER: A NATIONAL RESOURCE FOR MATERIALS ON WORK EVALUATION AND ADJUSTMENT

Arnold B. Sax and C. Thomas Allen

The Need for Information and Materials
The Information Service of the MDC
Research Utilization, and Development Component
Summary
References

THE MATERIALS DEVELOPMENT CENTER (MDC) is a program within the Department of Rehabilitation and Manpower Services at the University of Wisconsin—Stout, which has been established to serve as a national resource center for materials in work adjustment. The MDC is supported in part by a Research and Demonstration Grant from Social and Rehabilitation Service (DHEW). The purpose of the MDC is to collect, develop, and distribute information and materials which may be used to facilitate the development and improvement of work evaluation and work adjustment programs.

THE NEED FOR INFORMATION AND MATERIALS

Work evaluation and work adjustment are relatively new services which have undergone rapid expansion in recent years.

This growth was spurred first by passage of Public Law 83-565 in 1954 which authorized the expenditure of large sums to support the development of programs within rehabilitation facilities. An even greater boost came with passage of Public Law 83-333 in 1965 which authorized the use of evaluation services to determine if an individual has potential for vocational rehabilitation services. At the same time, rehabilitation services were expanded to include new groups such as public offenders and the socially deprived. Thus, the need was established for more facilities to provide work evaluation and work adjustment. Pending welfare reform legislation would have the effect of vastly expanding current needs for work evaluation services.

There is a great shortage of personnel trained specifically in work evaluation and work adjustment. Although three universities (University of Wisconsin—Stout, Auburn University, and the University of Arizona) offer graduate training in work evaluation, the number of students prepared in these programs is far below that needed to meet the expanding needs of the field. Short term training programs have been established but are still very limited in the number of participants that can be trained. As a results of insufficient training opportunities and standardized systems of evaluation and work adjustment, many practitioners have been forced to develop programs with little assistance from outside their facilities. Although this has resulted in the display of quite a bit of creativity in programs developed, it has also been somewhat inefficient and has led to the development of many marginally effective programs. Because there was no effective central source of information on programs that have been developed in facilities throughout the nation, many facilities' personnel have spent needless time in duplication of effort. This time would have been more effectively spent in modifying existing programs and evaluation procedures to meet the specific needs of individual facilities.

When the Graduate Training Program in Vocational Evaluation was established in 1967 at the University of Wisconsin—Stout (formerly Stout State University) considerable time and effort was spent collecting resource material. The methods used to collect these materials included a search of the literature, including journals, research reports, books, unpublished articles and direct written requests to over 2,000 rehabilitation facilities, visitation to numerous facilities; and advertisements in journals.

The search revealed several important factors. First, there is a serious lack of materials relating to work evaluation and adjustment that are appropriate for general distribution. Additionally, facilities' personnel often do not have the time, resources, or talent necessary to prepare descriptions of work evaluation and work adjustment procedures they have developed in such a way that other persons in the field might be able to replicate, adopt or modify these procedures to meet the specific needs of their facility. Third, there is a great need from rehabilitation facilities, other service programs, state agencies, training programs for preparation of rehabilitation personnel, and others for adequate access to materials currently available on work evaluation and work adjustment. As rehabilitation personnel became aware that materials were being collected by the graduate program at Stout, many individuals turned to the program for assistance in obtaining information on topics related to work evaluation and work adjustment.

The results of the search for materials and resultant requests clearly established evidence of the need for a national center for materials on work evaluation and adjustment. The Materials Development Center was established in July 1969 as a one-year pilot project under a Research and Demonstration Grant (RD-3040-GA-69) from Social and Rehabilitation Service. Activities of the first year were focused upon defining the needs of evaluators in the field and in planning programs to meet these needs. A questionnaire survey of evaluators in the field of rehabilitation served as a basis for most decisions concerning services which were needed. To adequately met the information needs of the field, it was determined that the MDC must pursue an active course in the development of materials, as well as the collection and dissemination of those materials now in existence.

In September 1970 the MDC began full operation under a five-year continuation Research and Demonstration Grant (12-P-55307/5) from Social and Rehabilitation Service. The functions of the MDC are divided into two major service components: (1) the Information Service, and (2) the Research, Utilization, and Development component. The primary target groups for MDC services are (1) rehabilitation facilities that serve state vocational rehabilitation agency clients and (2) state rehabilitation agency personnel who are primarily concerned with the provision, development and improvement of work evaluation and adjustment services in facilities. MDC publications and other services are available free of charge upon request by members of these target groups. Other facilities, training programs, and interested professionals may purchase MDC publications and services.

THE INFORMATION SERVICE OF THE MDC

The purpose of the Information Service is to provide a means through which practitioners may easily obtain information on topics related to work evaluation and work adjustment. The basic functions of this service are collection, classification, and dissemination. Loan copies of materials relevant to the needs of users of this service are made available.

The Information Service maintains the most extensive existing collection of information related to the topics of work evaluation and work adjustment. A systematic program has been established for continued collection of journal articles, speeches, manuals, research reports, publications from facilities and government sponsored programs, procedure descriptions, work sample descriptions and behavior rating scales.

In order to quickly and accurately identify and locate specific items of information from such an extensive collection of closely related materials, an information retrieval system has been established for use with all materials related specifically to work evaluation and work adjustment. In preparation for incorporating a document into the information retrieval system, the document must be carefully read to identify the specific topics covered. An abstract or descriptive summary is prepared which outlines the content of the document. Key concept terms (which are used later to identify documents for retrieval) are then assigned to the document. Due to considerable variation in the use of much of the terminology of work evaluation and work adjustment, the key concept terms must be precisely defined and used consistently within the information retrieval system. Some authors use different terms to refer to the same basic concept. Others may use a commonly used term to represent specialized meanings differing from the popular meaning of the term. All key concept terms assigned to any document reflect a particular concept as defined by the MDC.

The document is then assigned a code number for access to its location in the storage files. For each key concept term, there is a reference card which lists the code numbers of each document dealing with the topic. A second card file contains the bibliographic information, abstract, and key terms for each document entered into the information retrieval system. Material within the retrieval system can also be identified by author's name, title of the article or organization which published it.

As requests for information are received, the content of the request must be analyzed carefully and related to the key concept terms which are used in the information retrieval system. To aid in this process, those who seek information are asked to state the request as specifically as possible, pointing out why the information is needed and how it is expected to be used. An acceptable request might be, "Send information on the construction and development of a small engine repair work sample," or "We are trying to develop a behavior rating scale which will provide an avenue for report writing to describe a client's work related behaviors. What do you have in this area?" Such specific requests are relatively easy to deal with since it can quickly be determined if appropriate materials dealing with this topic have been filed in the information retrieval system. Other requests, such as "Send information on work evaluation," cannot be dealt with appropriately through use of the information retrieval system. Various publications discussed in a later section are available through the MDC that will provide basic information to help the individual more specifically describe the type of information he desires.

After the key concept terms relating to the request are chosen, the numerical code access number of each document dealing with the topic requested is identified. The abstract of each document is then reviewed in order to select those documents which appear to relate best to the needs expressed in the request.

Loan copies of the materials selected and other possible references on this topic are then sent to the person making the request. If the individual is not fully satisfied with the materials he has obtained, he may request the loan of other materials identified during the information search or modify the request to more specifically outline his needs.

For cases in which the individual seeking information does not indicate a rather specific problem area, the MDC has developed such publications as *Work Evaluation—An Annotated Bibliography: 1947-1970*. This publication contains references and annotations of over four hundred documents which are contained in the MDC collection and filed for use with the information retrieval system. After reading the entries of this publication, an evaluator can better realize the types of materials which are available and then formulate specific requests appropriate to his needs. Yearly supplements to the annotated bibliography are planned to keep readers abreast of new materials as they are published. A similar publication, *Work Adjustment—An Annotated Bibliography* should be ready for publication in the summer of 1972, and will be updated yearly by supplements.

All of the currently held materials relating directly to work evaluation and work adjustment have been annotated, assigned key concepts, and entered into the information retrieval system. The emphasis of activities is shifting from one of developing the information-retrieval system to one of promoting maximum utilization of the benefits it can provide. New literature can now be processed for entry into the system as soon as it arrives. A Selective Dissemination of Information (SDI) plan will be established. This plan automatically routes new literature on selected topics to interested professionals without need for specific requests.

In the planning stage is an additional analysis of the literature which will allow comparison of the sophistication of the material to the comprehension of the user, who may be a novice or an experienced person. Due to the limited number of MDC staff, the information retrieval system is open only to those indicated previously in this paper as our target group. In time we would hope to open this service to all concerned individuals.

In addition to providing professionals with fast and accurate access to the literature, the Information Service provides an equally important function within the MDC. Through familiarity with the available literature of work evaluation and work adjustment and with the analysis of the requests from practitioners, the Information Service is in an excellent position to identify specific areas in which materials should be developed. This information may be used to establish priorities for activities of the Research, Utilization, and Development component of the MDC. Also, this information may be used to identify needs for state-of-the art publications which can fill gaps and clarify the significance of existing literature to better meet the requests of those who make use of this service. If necessary funds are available, the MDC plans to add a new staff position in the fall of 1972. The primary duties of this person would entail the development of the state-of-the-art publications as mentioned above and to prepare packaged programs with how-to-do-it material on selected areas of concern. While it is recognized that there are serious limitations in the current literature of work evaluation and work adjustment, there is much that can be done to pull together information from existing research and reports of innovation service programs. The MDC staff believes that these publications and programs will report and consolidate information on available materials, hardware and techniques and provide emphasis for practitioners to further explore existing literature.

The Information Service also is active in disseminating a variety of materials published by the MDC. The MDC has established a Reprint Series to make available to practitioners valuable publications which are in great demand but are otherwise unobtainable. *The Pre-Vocational Unit in a Rehabilitation Center* by Henry Redkey and Barbara White, *Adjusting People to Work* by Dr. William Gellman and other members of the Chicago JVS staff, *Work Evaluation in Rehabilitation* originally published by Association of Rehabilitation Centers, Inc., and *Guidelines for Organizing Vocational Evaluation Units* developed by the Fourth

Institute on Rehabilitation Services are examples of the Reprint Series publications. The MDC also publishes a series of *Readings in Work Evaluation and Work Adjustment*. This series is made up primarily of publications on work evaluation and work adjustment that have not received wide distribution. Individual publications within this series will focus on such topics as work sample theory, construction of work samples, behavior rating scale theory and report writing. The Recommended Procedures series is a group of brief publications dealing with pratcical, how-to-do-it procedures also published by the MDC. Included in this series have been publications on procedures for simplifying a card filing work sample, procedures for simplifying the writing of an evaluation report, using industrial engineering techniques to develop industrially related performance standards for work samples, and suggested publications for developing a library of work evaluation and work adjustment materials within a rehabilitation facility.

Other MDC publications disseminated by the Information Service include the *Proceedings of the Decatur Seminar*, containing descriptions of seven evaluation units in the State of Illinois and the *Think Tank* which is a transcript of a conference at Stout State University in which definitions, goals and purposes of work evaluation and adjustment were discussed. The MDC acts as the national distribution center for the thirty in-service training units in rehabilitation known as *Studies in Continuing Education for Rehabilitation Counselors* (SCERC) which were developed by the Rehabilitation Department, University of Iowa. The Information Service also loans audio tapes of conference programs and meetings on the topics of work evaluation and adjustment. Materials and services available through the MDC and other sources are announced in the *MDC Information Newsletter*. The newsletter is sent to over 4,500 interested professionals in the United States as well as to approximately two hundred foreign facilities.

RESEARCH, UTILIZATION, AND DEVELOPMENT COMPONENT

As indicated by the results of the pilot year questionnaire survey and by daily requests to the MDC, practitioners seek not only the literature of work evaluation and work adjustment, but also a source of actual hardware (e.g., work samples) and procedures (e.g., techniques for identifying and changing work behavior problems, report writing formats). As mentioned earlier, many of the better materials and procedures developed in the field are seldom passed on to other settings. This is due in part to the fact that materials are not packaged in such a way to facilitate rapid adoption.

The effectiveness and extent of use of work evaluation and work adjustment procedures is dependent in many instances upon the degree to which specific and detailed information on using a procedure or technique is contained in training and orientation materials. Since work evaluation and work adjustment procedures generally involve a great deal of observation and recording of performance and work behaviors, specific direction on when and how to make observations should be given whenever possible. Unless directions are given for making effective and efficient observations, efforts to adopt materials before effectiveness may be assessed may be cut short due to excessive time investment by facility staff.

The Research, Utilization, and Development component of the MDC attempts to alleviate the problem of inadequately prepared material through the use of extensive field trial research of materials. Approximately 140 rehabilitation facilities, designated as MDC Cooperative Centers, have agreed to field test MDC materials and provide suggestions and information that is needed to be certain that materials are both effective and relatively easy to incorporate into existing service programs. Although some materials are originally developed by the MDC staff, the majority of the projects of this component of the MDC will deal with materials and procedures originally developed by others in the field and revised for national distribution by the MDC. It is further anticipated that the MDC Cooperative Centers will serve as utilization centers where developed material can be demonstrated to other centers.

The MDC can provide the resources necessary to refine and further develop materials to the point that they may be utilized by facilities on a national basis. The materials and procedures developed by the MDC should meet the following criteria: (a) meet very practical needs of many rehabilitation facilities; (b) possess an adequate research background, especially in terms of extensive field trial; (c) include orientation and training materials to facilitate implementation; and (d) be reasonably priced in order that even rehabilitation facilities with very limited budgets would be capable of adopting them. The activities of the Research, Utilization and Development Component of the MDC might best be understood in reference to the following review of several of the projects currently underway.

The MDC is currently engaged in the field trial of the first of a series of work samples, the MDC/VGRS Assembly Work Sample. This work sample, originally developed and used by the Cleveland Vocational Guidance and Rehabilitation Service, is intended to assess a client's potential for a variety of light assembly occupations. Although the MDC was interested in suggestions for possible improvements in the technical characteristics of the work sample, the primary concern was for the clarity and useability of information which should be contained in the user's manual. Several features of this work sample differ greatly from most work samples in current use. Standards for evaluating a client's performance of the work sample have been developed using Methods-Time-Measurement (MTM), a method which may be used to estimate the average competitive rate that might be found if the work sample task was actually performed in industry. To be validly compared with this performance standard, the client must perform the assembly operation using a standardized method. Repeated trials of the work sample should be used to provide the experience with the task to allow comparisons to the competitive rate standard. Data gathered during this field trial will provide a basic model for field trial of other work samples.

Most evaluators have heard of work evaluation system such as the TOWER, Thomasat, the Philadelphia JEVS Work Sample Battery, and the Singer/Graflex Vocational Evaluation System. However, most evaluators have never seen nor been exposed to specific information on the use of these systems. A slide-cassette program of each system has been developed to orient work evaluators to these materials. Descriptions of the purpose of each work

sample or system component accompanies pictures of the hardware. The purpose of this program is not only to acquaint professionals with currently available systems, but also to provide an
opportunity for evaluators to learn of various features that might
stimulate ideas for improvements within their own evaluation
units. The sound-cassette programs are made available on loan to
interested groups of professionals.

Also under development is a program which incorporates
basic orientation, training and evaluation for performing custodial work. This program is a modification of a similar program
developed and used by the Minneapolis Rehabilitation Center.
Slide-cassette programs have been developed which demonstrate
correct procedures for seven basic custodial activities. After a
client finishes each phase of training, his ability to perform the
actual tasks is assessed. Detailed information on observations that
are to be made of the client's work and criteria for evaluation are
provided for the evaluator. The project has been undertaken primarily to investigate the effectiveness and practical implications
of using basic training materials as an aid to evaluation.

The MDC is also engaged in projects designed to aid in the
identification, evaluation, and change of work behavior problems.
The MDC Behavior Identification Form has been developed to
aid in the identification and description of a client's work behavior problems. This form is designed to focus attention on
critical work behaviors and aid in the efficient recording of behavior observations in order that an individualized work adjustment program may easily be designed for a client or appropriate
criteria for selective placement may be identified. Additional field
trial of this form is needed to assure that training materials for its
use are appropriate for use by individuals new to work evaluation
and work adjustment. The purpose of this program is not simply
to provide another form for use in evaluation facilities, but more
to provide an effective training device which will help develop
skills in observing and recording behavioral information.

Related to work with the MDC Behavior Identification Form
the MDC is also preparing materials to orient facility personnel
to the use of behavior modification and modeling procedures as

techniques of work adjustment. The objective of this project is to develop training material on behavior modification and modeling which are both basic in nature and practically oriented. Most existing reference materials on practical applications of these techniques have been developed with the assumption that the reader is already familiar with the basic principles of these procedures. The materials will not deal with theoretical issues but rather practical applications of these procedures in work adjustment settings to bring about positive behavior changes.

SUMMARY

The Materials Development Center exists to assist practitioners in obtaining information and materials needed to develop and upgrade work evaluation and work adjustment programs. The MDC welcomes information on materials that personnel in the field feel might be helpful for others. Requests for assistance are always welcomed. If the MDC does not have the materials you are seeking, perhaps we can suggest where you might find them. Direct any requests to: Director, Materials Development Center, Department of Rehabilitation and Manpower Services, University of Wisconsin-Stout, Menomonie, Wisconsin 54751.

REFERENCES

Allen, C. and Sax, A. (Comps): *Selected Bibliography on Work Adjustment.* Menomonie, Stout State University, Department of Rehabilitation and Manpower Services, 1971.

Fry, R. (Ed.): *Work Evaluation: An Annotated Bibliography, 1947-1970.* Menomonie, Stout State University, Department of Rehabilitation and Manpower Services, 1971.

Fry, R., Genskow, J., Sax, A. (Eds.): *Proceedings of the Decatur Seminar.* Menomonie, Stout State University, Department of Rehabilitation and Manpower Services, 1971.

Gellman, W., et al.: *Adjusting People to Work*, 2nd ed. Jewish Vocational Service, Monograph No. 1, Chicago: Jewish Vocational Service, 1957.

Hoffman, P. (Ed.): *"Think Tank" Workshop on Work Evaluation.* Menomonie, Stout State University, Institute for Vocational Rehabilitation, 1969.

Little, N. (Ed.): *Guidelines for organization and operation of vocational evaluation units: Report No. 2 of the study committee on evaluation of*

136   *Vocational Evaluation for Rehabilitation Services*

vocational potential. Rehabilitation Services Series No. 67-50. Fourth Institute on Rehabilitation Services, Chicago, U.S. Department of Health Education, and Welfare, 1966.

Pruitt, W. and Pacinelli, R. (Eds.): *Work Evaluation in Rehabilitation.* Washington, Association of Rehabilitation Centers, 1969.

Redkey, H., and White, B.: *The Pre-Vocational Unit in a Rehabilitation Center — An Effective Tool For Evaluating Work Potential of the Handicapped.* Washington, U.S. Department of Health, Education, and Welfare, 1956.

PART THREE

VOCATIONAL EVALUATION
APPROACHES AND PROCEDURES

The Work Sample Approach to Vocational Evaluation

The Modapts Approach to Vocational Evaluation

The Work Evaluation Report

The Utilization of the Dictionary of Occupational Titles
    in Work Evaluation

Prevocational Evaluation

Scientific Observation in Work Evaluation

VII

THE WORK SAMPLE APPROACH TO VOCATIONAL EVALUATION

BERNARD ROSENBERG

Introduction

Emergence of Work Sample Approach

Specific Work Sample Approaches

The Vocational Evaluation Process

Vocational Evaluation Benefits to Client and Professional Team

Recommendations After Vocational Evaluation

The Tower Work Sample Approach

The Development of Work Samples

Format for Writing the Work Sample

Scoring Criteria

Follow-Up

Use of Pliers

References

INTRODUCTION

THE MOST difficult aspects of man is determining his present abilities, skills and potentials toward future vocational goals. There is no magic formula or method to assess aptitudes and human abilities. Throughout the years of man's existence, the identification of his skills has not been simple. Tests by themselves have been helpful, but their results alone have not provided the extensive information needed to solve all the problems or questions concerning man's future areas of occupational success. Results of tests can give only guidelines as to a level of ability which

139

may suggest possible areas of success, but it must be clearly understood that even the best test predictor can be considered only an
indicator of a good chance of success.

As early as 2200 B.C. the ancient Chinese invented the aptitude test and applied it to determine the qualifications of government personnel. The emperor of China used a practice of examining his officials every third year following which he either promoted or dismissed them from the service. At the beginning of the
Chan Dynasty in 1115 B.C. a formalized screening and examining
procedures for potential candidates for office were established. A
form of sample tests was used requiring skill and proficiency in
such arts as music, archery, horsemanship, writing, and arithmetic.
Confucius (551-478 B.C.) used a similar testing system for determining the qualifications of candidates for office.

In the early twentieth century Parsons, a pioneer in the vocational guidance movement, analyzed the job and the individual
and tried to match them in an attempt to predict the individual's
future vocational goals. Munsterberg conducted an experiment
on the use of aptitude tests with motormen of the Boston Elevated
Railway and is considered man's first attempt at personal selection for a specific job. Munsterberg also tried to relate the test
scores earned by workers on a job to the level of success they
achieved in that capacity. The First World War gave important
impetus to the testing movement when tests were developed by
the armed services to screen and utilize manpower more efficiently.
In the growing economy of the 1920's standardized aptitude tests
as instruments for the selection of personnel in business and industry came into greater use. Scores on tests were related to employed workers' performances and gave little consideration to the
individual differences of people. The interest in aptitude tests
steadily increased after the Second World War when there was
a need for an improved technique for the vocational guidance of
returning veterans. Hundreds of aptitude tests have steadily improved the accuracy and precision of our vocational predictions
of people.

When test and educational experts studied and analyzed these
aptitude tests after years of use, it was found that standardization

techniques varied with each author and the population to be tested. There appeared to be wide variations in the determination of objective criteria between the foreman's ratings, the worker's level of productivity, and the quality of the work performance. Most aptitude tests have low validation scores ranging between two and four which are far below acceptable standards. These low scores were due to poor test construction, extensive subjectivity of scoring criteria, and poor normative data. These aptitude tests proved most inaccurate for judging performance of the handicapped due to their slow response, limited life experiences, limited hand coordination, memory difficulties, behavior problems and visual impairments.

EMERGENCE OF WORK SAMPLE APPROACH

Recognizing the inadequacy of aptitude tests for the handicapped, the Institute for the Crippled and Disabled developed and established the work sample approach known as *guidance test class* in 1937. Work samples were developed from observations in industry. The work sample approach emerged from the need to establish a system of testing that gives due consideration to the needs of the handicapped. There was a need to project the handicapped into a realistic situation that would enable him to perform at his optimum level. The Institute for the Crippled and Disabled developed the concept of placing the handicapped client in a learning situation whereby he is taught how to manipulate or handle a hand tool or machine in an occupation as it occurs in industry. Work samples were structured around trades taught at the Institute.

A work sample is a mock-up or an abbreviated work activity that simulates and closely resembles the actual industrial operation as it occurs in industry. Work samples may be called *work tasks, job samples, simulated tasks, evaluation tasks, job evaluation tasks* or *prevocational tasks.* The approach attempts to bring to the client in evaluation the job essentials and major factors inherent in the actual functioning of a worker who is performing on that job. This simulation of an actual job projects the individual into an industrial situation of reality and thereby makes it more useful than aptitude tests. It can be used where aptitude tests are infeasible, such as, clients with language, educational, and cultural barriers.

Rehabilitation facilities use different types of work samples. Simulated tasks have been developed in occupational therapy programs where there is a medical emphasis, while workshops have stressed actual job samples pertaining to the subcontract work obtained from industry. Actual job samples still differ from actual work, since you cannot recreate the identical physical aspects of actual work such as noise, dust, odors, and pressures of industry. Job samples are geared to demonstrate the client's ability to function in a field of work, such as, industrial bench assembly, electronics, or clerical work. Actual work samples are closer to the criterion and have a likelihood of a practical face validity, since the client feels that he is performing real work as in industry.

Interest in work samples has been building up for many years in the field of vocational rehabilitation. The Hill-Burton Program or the Medical Facilities Survey and Construction Act was amended in 1954 and stipulated the expenditure of federal funds for the construction of diagnostic and treatment facilities, rehabilitation facilities, and nursing homes. This act recognized the important need that to serve the severely disabled client required special vocational evaluation techniques that were not being met by the prevailing psychometric tests. Psychometric tests were not geared to evaluate the severely involved multiply handicapped; the client with severe physical limitations; the client who never had been exposed to the world of work; and the severely retarded individual. Standardized tests were developed on a normal population and were not adapted for the handicapped.

In 1956 representatives of the U.S. Department of Health, Education, and Welfare approached the Institute for the Crippled and Disabled to develop a structured work sample approach and publish evaluation materials that would have application to the entire field of rehabilitation. All of these materials and the method for using them were organized into the Testing, Orientation and Work Evaluation in Rehabilitation (TOWER) System. The government stipulated in legislation that agencies applying for expansion grants were to develop prevocational evaluation programs around the use of specialized work samples patterned after the Institute's approach. The major reason for this stress on work samples was because handicapped individuals were performing poorly on aptitude tests in state programs due to the emphasis on speed and accuracy. Many handicapped individuals who had potential were rejected for services because the aptitude tests that were administered deemed them unemployable.

Rehabilitation agencies had a tendency to evaluate people through a trial and error approach. They would try an individual at a given occupation and if he succeeded, he would continue in that occupation. If he failed after a day's tryout, he would be given an opportunity in a different occupation. It was basically a hit-and-miss approach. If he had no specific interests, he was shifted into various training programs. If it were a workshop, he was tried on various subcontracts. Failing these activities, he was closed as unfeasible for rehabilitation.

SPECIFIC WORK SAMPLE APPROACHES

There is extensive interest in the field of vocational rehabilitation to improve the quality of the use of work samples as an appraisal device for predicting work skill and potential. During the past ten to twenty years there has been a proliferation of numerous work samples developed by many newly established vocational evaluation units at rehabilitation facilities. The work samples were developed by rehabilitation counselors, vocational evaluators, workshop supervisors, occupational therapists, and industrial art teachers on a subjective, impressionistic basis with little consideration given to the standards of industry. A variety of unique approaches to evaluation has emerged.

In 1951 Williamsport Technical Institute, Williamsport, Pennsylvania instituted a program for diagnosing clients over a period of four weeks during which time the students were tried out in various occupations in the training shops. They used a trial and error approach with no formal evaluation procedure.

The May T. Morrison Center for Rehabilitation in San Francisco, California, used work samples in 1958 to evaluate their clients' capacities to perform job tasks. There were twenty-five tasks used in clerical and sales, service, skilled and mechanical work, and semiskilled to unskilled manual work. They organized the tests according to major job families described in the *Dictionary of Occupational Titles.* Their experience has shown that using the reality situation or work sample method meets the need for a more thorough appraisal and accurate prediction of vocational capacities of individuals for whom other evaluation methods are not appropriate.

In 1959 the Cleveland Vocational Guidance and Rehabilitation Service (V.G.R.S.) Program hypothesized that actual job samples comprised of segments of industrial processes would be effective evaluative instruments for predicting job success. They compared Goodwill Industries Job Samples, TOWER System Job Samples, and V.G.R.S. Job Samples. They found that TOWER and V.G.R.S. Samples had an equal amount of success on specific jobs related to actual job samples. It was found that only one-fourth of the jobs held were directly related to the job sample counterparts. This limits the extent to which we can predict directly from an actual job sample task to its industrial job equivalent. It was felt that the primary asset of job samples is its face and concurrent validity.

In 1960 Highland View Hospital in Cleveland created an instrument designed to appraise cognitive-motor function on jobs performed in a sheltered workshop. The technique was designed to eliminate subjectivity of vocational appraisals of older chronically disabled individuals and to provide a baseline for meaningful interpretation of such results. A performance scale known as THOMASAT was constructed to evaluate psychomotor skills of the upper extremities. The test appraises eye-hand coordination, the ability to grasp, hold, stabilize and manipulate objects according to size, color and shape. The standardization is based on chronically disabled patients and appears to be a valid predictor of performance in a sheltered workshop catering to the needs of the chronically ill. The THOMASAT method has not been studied with other disabled populations or younger groups at other facilities.

The Veterans Administration hospitals use the manual arts approach to determine the vocational potentials of clients; they may include tasks in woodworking (cabinet making, wood turning, wood finishing, upholstering); electricity and electronics (radio, television, amateur radio transmission); mechanics (fine mechanics, watchmaking, auto mechanics); machine shop and sheet metal works, decorative metal work (art metal, jewelry, casting); photography and photo oil coloring; fine and commercial arts; needle trades; and blue print reading and drafting. An attempt is made with these activities to evaluate the client on any level in a wider range, and in one vocational area. The major drawback of this approach is the lack of standards with which to judge the client's skills according to the performance required by industry.

Workshops for the mentally retarded use a combination of several approaches. A series of work samples is administered to each new client during his first seven weeks in the workshop. The samples are selected as evaluation tests from hundreds of contract jobs that had been performed in the workshop over the years. They include a variety of aptitudes, abilities and skills usually required in simple industrial operations. An important aspect of this evaluation is repetition and learning experiences of efficiency and productivity. The retarded client does each of the work samples three times. Detailed records are kept of the time taken to complete the task at successive sessions. On the average there is a three-day interval between trials of the same tasks. Individual rates for initial learning (first trial performance), rate of improvement (second trial performance), and ultimate efficiency (third trial performance) are computed. Observations made during the evaluation include work discipline, productivity and self-direction, initiative, and appearance, as well as the ability to use public transportation, handle money and the telephone. The evaluation is continued informally as part of the personal adjustment training program which usually follows the regular evaluation. The client is studied to determine potential ability for some type of unskilled service job, such as, messenger or bus girl.

Memphis Goodwill Project (RD490) was based on the prototype project of the Institute for the Crippled and Disabled. The project served cerebral palsied, other brain damaged, and mentally retarded clients. All clients received two weeks or more of Job Sample Tests and three weeks of Work Habit Tests. The Job Sample Tests were designed from practical everyday materials characteristic of the working world. Reading, for instance, was tested by use of city maps, telephone directory and newspapers. They used activities such as grocery store stock, filling orders from sales slips, and stocking shelves with canned goods. The results were not graded by standard methods but were weighted according to their vocational value. Job samples were table tests where the work was judged both as to the quality and as to the time required to perform the task. Work Habit Tests were given for the purpose of determining job readiness. Clients were sent to work stations in Goodwill's training classes, such as, small appliance repairman's helper, upholsterer's helper, sales floor helper, belt sorter and cafeteria helper.

Since December, 1958 the Philadelphia Jewish Employment and Vocational Service (J.E.V.S.) has been working on a series of graded industrial tasks which are used for assessing the abilities of clients. Through the Manpower Development and Training Act, the U.S. Department of Labor negotiated a work sample project with J.E.V.S. in the early 1960's. They developed in 1963-1965 a series of work samples for use in serving disadvantaged youths. A series of twenty-eight work sample tasks were structured to measure potential skills in fourteen general industrial categories: assembly-disassembly, bindery, clerical, display and printing, electrical, industrial housekeeping, layout design and drafting, mailroom, mechanical, packing, sorting, structural development, textile and tailoring, and metal work. A client begins the two week battery with the simplest of twenty-eight work tasks—the assembling of three sizes of nuts, bolts, and washers. In successive tasks of increasing complexity, the client is required to do such things as: letter signs, couple sections of pipe, solder a square of tin, take apart and reassemble a step ladder, a door lock and a telephone, perform varying electrical tasks, sort colored tiles, weigh letters and boxes and compute postage rate, cut and baste a blouse pattern, among others. Each work sample is rated for time and quality on a five point scale for nine aptitudinal factors: G (general intelligence), V (verbal ability), N (numerical ability), S (spatial relations), P (form perception), Q (clerical ability), K (motor coordination), F (finger dexterity) and M (manual dexterity). These work samples are directly related to *worker trait group* arrangements in the *Dictionary of Occupational Titles.*

In the past few years the Jewish Vocational Services (J.V.S.) in Newark, Detroit, and New York have patterned their evaluations around the Philadelphia J.E.V.S. work sample series. In addition, this approach has been adapted by the Department of Labor in over forty cities to serve the needs of the socially and culturally deprived and is still being tested on an extensive basis.

Recently, there has emerged a system of vocational evaluation known as *The Singer-Graflex Vocational Evaluation System* developed by the Singer Corporation. This approach utilizes an audio-visual teaching machine to present programmed instructions on how to perform on specific work tasks. Work tasks have been developed in ten occupational areas; basic tools, bench assembly, drafting, electrical wiring, plumbing and pipe fitting, carpentry and woodworking, refrigeration, heating and air-conditioning, soldering and welding, office and sales clerk, and needle trades. Each occupational area has a work station containing a teaching machine with film strip, synchronized tape cassette, and the specific tools and supplies required to complete the work task. The Singer-Graflex System is being field tested at several facilities and normative data is being collected to establish its scoring criteria.

THE VOCATIONAL EVALUATION PROCESS

Work samples are utilized in a process known as vocational evaluation. Vocational evaluation is a process that attempts to assess the individual's physical, mental, skills, abilities and personality behavior in an effort to determine his present and future work potential and adjustment. The process pinpoints the client's strengths, weaknesses and level of overall vocational functioning. It is basically a diagnostic tool that observes behavior, predicts vocational training and placement potential, and attempts to effect change in a client's self-concept through a structured and concrete treatment plan. Vocational evaluation helps the client reach a level of dignity and ultimate acceptance as a productive member of society. Work is an essential goal of assessment and gives meaning to all processes leading to this objective.

A Vocational Evaluation Unit should concern itself with the following objectives:

(1) A determination of the client's current level of skill, work habits, physical capacities, interests, and abilities through a system of work sample testing in the major occupational areas of clerical, skilled, semiskilled, unskilled and service occupational groupings.

(2) An assessment of the client's attitudes, motivation, and vocational goals through a specified period of time of observing his performance in an actual work situation.

(3) An appraisal of the client in interpersonal relationships with his peers, supervisors, and teachers.

(4) A means of helping the client develop proper work habits, work tolerance, and work confidence in a simulated work environment.

Vocational evaluation is designed to serve and assist those insecure and nonverbal clients who cannot make it into training or employment through the usual means; those clients who have doubts and questions about their skills and abilities; those clients whose disability or physical limitations prevent return to their former occupation; marginally employed clients who need clarification of their level of skills and work potentials; those younger age group of clients (fourteen and up) who have not had meaningful work experiences prior to onset of disability; and older age group of clients (fifty and up) whose abilities may be channeled toward gainful employment.

VOCATIONAL EVALUATION BENEFITS TO CLIENT AND PROFESSIONAL TEAM

Through exposure to work samples in the vocational evaluation program the client has a mirror of his specific vocational assets and clarification of his readiness to go to work. As the client goes through a series of work samples, he is required to use his hidden abilities and potentials in a way that is meaningful to him and enables him to complete the work sample at his own pace. The reality of work is continually before the client and enables him to discover his basic abilities and limitations.

The results of the evaluation can assist the physician in determining the client's physical capacity to go to work, his work tolerance, ability to travel daily, and the extent of physical limitation. It provides guidelines for suitable vocational areas and may indicate the need for further medical treatment. For clients with prosthetic or orthotic devices, it uncovers problems in adapting to vocational tasks. Does he use the prosthetic device to manipulate tools and machinery? How long can he stand in an occupation which requires constant standing? Does he know the signs of approaching fatigue?

For the psychologist the vocational evaluation unit offers information on the client's ability to get along with people, supervisors and peers; the client's acceptance or rejection of his disability, his motivation to go to work; his adjustment, work behavior, his personality, and intellectual potentials related to specific occupations and work.

The social worker gains insight into the client's family and financial problems which may surface when trade training and work are discussed. A careful record of attendance and punctuality may be an indicator of social, home or welfare problems which hamper the client's ability to function and adjust to the work setting. His interests may be hindered by concern over who is watching his children, if his wife is working or who is taking his children to school or clinic?

The vocational rehabilitation counselor gains a wealth of knowledge through vocational evaluation; he gains insight into the client's skills, aptitudes, educational level, occupational readiness, work habits, interests, work tolerance, motivation and the client's future vocational goals and objectives. While undergoing vocational evaluation, clients are seen by a vocational rehabilitation counselor for supportive counseling. For some clients intensive daily services are required to reinforce the vocational activities and proper adjustment to work. The counselor helps the client integrate the vocational evaluation findings into a meaningful and realistic plan. He reviews with each client his performance and progress, attempting to arrive at a goal consistent with his abilities, interests, capacity for work and job opportunities in the community.

The vocational evaluator plays a key role in determining the future of the client. The evaluator is in the best position to rate the client through observations and standards of functioning. He is responsible for assessing the following:

1. Work aptitudes of the client.
2. Dexterity and abilities with hands, tools and machinery.
3. Work tolerance related to standing, sitting and frustration level.
4. Work habits; neatness, industriousness, relationships with supervisors and clients, attendance and punctuality.
5. Comprehension of written and oral instructions.
6. Attitudes toward work, disability, and reaction to work environment.
7. Personal appearance, grooming, and dress.
8. Potential for vocational training and placement.
9. Independence in daily living.
10. Need for medical, psychosocial, and vocational services to alleviate existing client problems.

RECOMMENDATIONS AFTER VOCATIONAL EVALUATION

After a client completes a three to seven week vocational evaluation program that varies according to the client population, results might indicate any of the following:

1. Potential skills for vocational training in trade and business areas in the skilled, semiskilled, unskilled or clerical areas.
2. Referral to a sheltered or industrial workshop for training, work conditioning, work tolerance improvement or an accelerated production program to build up speed.
3. Placement of the client in his previous or related occupation or an area commensurate with his skills.

4. Referral to a medical treatment program for further improvement of hand coordination, work tolerance and ambulation.
5. More advanced college or technical training related to the client's academic potential.
6. Remedial academic and language training to reduce basic deficiencies for employment.
7. Referral for psychosocial services to reduce personality and family problems which might hamper employment.
8. Closure due to disinterest, lack of motivation, or severe medical or emotional problems which rule out any future vocational goals.

THE TOWER WORK SAMPLE APPROACH

The TOWER System developed the work sample as a means of predicting the vocational skills of handicapped clients at the Institute for the Crippled and Disabled. The Institute designated its testing approach the *TOWER* System, the acronym for Testing, Orientation, and Work Evaluation in Rehabilitation.

TOWER is a system of reality testing which utilizes scientifically evolved and tested work tasks in a simulated work environment. It may be used alone or in conjunction with standardized aptitude test batteries, and is particularly useful for evaluating the vocational potential of handicapped persons.

The TOWER System includes fourteen broad areas of vocational evaluation: clerical, drafting, drawing, electronics assembly, jewelry manufacturing, leathergoods, lettering, machine shop, mail clerk, optical mechanics, pantograph, sewing machine operating, workshop assembling, and welding. Each area covers a number of related occupations for a total of more than one hundred different tasks or tests. For each there are qualitative and quantitative criteria developed in accordance with industrial requirements and standards.

During the evaluation the client is tried at a number of jobs representing all phases of an occupational area. For example, to determine hand dexterity for jewelry work, he is exposed to jewelry filing, tracing, piercing, plier work, cutting, soldering and polishing. If a client fails to perform effectively on one of the simpler sequences, he may be given no further tests in this area. In most occupational areas the last test in a given occupation involves the use of every tool from the preceding tasks. When he is confronted with a task involving a basic hand tool, the client is shown how to manipulate the tool in the execution of a purposeful task through written and oral instructions. Demonstration techniques are used, and there is ample opportunity for practice. Once the client is acquainted with the use of this tool, he is given a task to perform which, in turn, is rated. This approach guides him through various activities and helps him avoid mistakes.

The TOWER vocational evaluation program facilitates the observation of other factors which are significant in the measurement of work potential. Work habits and work tolerance are determined through exposure to meaningful tasks. Pertinent aspects of the client's personality are seen in this permissive atmosphere while he is participating in the evaluation process. When he undertakes many jobs over an extended period, flexibility and pliability are demonstrated. If a client has physical difficulties, appropriate devices can be applied to improve his functioning.

TOWER System Evaluation Categories of Work Samples

CLERICAL
1. Business Arithmetic
2. Filing
3. Typing
4. One-hand Typing (Alternate)
5. Payroll Computation
6. Use of Sales Book
7. Record Keeping
8. Correct Use of English

DRAFTING
1. T-Square Triangle
2. Compass
3. Working Drawing
4. Drawing to Scale
5. Geometric Shapes

DRAWING
1. Perspective
2. Forms, Shapes, and Objects
3. Shading, Tone, and Texture
4. Color
5. Free Hand Sketching

ELECTRONICS ASSEMBLY
1. Color Perception and Sorting
2. Running a 10-Wire Cable
3. Inspecting a 10-Wire Cable
4. Lacing a Cable
5. Soldering Wires

JEWELRY MANUFACTURING
1. Use of Saw
2. Use of Needle Files
3. Electric Drill Press
4. Piercing and Filing Metals
5. Use of Pliers
6. Use of Torch in Soldering
7. Making Earrings and Brooch Pins

LEATHERGOODS
1. Use of Ruler
2. Use of Knife
3. Use of Dividers
4. Use of Paste and Brush
5. Use of Scissors and Bone Folder in Pasting
6. Constructing Picture Frame
7. Production Task

LETTERING
1. Lettering Aptitude
2. Alphabet and use of T-Square
3. Use of Pen and Ink
4. Use of Lettering Brush
5. Brush Lettering

MACHINE SHOP

1. Reading and Transcribing Measurements
2. Blueprint Reading
3. Measuring With a Rule
4. Drawing to Measurement
5. Metal Layout and Use of Basic Tools
6. Drill Press Operation
7. Fractions and Decimals
8. Measuring with the Micrometer Caliper
9. Mechanical Understanding

MAIL CLERK

1. Opening Mail
2. Date-Stamping Mail
3. Sorting Mail
4. Delivering Mail
5. Collecting Mail
6. Folding and Inserting
7. Sealing Mail
8. Mail Classification
9. Use of Scale
10. Postage Calculation

OPTICAL MECHANICS

1. Use of Metric Ruler
2. Use of Calipers
3. Lens Recognition
4. Lens Centering and Marking
5. Use of Lens Protractor
6. Hand Beveling and Edging

PANTOGRAPH ENGRAVING

1. Introduction to the Engravograph (Pantograph) Machine and Determination of Aptitudes for Setting Pantograph Arm Ratios
2. Setting up, Centering Copy and Determining Specified Ratios
3. Use of Workholder and Adjustment of Cutter
4. Setting up and Running Off a Simple Job

SEWING MACHINE OPERATING
1. Sewing Machine Control
2. Use of Knee Lift and Needle Pivoting
3. Tacking and Sewing Curved Lines
4. Upper Threading
5. Winding and Inserting Bobbin
6. Sewing and Cutting
7. Top Stitching

WELDING
1. Measuring
2. Making a Working Drawing
3. Identifying Welding Rods
4. Use of Acetylene Torch
5. Use of Rods and Electrodes
6. Use of Torch and Rods
7. Measuring and Cutting Metal
8. Soldering

WORKSHOP ASSEMBLY
1. Counting
2. Number and Color Collating
3. Folding and Banding
4. Weighing and Sorting
5. Counting and Packing
6. Washer Assembly
7. Inserting, Lacing, and Tying
8. Art Paper Banding

THE DEVELOPMENT OF WORK SAMPLES

A major issue in establishing a vocational evaluation unit is the determination of suitable work samples to be used in evaluating clients. It is essential that an agency consider three factors:

a) Population to be served
b) Occupations feasible for the population
c) Placement and future job opportunities

The basic purpose of a work sample is to predict skills, aptitudes, and potentials for vocational training and eventual entry into a job. In order to determine specific occupational areas for clients in the vocational evaluation unit, due consideration must be given to the client population. Several questions about the client population must be answered; What is the age range? What is the intelligence level? What are the physical limitations? What is the approximate reading and arithmetic level?

A survey of local industries should be undertaken to determine specific occupations that meet the needs of the client population mentioned above. The survey should elicit occupational information that would uncover extensive data on the specific requirements of the occupation, the vocational training resources in the community, and the overall job placement possibilities for the present and future. Further placement information might be obtained through the *Occupational Outlook Handbook,* the local state employment service and the vocational rehabilitation office. In selecting an occupational area one must consider the adaptability of this area to work sampling, the tools and materials required, the space and equipment necessary for implementation.

Extensive information on industries and occupations can be obtained through the *Dictionary of Occupational Titles,* interviews with supervisors, foremen and workers in industry. Placement information can be obtained through trade papers, newspaper ads and private and public employment agencies. The ideal method for work sample development should include all of these techniques of learning about occupations, however, the most accurate and efficient method is the job analysis approach.

The job analysis approach provides for the actual observation of an occupation as it occurs in industry. It is a detailed step by step breakdown of the job. Specific information is obtained through a *Job Analysis Formula.* The formula answers five basic questions: "What a worker does?" "How he does it?" "Why he does it?" "When he does it?" "What are the skills involved in performing the task?"

Specific components of a job analysis should include the following twelve items:

1. Job Title — (This should be the title indicated by the fore-

man and/or worker in that industry and geared to the *D.O.T.* title)

2. Industry, Plant, Department — (This identifies where the job is found and location of the job which was analyzed)

3. Number Employed — M_____   F_____

    (This information is necessary for determining the importance of the job as it relates to the number employed in it)

4. *D.O.T.* Title and Code Number — (For classifying the occupation)

5. Work Performed — (This is a narrative descriptive statement of the actual tasks performed by a worker. It is an exact concise statement of what the worker does, how he does it, why he does it, and with what he does it. Each item is begun with an action verb. Each item may be rated as to complexity such as A, B, or C, and the percent of time spent on each item may be noted. Each task is described in the order in which it occurs.)

6. Experience: None_____   Acceptable_____

    (This describes need for prior experience if job requires it)

7. Training Date: Minimum Training Time
    a) Experienced Workers
    b) Inexperienced Workers
    (This gives the training time required on the job)

8. Responsibility — (How much is required in terms of responsibility for the work of others, for equipment, for material, for safety, for cooperation of others, for handling money, etc.)

9. Skill Requirements — (This is a detailed analysis of manual dexterity, eye-hand coordination and motor functions required of a worker for successful performance on the job)

10. Equipment, Materials, and Supplies — (This consists of the tools, materials, machines, and other devices used in performing the job)
11. Physical Demands — (This describes the physical requirements of the job)
12. Work Environment — (This consists of the specific working conditions involved on the job)

Job analysis of an occupation should be performed at several similar firms to determine whether there are any different procedures between employers. Once the job analysis at these firms has been completed, the design of the work sample begins with the specific selection of job tasks that are to be incorporated. Selection of tasks should follow the sequence of the job task as performed on the job. This sequence of job tasks is written up in simple language for use by the client and the evaluator.

FORMAT FOR WRITING THE WORK SAMPLE

The final complete write-up of the work sample should include information of use to the evaluator and the client. A series of work samples in a specific occupational area should have an introductory information sheet that orients the user of the work sample as follows:

Orientation:
1. The purpose of the work sample.
2. A simple description of what an employed worker does in his occupation.
3. A statement of placement possibilities and where these job opportunities may be found.
4. A list of related and allied placement possibilities to the work sample through the *Dictionary of Occupational Titles, Part II* and *Supplement*
5. Description of work environment and key job factors for employment.

Preparation:
This section should assist the evaluator by describing the types of materials, tools, and apparatus to be used in the work sample. Special precautionary suggestions to administer this work sample should be offered.

The work sample instructions given to the client should include the following:

1. The purpose of the work sample.
2. A list of materials, tools, and apparatus.
3. Simple step by step written instructions with illustrations and diagrams advising the client how to proceed in stages to perform the required work sample.
4. A practice period should be presented to enable the client to understand the instructions and skill necessary to function on the work sample.

It is essential that the instructions be written on a level understood by the client. If the specific occupational area under consideration requires reading ability or the ability to follow diagrams, such procedures should be incorporated in the work sample instructions. If the occupational area does not require a certain level of reading ability, the work sample should be demonstrated to the client on a verbal basis. Work samples should not be contaminated with reading prerequisites since this factor of comprehension may eliminate clients who possess the skills and dexterity required in this occupation.

All work samples should be administered to the client in a uniform manner for the development of standards of performance. The evaluator must recognize a good finished product and how it relates to a specific vocational objective. Performance must be rated at various levels: superior, above-average, average, below average and inferior. Discrimination of ratings enable the evaluator to pinpoint the client's level of training needed and eventual goals to be reached. Scoring criteria should be based on the qualitative and quantitative standards of work performance as it occurs in industry.

SCORING CRITERIA

Though there has been a proliferation of vocational evaluation programs utilizing work samples established throughout the country, there has been relatively little done to structure and standardize these work samples. Few agencies have related these work samples to the requirements of the local community and occupations prevalent in that area. Most work samples utilized at facilities are tasks obtained from workshop subcontract activities. The work samples chosen by a facility should represent the realistic demands of an occupation performed in industry with potential for ultimate employment. Most work samples are selected through the vocational evaluator's judgment regarding jobs in which the handicapped might perform in industry. These vocational evaluators have placed little reliance upon the judgment of industry and based work samples on their own experiences. The selection of work samples should be based upon the evaluator's general understanding of the vocational needs of his client population and should be relevant to his client's interests, abilities, and skills.

The administration of work sample tests should not be an end in itself. Work sample tasks should never be given simply for the sake of information taking. Each work sample should be administered for a specific purpose and used to help the client determine his future vocational goals.

Since work sample tasks are predictors of a client's future vocational functioning, it is essential that proper scoring criteria be developed for each work sample. It cannot be done on a subjective basis, but must be based on an objective determination from industry. The more the work sample simulates the way it is performed in industry, and scored through their standards, the closer the work sample reaches reality standardization, and face validity.

The most essential step in work sample development is scoring the results of the completed product or scoring criteria. A client's performance can be evaluated by comparison to the performance of a beginning or entry worker or a new trainee in an occupational field. The scoring standard might be described by the number of items completed correctly, speed required to complete the task, and quality of work performed. This scoring might be presented in percentile ranks or standard scores.

Once the initial work sample is completed, there is a need to contact the employers where the job analysis was performed to review the entire test and scoring criteria. Employers should be encouraged to have their employees tried on this initial work sample. Employees should be both entry and experienced workers. This employer-employee review provides a realistic and practical opinion of the feasibility of the work sample. Specific recommended changes of instructions to the client and scoring criteria will enhance the practical application of the work sample. The work sample is then administered to the client population in the new form as suggested by the employer.

FOLLOW-UP

Through extensive exposure of the work sample to your clients in the actual evaluation setting, sufficient data will be obtained to justify further use and implementation. Work sample development is a continuous ongoing process and can only be further tested by a follow-up of the clients into training and placement. This practical validation will strengthen the use of this work sample on a regular basis as part of the vocational evaluation program.

JEWELRY TEST No. 6

OBJECT: To test aptitude in use of pliers.

MATERIALS: Brass wire.

TOOLS: Flat nose and round nose pliers, shears, steel ruler, files.

READ ALL INSTRUCTIONS CAREFULLY BEFORE STARTING TO WORK

1. An essential part of Jewelry work is the ability to bend and twist wire into various designs and patterns. It requires good vision, patience and a desire to be creative. Care must be used not to squeeze too hard with the pliers, as the wire is easily marked or scarred.

2. Using flat nose pliers, bend a piece of wire to make a right angle, ½″ from end of wire—hold pliers tightly. Wire can be bent up with fingers, or ruler.

   Move pliers ½″ and make another right angle bend.

   Now make a third such angle, so that wire will be formed into a square.

   Snip off excess wire.

   Note—you can spot the ½″ places with a pencil mark first before starting bending. Last side should be a fraction less.

   Check angles and sides to assure that your job is as neat as possible, with square angles and straight sides. The open end will be soldered together later, so make sure that the ends meet snugly (file if necessary)

   like this →   **not** like this. →

   Make three more squares.

3. Bend wire to form a double square, with ¼″ sides.

   Sharp angles and straight sides.
   Make one more double square.

4. With round nose pliers, bend and form a circle, ½″ diameter. Start at one end of the wire and make a very slight bend. Shift the pliers a little and bend another slight curve. Keep shifting the pliers and continue bending to form a circle. Check the size carefully and frequently as you go. When the circle is completed, snip off extra wire and have the ends fit tightly. Make another circle of the same size.

Jewelry Test No. 6 — Page 2

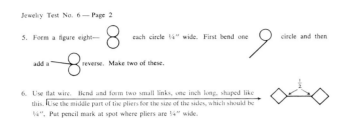

5. Form a figure eight— each circle ¼" wide. First bend one circle and then add a reverse. Make two of these.

6. Use flat wire. Bend and form two small links, one inch long, shaped like this. Use the middle part of the pliers for the size of the sides, which should be ¼". Put pencil mark at spot where pliers are ¼" wide.

7. Using round wire, make two links, with circles ¼" in diameter.

8. The principles of plier work and wire bending are often applied in decorative work, and in making initials and monograms.

   Some letters, such as C and S, require only one piece of wire. Others like L and V need two pieces of wire. The letters H and A are examples of those needing three pieces. E and W need four pieces.

9. You are to make the following letters, measuring and cutting the wire (ROUND) according to the size of the letters shown below. Keep the letters you make. In the next test you will solder them together.

J E W E L R Y

HAVE YOUR WORK APPROVED

RATING	QUALITY STANDARDS	PERFORMANCE RATE
Superior	Designs are nearly all exact; corners are square and at correct angles; circles flow smoothly and show no plier marks; letters are exact.	60 minutes or less
Above Average	One-half of designs are exact and all are within tolerance; corners square and at correct angles; circles flow smoothly and show no plier marks although they may have 1 or 2 flat spots; three-fourths of letters are exact and rest are within tolerance.	60 to 75 minutes
Average	Designs are within tolerance except 3 or 4 which are too large; corners slightly rounded instead of square; circles are within tolerance but show several flat spots; one-half of letters are exact and the rest are within tolerance.	75 to 90 minutes
Below Average	One-half of the designs are out of tolerance and none are exact; corners are generally rounded; circles and curves are uneven, having a series of flat bends instead of flowing curves; letters are not within tolerance.	90-120 minutes
Inferior	All designs out of tolerance; squares out of proportion with sides of different lengths; circles and letters are very large and almost unrecognizable.	120 minutes or more

SCORING CRITERIA

Test No. 6   Tolerance 1/32″

USE OF PLIERS

This Test measures the client's aptitude in the use of pliers to shape brass wire. The work task specified here requires that the plier holding hand enjoy a broad range of motion. The client must possess and be able to demonstrate an effective sense of spatial relationships. In the course of this task, he is called upon to use different tools and materials than those with which he has had experience in previous tests. The performance of this work task provides the evaluator with a useful opportunity for observing the client's concern with the finished product. Moderately high levels of neatness and precision characterize acceptable performance in this type of work and more frequently than not, will result from care and attention being paid to the work. Observe the specified tolerance in using the appropriate evaluator's scoring aid to determine the applicable quality standards level.

Special Preparation:

Either round or flat wire may be used for making the designs specified in this test. It is preferable to use flat wire for the straight side, sharp cornered designs, and round wire for the execution of those having curved lines. If the client exhibits a desire to use more than one type of wire in the course of executing a good design, permit him to do so. The evaluator should be aware of the fact that, in general, it is preferable to use only one type of wire in making a specific item although a good sense of design may result in a combination of types of wires which adds to the item's attractiveness.

REFERENCES

Ghiselli, E.E.: *The Validity of Occupational Aptitude Test.* New York, Wiley, 1966.

Harris, W.M., Miller, M.J. and Merritt, T.E.: *Placement of the Cerebral Palsied and Others Through Evaluation and Training.* V.R.A. Project-490, Memphis Goodwill Industries.

Hoffman, Paul: *Think Tank Workshop on Work Evaluation.* U.S. Department of Health Education and Welfare, 1969.

Institute for the Crippled and Disabled: *TOWER: Testing, Orientation and Work Evaluation in Rehabilitation.* New York, 1967.

McLaughlin, K.F.: *Interpretation of Test Results.* U.S. Department of Health, Education and Welfare, 1964.

Neff, Walter F.: Problems of Work Evaluation. *Personnel and Guidance Journal,* March 1966.

Overs, Robert P.: *Obtaining and Using Actual Job Samples in a Work Evaluation Program.* Cleveland, Vocational Guidance and Rehabilitation Services, 1964.

Philadelphia Jewish Employment and Vocational Service: *Final Report: A Study of the Need for Work Adjustment and Social Work Assistance for the Long Term Unemployed,* 1967.

Redkey, H.: The function and value of a prevocational unit in a rehabilitation center. *American Journal of Occupational Therapy, 11:*20, 1957.

Rosenberg, B. and Usdane, W.W.: The TOWER System: vocational evaluation of the severely handicapped for training and placement. *Personnel Guidance Journal, 42:*149, 1963.

Sakata, R. and Sinick, D.: Do work samples work? *Rehabilitation Counseling Bulletin, 8* (4), 1965.

Thomas, C.W., Izutsu, Si, and Spangler, D.P.: *The Thomasat.* Cleveland, Highland View Hospital, 1961.

Teng, S.Y.: Chinese influence on the eastern examination system. *Harvard Journal of Asiatic Studies, 7:*267, 1943.

U.S. Office of Vocational Rehabilitation: *The Pre-Vocational Unit in a Rehabilitation Center,* Washington, 1955.

Vocational Guidance and Rehabilitation Services: *Obtaining and Using Actual Job Samples in a Work Evaluation Program.* V.R.A. Project RD-412, final report 1959-1964. Cleveland, 1964.

Wegg, Lillian S.: The essentials of work evaluation. *American Journal of Occupational Therapy. 14:*65-69, 1960.

VIII

THE MODAPTS APPROACH TO VOCATIONAL EVALUATION

Bruce C. Hume

Measurement of Productivity
Time and Motion Studies
Definitions of Predetermined Time Standards
The Modapts System
Modapts Equipment

MEASUREMENT OF PRODUCTIVITY

Ergonomists, industrial engineers, method engineers and time study engineers all belong to the branch of engineering science aimed at improving productivity in industry. The role of this group is adequately defined. The major aim is to increase the efficiency of the man/machine unit by the speed and accuracy of his performance.

The engineer can then work with clearly defined criteria. Research provides general principles, basic measurement of human and physical capacities, and techniques for evaluating the facts on human performance by various factors of machine design and working environment. The problem is one of fitting both the man to the machine and the machine to the man.

With the disabled worker, we have the same intense problem —we must define the physical and psychological capacity of the disabled before any equipment or machine design can take place.

At Centre Industries, Sydney, Australia, the problem of objectively measuring the ability and potential of the disabled has been the subject of a study by the engineering and rehabilitation team.

Centre Industries is a commercial manufacturing facility providing effective paid employment to a wide range of severely disabled cerebral palsied and other physically disabled persons. Equipment manufactured includes: a range of telephone relays and completed relay sets for automatic telephone exchanges, as well as control units for teleprinters, broadcasting amplifiers, electronic test equipment and sophisticated plug-in circuit modules; glass encapsulated semiconductor devices (diodes); and microwave transmission equipment. At the present time, 850 people are engaged in this work, three hundred of whom are severely physically disabled.

Manufacturing departments include a Primary division where basic components are manufactured from raw materials. Powered foot and hand operated presses blank, pierce and form metal components; lathes and milling machines cut and turn; drills and tapping machines drill and tap holes; moulding machine produce plastic components. A Secondary production division includes coil winding and assembly departments—coils are wound on high-speed coil winding machines; completed relays are assembled from coils and components manufactured in the Primary division; wiring forms are loomed and relay sets are wired, tested, inspected, packed and shipped.

Service functions to control and assist this manufacturing complex include production planning and control, stores and stockkeeping, personnel management, accounting, quality control and engineering. Engineering departments include product design, electronic, electrical, mechanical and methods and time study. These engineering disciplines employed in the design, development, training and control of manufacturing are extended into the training and rehabilitation of the disabled work force. On entry into this industrial environment, the disabled are placed into the Training Unit, a section of the factory set up with representative apparatus and functions used through both the Primary and Secondary divisions. Initially, the disabled operators are tried on a series of preselected operations to gain an initial profile of their skills.

Detailed assessment is carried out only after the operator has settled into the industrial environment and adjusted to the new way of life. First, he must become familiar with the demands of work, the requirement of the job, the time allowed to perform the job and the payment for the job performed and, most importantly, learn how to live in the world of work.

In our early human engineering work with the disabled, we found it impossible to evaluate in sufficient depth the capacities and limitations of the disabled and the machine to assess work potential.

The provision of effective job placement and training of the severely disabled is dependent on adequately detailed assessment of work capacity and inherent ability. It is simply not good enough to rely on observation studies of the disabled at a work station to provide this detail.

TIME AND MOTION STUDIES

In order to gain this adequate detail, micromotion film studies (of the disabled at work) were commenced and laboriously examined, frame by frame to build up profiles of work capacity and capability. Although expensive and time-consuming, film analysis revealed in measured time any unwanted and problem motions that cannot be detected by visual observations.

It was obvious from this work that a method was needed to measure the effectiveness of the disabled in performing work motions along with the ability to perform the sequences of such motions.

Production has been described as a function of the methods used to accomplish specific tasks and method defined as a sequence of motions logically performed in a definite order to produce the desired effect on the workpiece or the placement of the body members.

DEFINITIONS OF PREDETERMINED TIME STANDARDS

Predetermined time standards describes work related motions of human operators and classifies these into a limited and discrete set of descriptive categories and further provide productive norms for each of these categorized motions. Once elemental motions are identified, a standard time can then be established to assess individual performance and provide productive norms for the task being studied.

Another criteria in these systems that should be mentioned here is that the productivity of an operator is not only dependent on the speed of performing the motion patterns but rather by the manner or method in which the job is carried out.

> The basic key to all predetermined time systems if the fact that variations in the time required to perform the same motion are essentially small for different workers who have had adequate practice.

It follows that, given sufficient learning or instruction, the difference between the very best or very poorest performers will be negligible. Where the differences are not negligible, then there are other sources of variables which need to be located.

Predetermined time systems classify these variables into classes of fit, (loose, close, exact), symmetry, position, ease of handling, and so on.

THE MODAPTS SYSTEM

The predetermined time system is an empirical system of variables, and validity of such systems can only be confirmed at this time by their widespread usage. MODAPTS is one of the systems relating time to movements of the parts of the human body. MODAPTS (*MOD*ular *A*rranged *P*redetermined *T*ime Standards), a recently developed Australian system, has the following original features:

1. That all values are expressed in modular form rather than in units of time of *standard time*.
2. That the system of classifying movements is such that the actual number of units of human activity represented by each classification is contained in its short description and identification.
3. That the units selected for the MODAPTS system distinguish between general movements of the fingers, hands, and arms through space, and the terminal movements of the

body member in close proximity to the work being performed.

4. That the presentation of the data is in a visual form, capable of being memorized as a picture, whilst all previous presentations were in the form of tables of words and figures.

5. That, on account of 1, 2, 3 and 4, the design of the MODAPTS system enables it to be applied without recourse to any tables of values.

The major virtue of MODAPTS, however, is its simplicity.

c

The basic work unit used is a simple finger movement, with the finger doing nothing very special. All other activities are expressed in terms of this finger movement or module, which has a value for quick planning of one-seventh of a second. There are only eight different values of activity, or multiples of the basic module —0, 1, 2, 3, 4, 5, 17 and 30. These values are applied to only twenty-one types of activity derived from movements of the fingers, limbs, body and eyes.

An unusual break with convention is the application of a zero value to certain portions of the activity—for instance, in what is called *obtaining control* by finger or hand contact (say, to slide an object along the bench) no time value is allotted to obtaining control because this has already been paid for in the time allotted to the finger and associated movements. In other systems this form of obtaining control is given a value.

The classifications also cover activities such as lifting, walking, accurate placement, pedal operation, etc., with suitable module values, while appropriate combinations enable measurement to be made of almost any likely work situation.

MODAPTS EQUIPMENT

Equipment has been designed, developed and manufactured at Centre Industries based on these MODAPTS functions. Seventeen pieces have been developed and tested as follows:

1. *Move Board:* This equipment is used for the assessment of the ability to perform forearm moves, whole arm moves

and extended arm moves. The test assesses the ability to perform these movements in four directions: *viz.,* forward; forty-five degrees to the side; and vertical. Equipment comprises a six-feet by two-feet board with two outrigger extensions into which twenty-eight microswitches mounted as six-inch centers from side to side are wired to two programmable banks of push buttons. This circuit is connected to an electronic timer and counter unit. The timer and counter unit allows time cycles from .1 to .5 of a minute to be selected for the duration of the test.

The test consists of inserting the buttons into the desired microswitches and the interval of time taken for the forearm or whole arm or extended arm to travel over the distance can be measured. Normalized time in .1 of a minute requires sixteen moves for the forearm, twelve for the whole arm, and nine for the extended arm. Data from this test shows us the speed of arm movement and the range of arm movement and allows determination of the preferred work station for the disabled operator.

2. *Finger movements:* Equipment has been designed to measure movement including vertical and rotary finger movements.

Vertical finger movements are measured by a hinged steel plate actuating a microswitch and connected to the electronic timer.

Normal time (.1 minute) = twenty-three movements

To test rotary finger movements, two microswitches have been mounted in a steel box and these are actuated by a cam shaft which, in turn, is operated by the external 1-inch knob with peripheral travel of ¾ inch. This unit again is attached to the counter and timer and the time measured in moving thumb and forefinger forward and backward on the knob. This test is carried out in three positions; with the knob pointing forward; to the side; and upward.

Normal time (.1 minute) = twenty-three movements

3. *Wrist movements:* These are done as wrist joint movements resulting in movements of approximately two inches. Two classified movements are measured; *viz.,* (a) hori-

zontally sideways movement, and (b) rotary movement.

Normal time (.1 minute) = twenty-three movements

(a) Horizontally opposed microswitches are actuated by a sliding carriage interposed between them. The hand resting on the carriage with a locating peg between the second and third finger enables the time interval to be recorded in sliding the carriage between the two microswitches.

(b) The wrist movement of a rotary nature is similar to that for the 1-Mod rotary movement in the fingers except that the operating knob is two inches in diameter.

4. An activity operation test that embodies a sequence of motions measuring simple thumb and forefinger *Get* movements with forearm moves and low conscious control *Puts,* consists of a central bin and interchangeable chute units located each side of this bin.

The tests here include the two sizes of pieces to be handled from the chute location into the bin. These pieces are two inches by one inch diameter aluminum tube and ¾-inch aluminum cubes. In addition to the chute arrangement, a peg board is also in use that holds these components in an upright position. This operation is performed with left hand and right hand and measures the ability to get the components, remove them to the central bin and release. Right hand, left hand and simultaneous sequence motions are measured.

Normal time group motion = .15 minute per ten pieces

5. Another sequence test measures *Get* movements involving more than one simple forefinger movement. The components used as the test pieces are components selected from the actual work situation and require additional selection from a jumbled stock.

Normalized time = .19 minute for ten pieces

6. Another sequence test series measures placement *(Put)* ability. The first test requires one simple positioning associated with forearm moves. Equipment comprises a turntable with a lock pin enabling a location of one of three test positions. Three sized pieces have been selected, 1¾ inches square, ¾ inch square and 5/16 inch square that enables

the measurement of the ability to place objects over suitably sized locating pins.

Normal time = .19 minute for ten pieces

7. *More than one positioning* is measured by the use of pegged plate holding eight test pieces. The test pieces are sectioned and require one additional degree of difficulty for satisfactory location over the terminal pin.

Normal time = .21 minute for eight pieces

8. *Eye use and decision making:*   Test equipment here consists of a chute attached to a landing bar extended at right angles to the chute. Components used are twelve aluminum slugs 1¼ inches by 1½ inches by 1-inch thick, six of which carry a plain label squarely placed on one face and the other six carrying the same label fixed seven degrees off square. A solenoid control plunger pin controls release of each block from the chute as the previously examined blocks are pushed aside. The test requires a decision to be made on which block appears from the chute and the action taken to push the block left or right.

9. *Pronation - Supination:*   A spade-shaped handle attached to a shaft carrying a pointer and spur gear calibrates range of supination and pronation of the wrist. The spur gear meshes with a rack which carries a stylus transferring the shaft movements on a moving chart and the range of movement is thus recorded.

10. *Palmar grasp and pincer grip:*   Tests are carried out using a specially designed hand piece shaped to accommodate the fingers and wrist linked in such a way that applying pressure transmitted to a silicon strain gauge is amplified on a solid state amplifier providing readings in mivro-amps as pressure is applied to the test pieces. The meter readings are converted into pounds pressure being applied.

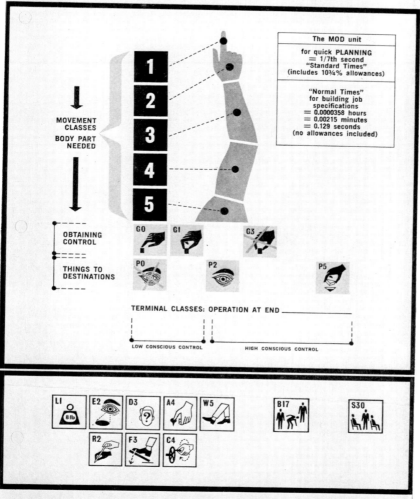

MODAPTS

MODular **A**rrangement of **P**redetermined **T**ime **S**tandards

MOVEMENT CLASSES
BODY PART NEEDED

The MOD unit

for quick PLANNING
= 1/7th second
"Standard Times"
(includes 10¾% allowances)

"Normal Times"
for building job
specifications
= 0.0000358 hours
= 0.00215 minutes
= 0.129 seconds
(no allowances included)

OBTAINING CONTROL

THINGS TO DESTINATIONS

G0 G1 G3

P0 P2 P5

TERMINAL CLASSES: OPERATION AT END

LOW CONSCIOUS CONTROL   HIGH CONSCIOUS CONTROL

L1 E2 D3 A4 W5 B17 S30

R2 F3 C4

THE AUSTRALIAN ASSOCIATION FOR PREDETERMINED TIME STANDARDS AND RESEARCH

Other equipment developed enables measurement of capacity in operating machine levers and ankle flexion.

This test battery administered provides a profile of *efficiency and effectiveness* of the individual in performing work-related motions.

A MODAPTS observation study is also carried out on the actual work tasks performed at Centre Industries and modular classifications of function and time value allotted to each task.

The *cross match* of the profiles of the disabled and the task then point out the discrepancies that enable the direction of job training and the rehabilitation program, including:

1. Modification of the work station, work components, and machine members to suit the disabled person's ability. This can mean the deletion, combination or manipulation of work elements within the task with the aim to eradicate unwanted or useless motions substituting more efficient motions by the repositioning of control levers, workplace layouts and production components.

   This study also indicates the necessary mechanical aids and devices required to enable the operator to perform the task at his maximum potential.

2. Guidelines to medical services and the plannings of remedial therapy.

3. Establishment of a *learning curve* to measure comparable efficiency of the disabled at the decided work place.

4. Provision of basic data to assist research and development aimed at solving some of the basic problems confronting the severely disabled.

5. The ability to reassess the success or otherwise of the results of the training and rehabilitation program.

6. The program of assessment described herein for job tasks in an industrial setting should be employed to measure the capacity and capability of the disabled child in an educational and prevocational setting.

The common failing of all assessment programs must be the inability to measure human ingenuity. We can never forget that the disabled themselves, once effectively placed in employment, provide us through reassessment and follow-up the direction our work should follow.

IX

THE WORK EVALUATION REPORT

CHARLES SMOLKIN

Introduction

Survey

Organization

Smolkin Narrative Report Writing Format

Discussion

Summary and Recommendations

Implications

References

INTRODUCTION

A LTHOUGH EFFECTIVE REPORT WRITING is one of the critical deficits in many otherwise effective work evaluation programs, this chapter is not meant to mitigate the objective anxiety necessary for conscientious reporting. A realization of the impact that a work evaluation report can have on the life of a handicapped individual makes continuous self-evaluation by work evaluators a necessity. Services that a client will receive, or the lack of them, are many times the result of the several hundred words that comprise a work evaluation report.

The anxiety that breeds thoroughness, creativity and objectivity is a necessity for growth and change. The anxiety that hampers these assets has its roots in the defensiveness and conceit that cause conflict among workshops, among agencies and facilities, and among colleagues. Of course, the ones who suffer are the clients who have reports written on their potentialities when these potentialities are influenced by extraneous factors that affect the objectivity of evaluators.

The report format offered in this chapter is a time saving device that frees the evaluator from the drudgery of repeating the same statements over and over again. This energy should be spent better in thought about the implications of the new and unique information gathered on each client. Competent use of this format should lead to a highly structured, yet uniquely individualistic and productive report on each client.

SURVEY

Incredibly, many facilities and workshops determine the needs of clients and referring agencies without first contacting them. This interaction will establish a basis for effective report writing. Because a work evaluation report reflects the objectives of a program, it will not be utilized if its contents are not consistent with the needs of the community to be served. The first step in effective work evaluation reporting must be a survey of those who will be utilizing the report. Too many times recommendations are not followed because of a breakdown in communication between the resource and the referring source. Because the facility will probably suffer from a lack of referrals, clients who need direction will not be served because of a conflict they had no part in creating.

When Sinai Hospital began its program, vocational rehabilitation counselors were invited to the facility. Much time was spent in the exchange of ideas. The types of information that any work evaluation program will need in order to report effectively are:

1. Why do counselors refer clients for work evaluation?
2. What types of information do they wish?
3. Generally, what is the orientation of these counselors (academic or functional) ?
4. What types of positive experiences have the counselors had?
5. Do the ideas presented seem as if they are consistent with these positive aspects?
6. If not, how can they be modified?
7. What types of negative experiences have these counselors had?
8. How can the facility avoid causing similar conflicts?

9. Also, will the counselor be willing to modify his ideas if a continuous dialogue is established?

A wide variety of rehabilitation counselors from different areas (inner city, rural, suburban, educational, etc.) should be contacted so that the agency providing the service will not get a narrow view of needs. Effective reporting cannot be done when work evaluators do their job in isolation. Of course, the same effort towards establishing lines of communication must be made within the work evaluator's own facility. He must be in continuous contact with administration and other disciplines so that the rehabilitation team has its foundation in team work and mutual confidence.

Knowledge of the labor market is another essential for report writing. It is absurd to recommend training or jobs that do not exist within a reasonable distance from the client's home, except in special circumstances. The employment service should be visited and the labor situation reviewed with its staff. Some of the counselors can arrange visits to various training schools and facilities.

An important tool in gaining knowledge for effective reporting can be the state Vocational Evaluation and Work Adjustment Association. This affords the opportunity to discuss objectives with other work evaluators from different facilities and workshops. Visits to factories and job sites should be made to gain first hand knowledge about the requirements of particular occupations. This further emphasizes the need to report from reality based, practical first hand experience. Once the credibility of a work evaluator is tarnished because of his innocence about the requirements of the job market, his expertise is most difficult to reestablish.

ORGANIZATION

Preparing a quality report is an important and demanding responsibility. The structure and organization of a work evaluation report will play a major role in the amount of utilization of a particular work evaluation program. Because of the difficulty that many evaluators have in phrasing their findings and in determining the extent to which detailed information is needed, the *Smolkin Narrative Report Writing Format* was created to be used as a helpful tool in alleviating those problems.

The following sections will present the *Format* interspersed with samples taken from an actual report followed by a discussion of the foundation for the inclusion and structure of each of its components.

SMOLKIN NARRATIVE REPORT WRITING FORMAT

The evaluator will give the name of the client and rating of punctuality. The secretary will fill in the other information.

Date:6-26-71

Evaluation Period: 5-29-71
to: 6-24-71

Client: Young, Allan
Date of Birth: 10-18-48

Days Absent: 0
Punctuality: Excellent

BACKGROUND INFORMATION:

1. _____ was admitted to Sinai Hospital, Department of Rehabilitation Medicine for Vocational Evaluation on _____. (He, She) was referred for vocational evaluation in order to _____.

Mr. Young was admitted to Sinai Hospital, Department of Rehabilitation Medicine for Vocational Evaluation on May 29, 1971, with a congenital disease of the spine which makes it necessary for client to be confined to a wheelchair. Mr. Young was referred for vocational evaluation in order to evaluate the vocational implications of being wheelchair bound and the concomitant problems with transportation to and from work and possible architectural barriers. Although client suffers from congenital incontinence, this did not appear to be a problem during the evaluation process.

2. A review of client's educational history reveals that (he, she) has _____.
Vocationally, client has worked as a _____.

A review of client's educational history reveals that he is a high school graduate. Vocationally, client has worked as a general school maintenance man during summer vacations. Also, he has worked in the school library as a library assistant.

PSYCHOLOGICAL TEST INTERPRETATION:

3. Non verbal intelligence testing indicates that client functions within the _____ range of intellectual classification on the Revised Beta Examination and the _____ range of intellectual classification on the Culture Fair Intelligence Test. Client's performance on the arithmetic section of the Wide Range Achievement Test indicates that (he, she) has mastered the basic arithmetic skills needed at the _____ grade level. When total reading assets are given consideration, client appears to be reading at the _____ grade level on the Nelson Reading Test; the maximum level measured by this test is the 10.5 grade level.

Non-verbal intelligence testing indicates that client functions within the high average range of intellectual classification on the Revised Beta Examination and the high average range of intellectual classification on the Culture Fair Intelligence Test. Client's performance on the arithmetic section of the Wide Range Achievement Test indicates that he has mastered the basic arithmetic skills needed at the 6.7 grade level. When total reading assets are given consideration, client appears to be reading beyond the 10.5 grade level on the Nelson Reading Test; the maximum level measured by this test is the 10.5 grade level.

4. According to the General Aptitude Test Battery, _____

_____.

The more specialized Purdue Pegboard shows that client possesses _____ ability to assemble small parts. _____ scores on the General Aptitude Test Battery enable (him, her) to meet _____ of the occupational aptitude patterns. Examples of individual occupations listed within these patterns are as follows:

_____

_____

The above job recommendations are made with the knowledge that aptitude tests, in general, do not compensate for disability. They are used as a means of widening vocational horizons and in the consideration of potential worksample areas.

(If no patterns are met, the evaluator will have to dictate that this should not be typed) .

According to the General Aptitude Test Battery, Mr. Young possesses average general intelligence, verbal aptitude, numerical aptitude, spatial aptitude, form perception and clerical perception. Client's finger dexterity is low average, while his manual dexterity is rated inferior. The more specialized Purdue Pegboard shows that client possesses average ability to assemble small parts. Mr. Young's scores on the General Aptitude Test Batery enable him to meet a number of occupational aptitude patterns. Examples of individual occupations listed within these patterns are as follows: Chemical Laboratory Technician, Chemist Assistant, Laboratory Assistant, Collection Clerk, Food Checker, Receptionist, Reference Clerk, Sales Person, Automobile Mechanic, Meat Cutter, Retail General, Merchandise Manager, Proof Reader, Balance Clerk, General Office Clerk, Cost Clerk, Inventory Clerk, Posting Clerk, Electronics Assembler, Sheet Metal Worker, Control Clerk, Customers Examiner, Garmet Packer, Order Clerk, Material Coordinator, Central Office Operator, Information Operator, Telephone Operator, Electrician, Radio Repairman, Television Repairman, Balance Assembler, Banking Adjuster, Tailor Mechanisms Assembler and General Repairman. It is obvious from this list of possible jobs that client has extensive vocational potential, although he is confined to a wheelchair. The above job recommendations are made with the knowledge that aptitude tests, in general, do not compensate for disability. They are used as a means of widening vocational horizons and in the consideration of potential worksample areas.

5. When considering objectively measured personality factors on the Sixteen Personality Factor Test, one gets the pitcure of _____

_____

This objective picture is _____ consistent with the more subjective evaluation observations over a _____ week period. The Picture Interest Inventory, a nonverbal measure of vocational interests, indicates a significant interest for _____

_____and a disinterest for _____

_____

When considering objectively measured personality factors on the Sixteen Personality Factor Test, one gets the picture of a practical, conventional and hard-to-fool individual. This objective picture is consistent with the more subjective evaluation observations over a four week period. The Picture Interest Inventory, a nonverbal measure of vocational interests, indicates a significant interest for business and computational occupations and a disinterest for natural jobs (farming, ranching).

6. Orthorater scores show that client's binocular acuity is _____ when viewing far objects and _____ when viewing near objects. Monocular acuity with the right eye is _____ for distant objects and _____ for near objects; while it is _____ for distant objects and _____ for near objects with the left eye. Phoria testing shows that client's ocular muscles are _____ in balance and _____ deviate from the correct position for binocular vision. Client possesses _____ depth perception and _____ color vision. In general, orthorater scores indicate that client's eyes are suitable for the performance of _____ occupations.

Orthorater scores show that client's binocular acuity is 20/25 when viewing far objects and 20/18 when viewing near objects. Monocular acuity with the right eye is 20/22 for distant objects and 20/20 for near objects; while it is 20/20 for distant objects and 20/18 for near objects with the left eye. Phoria testing shows that client's ocular muscles are in balance and do not deviate from the correct position for binocular vision. Client possesses inferior depth perception and excellent color vision. In general orthorater scores indicate that client's eyes are suitable for the performance of most occupations.

7. Because of client's performance on the psychological testing segment of vocational evaluation and expressed interests, (he, she) was given tryouts on worksamples related to _____

_____.

Because of _____.

Because of client's performance on the psychological testing seg-

ment of vocational evaluation and expressed interests, he was given tryouts on worksamples related to clerical, computational, drafting, electronics, jewelry manufacturing and machine shop occupations. Because of an expressed interest in the library field, Mr. Young was placed at an on-the-job tryout in the Medical Library of Sinai Hospital.

WORKSAMPLE CLARIFICATION-PERSONALITY VARIABLES:

a. An exploration of worksamples related to clerical and computational occupations presents a _____ picture. Client's aptitude on basic arithmetic problems is _____. (He, She) exhibits _____ potential for learning bimanual touch typing, while (his, her) ability to prepare a relatively simple type of payroll record is rated as _____. On the worksample which measures client's ability to pay close attention to detail, while working with and making entries of small and precisely formed figures in conjunction with the use of an adding machine client is rated as _____. Client's aptitude in the correct use of the written English language is rated as _____. (He, She) exhibited _____

_____

while performing these worksamples. Job opportunities represented by these evaluations range from such entry positions as file clerk and messenger to more skilled work, such as college trained accountants, secretaries, typists and bookkeepers. The results of clerical and computational worksamples show that (he, she) can be considered for the following jobs: _____

_____.

An exploration of worksamples related to clerical and computational occupations presents a mixed picture. Mr. Young's aptitude on basic arithmetic problems is below average. He exhibits below average potential for learning bimanual touch typing, while his ability to prepare a relatively simple type of payroll record is rated as average. On the worksample which measures client's ability to pay close attention to detail, while working with the making entries of small and precisely formed figures in conjunction with the use of an adding machine, client is rated as above average

Client's aptitude in the correct use of the writen English language is rated as average. Mr. Young exhibited superior aptitude in filing according to code number and chronological order, while his alphabetical filing ability is average. Job opportunities represented by these evaluations range from such entry positions as file clerk and messenger to more skilled work, such as college trained accountants, secretaries, typists and bookkeepers. The results of clerical and computational worksamples show that Mr. Young can be considered for the following jobs: File Clerk, Cashier, Timekeeper, Shipping Clerk, Parts Clerk, Library Assistant and Telephone Order Clerk.

b. Worksamples related to drafting occupations indicate that client possesses general aptitude rated at the _____ level. On the worksample constructed to measure client's aptitude for handling various drafting instruments, (he, she) achieves at a _____ level, while (his, her) ability to use a compass and bow divider is rated as _____. On the worksample which measures the basic principles of mechanical drafting while client is making a working drawing of a square prism, (he, she) performs at a _____ level of achievement. Client shows _____ aptitude for making a complicated scale drawing during the completion of a layout from a rough draft. While drawing many geometrical shapes which evaluate the adequacy of the client's space relations perceptual ability, (he, she) performs at a _____ level. Entry jobs in this area are usually as a tracer, copyist, detailer, or a junior draftsman. Client reacted to these worksamples in a _____

_____

(He, She) could be recommended for the following jobs: _____

_____

Worksamples related to drafting occupations indicate that Mr. Young possesses general aptitude rated at the average level. On the worksample constructed to measure client's aptitude for handling various drafting instruments he achieves at an above average level, while his ability to use a compass and bow divider is rated as average. On the worksample which measures the basic principles of mechanical drafting while client is making a working drawing of a square prism, client performs at an average level of achievement. He shows average aptitude for making a complicated scale drawing during the completion of a layout from a rough draft. While drawing many geometrical shapes which evaluate the adequacy of the client's space relations perceptual ability, he performs at an average level. Entry jobs in this area are usually as a tracer, copyist, detail or a junior draftsman. He reacted to these work-samples in a positive manner although he prefers other types of work more. He could be recommended for the following jobs: Blue Print Maker, Pattern Maker, Civil Draftsman, Detail Draftsman and Drafting Clerk.

c. On worksamples related to the jewelry manufacturing area, client exhibits _____ ability. Client's aptitude for using a standard jewelers saw frame is _____, while (his, her) ability in the use of jewelers needle files is _____. Client is rated as _____ in the use of an electric drill press and in the execution of fine detail work with a jewelers saw. Client's ability while using pliers to shape brass is rated as _____. Client reacted to these worksamples _____. With training (he, she) could be recommended for the following jobs:

On worksamples related to the jewelry manufacturing area, client exhibits above average ability. His aptitude for using a standard jewelers saw frame is above average, while his ability in the use of jewelers needle files is above average. Client is rated as above average in the use of an electric drill press and in the execution of fine detail work with a jewelers saw. His ability while using pliers to shape brass is rated as above average. With training he could be recommended for the following jobs: Chain Maker, Ring Maker, Watchband Assembler, Surgical Instrument Maker and Tool Grinder.

d. Results of worksamples related to electronics assembly jobs indicate that (he, she) has _____ aptitude in running a small cable harness of the solid color wires, while (his, her) ability to make tight nonsliding neat knots in lacing is rated as _____. A large percentage of electronics industry workers are engaged in assembly tasks. They are employed in the manufacture of such devices as radios, television sets, radar, telephone and telegraphic equipment, recording devices and guided missile components. Because of _____ accomplishment on these worksamples (he, she) is recommended for the following jobs: _____

_____.

e. Results of worksamples related to machine shop occupations present a _____ outcome. Client shows _____ ability for reading and transcribing measurements, _____ ability in relating surfaces and edges of a three dimensional drawing to a two dimensional drawing and _____ ability to measure accurately with a ruler. On a worksample which measures client's ability to draw to indicated numerical dimensions, (he,she) performs at a

_____.

rate. On the evaluation that measures client's ability to transfer a layout of a working drawing to a piece of metal while using hand tools to shape this metal, (he, she) performs at a _____ level. Client achieves at a _____ level while operating a drill press to drill holes in a prepared metal blank. (His, Her) ability to understand and apply basic arithmetical processes such as are required in routine machine shop practice is rated as _____. Client uses a micrometer caliper in measuring the thickness of plastic objects at a _____ performance standard. The principle job of most machine workers is the operation of machine tools, such as lathes, grinding machines, drilling and boring machines, millers, shapers and planers. (He, She) reacted to these worksamples _____

_____.

(He, She) is recommended for training for the following jobs: __

_____.

The results of worksamples related to machine shop occupations present a negative outcome. Although client's ability to read and transcribe measurements is superior and his use of tools in metal layout is above average, his use of a micrometer is inferior. His ability to use fractions and decimals is also inferior. Because of a below average summary rating in this area, no vocational recommendations can be made.

f. On worksamples which measure client's aptitude in the performance of work tasks representative of light assembly collation and packaging operations common to much of industry, he performs on _____ level. Placement opportunities related to this area of evaluation include tasks in which the worker completes a multifaceted assembly or collation alone, as well as tasks in which (he, she) takes a position on an assembly line while repeatedly performing one step or task which is preceded or followed by other tasks executed by fellow workers. Because of _____ achievement in this area, he is suited for the following jobs: ____

(His, Her) reaction to these worksamples would indicate _____

g. Actual on-the-job tryout

Because of client's repeated expressions of a desire for library work, he was placed within the Medical Library of Sinai Hospital. The head librarian makes the following recommendations about Mr. Woung's abilities: His clerical ability is satisfactory without further training, although his typing should be improved. She states that this ability is fair but not quite what would be expected of a library assistant. Being confined to a wheelchair hampers Mr. Young's use of library materials on high shelves. He will be unable to get to all areas of a library if the conditions are crowded. He and a prosepctive employer will have to evaluate the library carefully before offering or accepting employment. She thinks that Mr. Young will be feasible for placement as a library assistant if selective placement is made. Mr. Young's personal preference is to work in a general rather than a technical library. This feeling is motivated by the fact that he feels ignorant of technical terms.

SUMMARY AND RECOMMENDATIONS:

8. When considering relevant medical data, one gets the picture of a _____.
When one takes into consideration client's work personality, it can be concluded _____

Medical reports indicate that Mr. Young will continue to be confined to a wheelchair because of a congenital disease. During the evaluation process client has proven himself to be a mature and conscientious worker. He demonstrates multiple abilities and multiple vocational recommendations are made within the body of this report.

9. In considering vocational planning, _____

_____.

It is therefore recommended _____

_____.

In considering vocational planning, one must consider that client's primary interest is in the working within a library. A recommendation is made that selective placement be considered in this field. Client will have to receive some short term (six or eight weeks) intensive typing training to fulfill the requirements of a library assistant's position. Of course, transportation will be a problem no matter which area of vocational endeavor is selected.

10. Any additional information will be dictated by the evaluator.

Although client prefers the library area, the rehabilitation counselor will find it worthwhile to have Mr. Young visit a watchmaking training program or factory and a jewelry manufacturing facility.

DISCUSSION

The significant factors in each section of the report are discussed below.

Background Information

The critical point to remember in supplying background information to a referral source is not to parrot page after page of the same information as received. This gives the referring agency the impression that they are only getting what they have already submitted and leads to such statements as "why did I need to refer there? or "I already knew everything the report stated." Because background information is the first stimuli read by the referring person, it can establish positive feelings about or an aversion to what follows in the report.

The objective in this section of the report is to establish the functional, vocational implication of the client's disability in non-technical terms and to transmit any new information gathered. The reader should recognize that the actual report does not follow the format exactly, and the length of the blank line is not meant as a limiting factor (whether dictated or written). Much information can be fit easily into the Format though changes should be made to meet the needs of a particular client. For instance, in paragraph two, the space after "Vocationally, client has worked as a . . . " seems to be consistent with this client's limited work background. The same information might require seven or eight lines of past work history for a client with a more extensive background.

Psychological Test Interpretation

Before psychological tests are used for vocational prediction, the work evaluator must realize the limitations that these tests have as such a tool. They should be used in search for potential areas of vocational productivity rather than as a selection device. Each test should be researched through Mental Measurements Yearbooks Buvds 1965), manuals and publications. Although cation and client population might dictate the utilization of other useful, these instruments are not endorsed for every program. Lo-tests or techniques.

In paragraph three, it can be seen that one of the tests selected is the Culture Fair Intelligence Test (Cattell and Cattell, 1960). In a recent publication (Smolkin, et. al., 1970), it was concluded that this is really a misnomer. This test requires using pencil and paper, starting from the left side of the page and supposes the desire for achievement in a testing situation. On the other hand, nonverbal stimuli are a more equitable way of arriving at intelligence estimates for certain populations than verbal or numerical tests. For this reason, it was stated that a more accurate name for the test would be the Culturally More Fair Than Verbal or Arithmetic Intelligence Test. This is stated to emphasize the limitation of the instruments used. For if it were felt that psychological testing was by itself an effective means of vocational prediction, there would be no need for worksamples and on-the-job tryouts. If this were true, work evaluation probably would not exist; and people would continue to feel secure in predicting vocational success from psychological evaluations.

In paragraph four, the last sentence reenforces the particular limitations of testing for the handicapped, so that the referral source can place the data in perspective. Actually, the steps in work evaluation were published by Nadolsky (1971), emphasizing the use of a variety of procedures to eventually predict a feasible area of vocational endeavor.

In paragraph five, the Sixteen Personality Factor Inventory (Cattell and Eber, 1964) is utilized as a means of having an objective comparison with more subjective clinical observations over the period of the work evaluation. This should have some future research value.

Paragraph six on the Orthorater is included so that intellectual limitations will not be confused with visual problems. The information is divulged in layman's terms so that the referring source will not be intimidated. Professional consultation is recommended if a previously unknown visual problem is discovered.

Paragraph 7 is included within the psychological test section in order to emphasize the process orientation of work evaluation. Each client is given the opportunity to express which areas of work he wishes to encounter during the evaluation process. Emphasis is also placed on the potentials discovered during the psychological testing segment. One can see that the impression of worksample selection without foundation is not transmitted to the referral source because of the logical progression towards worksample utilization.

Worksample Clarification - Personality Variables

Although many work evaluators separate the objective worksample results from the clinical evaluation of personality, this is not done at Sinai. It is felt that this is an artificial separation, in that these personality traits are generally observed during worksample administration. Furthermore, an employer does not separate the personality of an employee from production. Workers who are dependable and conscientious, but have some production limitations, tend to stay employed while those who are productive, yet undependable, tend to be fired. In this way, the referral source can have the opportunity to grasp the interrelationship between the client's temperament and ability.

Two other points should be discussed about this section of the Report Format. First, this client was only administered worksample areas (a), (b), (c), and (e) and not all of them. Because there was a great deviation from client's achievement on worksample area (e) and the Format, the structure was suspended by the evaluator and an independently constructed paragraph was substituted. This shows that the evaluator is not rigidly tied to the Format and that each client is administered the worksamples that are relevant to his abilities and interests and not administered each worksample simply because it exists.

Secondly, much of the structure in the wording of the worksample areas comes directly from the material supplied within the TOWER System. This is a way of indicating that the *Smolkin Narrative Report Writing Format* was not created in a vacuum. Many people, not even remotely connected with the Department of Rehabilitation Medicine at Sinai Hospital of Baltimore, have made immense contributions to the report form. Work evaluators aware of the progress made at other facilities can increase their own potential for creativity.

Because working at a community hospital gives the work evaluator the opportunity to utilize many work areas, in that the hospital is like a city containing its own laundry, storeroom, accounting department, print shop, housekeeping department, etc., the opportunity exists to place the client with actual workers in areas of potential shown on testing and worksamples. This gives the opportunity to ascertain whether vocational predictions are consistent with the reality of an actual work situation. Also, the work evaluators are continuously in contact with employers and workers, thus keeping their perceptions reality oriented. Of course, while not having exactly the same situation, most other facilities have work areas and workshops that can be utilized in a similar way.

It should be noted that great effort is made to include the perceptions of the work supervisor in paragraph (g). This is based on the following hypotheses:

1. Work has to be appropriate to be therapeutic.
2. Work supervisors have much to offer clients in the way of support and criticism.
3. Work supervisors need the support and guidance of professional staff members in utilizing their assets constructively.
4. Referral sources have great respect for the recommendations of actual workers when given proper weight in work evaluation reports.

SUMMARY AND RECOMMENDATIONS

Medical information is reviewed; client's potentials are restated and his interests and reactions are considered in this section. The plan that will be necessary for the implementation of recommendations (direct placement, training, further education, etc.) is discussed.

IMPLICATIONS

There can be no implications for effectiveness in this or any other report format if recommendations are not proven dependable or are not followed by the referral source. For this reason, a continuing follow-up process utilizing the telephone (during both the day and in the evening) (has been instituted at Sinai.) in order to contact client and counselors about the results of the work evaluation. An article published by Smolkin, Long, and Cohen (1970) showed that 70 percent of recommendations were followed and those that were followed were proven to be 89 percent accurate in the proper placement of clients. Unpublished data continues to substantiate these findings.

Experience has shown that this structured, yet flexible approach to report writing, saves a great deal of time and leads to a highly productive relationship with referral sources. The report is extensive and easily understood. While not shown, raw testing and worksample data are attached to the report so that the referral source can supply complete information to other professionals who may utilize the data for the benefit of the client. By supplying such extensive information, referral sources may utilize the presented material in most creative ways and find appropriate placements that are not actually recommended in the report but are based on the data supplied. By having such a thorough mechanism of reporting, the potential for productive outlets for the client tends to multiply as professionals utilize the information. Each will bring his own unique background and experiences to the data in addition to that reported by the work evaluator.

REFERENCES

Buros, O.K. (Ed.): *Mental Measurements Yearbook.* New Jersey, Gryphon Press, 1938-65. 6 vols.
Cattell, R. B. and Cattell, A.K.S.: *IPAT, Culture Fair Intelligence Test.* Champaign, Inst. Pers. Abil. Test, 1949, 1957, 1960.
Cattell, R. B. and Eber, H. B.: *IPAT, Sixteen Personality Factor Questionnaire.* Champaign, Inst. Pers. Abil. Test, 1957, 1964.
Materials Development Center: Recommended Procedure — *Smoklin Nartive Report Writing Format,* Menomie, The Department of Rehabilitation and Manpower Services, School of Education, Stout State University, 1971.
Nadolsky, J. M.: *Development of a Model for Vocational Evaluation of the Disadvantaged.* Alabama, Auburn Duplicating Service, 1971.
Smolkin, C. and Cohen, B. S.: Vocational evaluation and the stroke patient: a discovery of self. *Maryland State Medical Journal, 20:*60-62.
Smolkin, C., Long, J. and Cohen, B. S.: The effectiveness of vocational evaluation in the rehabilitation process. *Maryland State Medical Journal, 19:*95-96, Nov. 1970.

X

THE UTILIZATION OF THE DICTIONARY OF OCCUPATIONAL TITLES IN WORK EVALUATION[1]

CRAIG R. COLVIN

The Evaluation Process and The *DOT*

Understanding The Dictionary of Occupational Titles *(DOT)*

Volume I of the *DOT*

Industry Designation

Volume II of the *DOT*

Occupational Group Arrangement (OGA)

Worker Trait Arrangement (WTA)

Handling .887

Qualifications Profile

A Supplement to the *DOT*

Putting it all Together

Vocational Report

Psychological Report

Summary

References

IT IS UTTERLY impossible for an individual to keep abreast of all the variables or ramifications surrounding the innumerable jobs within occupational categories; therefore, he must rely on references to bridge the gap between his personal knowledge of specific

[1]Acknowledgment is extended to Robert J. Brown, Associate Manpower Administrator for U.S. Training and Employment Service, for allowing segments of the *DOT* to be reprinted in this chapter.

195

jobs and those jobs totally unfamiliar to him. The *Dictionary of Occupational Titles (DOT)* is one such source which should and can become an indispensable tool for professionals working with clients toward vocational selection.

Fundamental considerations must be dealt with prior to, and in some instances, during client evaluation. The counselor or evaluator must examine the client to determine whether or not he envisions himself capable of performing work and its related activities. If an individual does not see himself capable of working, much time and effort spent in evaluation will be fruitless. If such a situation is evident it is necessary for the counselor to re-direct his initial efforts toward the objective of letting the client *see himself* as a productive member of some occupational work force. The necessity of counseling coupled with appropriate reinforcement may be required to provide the insight needed by this client.

Even though the counselor may experience some difficulty in motivating the client—or more appropriately getting the client to motivate himself toward considering work as a basic ingredient of life—there will be occasions where all is for naught; i.e., the client will *never* be considered a candidate for the labor market. Yet, such a decision should not be made until all intervening variables have been examined.

With this in mind it is manditory that a realistic appraisal of occupations be made in placing a client on a job or in a specific training area which will prepare him for some type of work. The client's physical demands, worker requirements, working environment, interests, etc. must be evaluated in relation to various occupational categories. *All* variables must be considered before the final commitment has been made. Therefore, the following material should be considered as an effective and efficient device to be used to aid workers in their search for understanding the many factors associated with specific jobs or the general variables surrounding occupational areas of work.

THE EVALUATION PROCESS AND THE *DOT*

Vocational evaluation is a process that attempts to assess the individual's physical and mental skills and abilities as well as his personality and behavior in an effort to determine his present and future work potential and adjustment. This process does attempt to find his strengths and weaknesses as well as his level of overall vocational functioning. The evaluation process is a diagnostic tool through which the trained evaluator observes behavior, predicts vocational training areas and, in turn, the client's placement potential (Cull and Colvin, 1972a). Further description as well as the objectives of a work evaluation unit are given in this book in Rosenberg's chapter.

In looking at the evaluation process and the use of the *DOT*, three questions must be considered:

1. What population is to be provided services;
2. What occupations are feasible for this population;
3. How can placement be achieved at the conclusion of evaluation, training, or extended work adjustment?

Evaluation, taking into consideration these three questions, is only valid as a process when it prescribes possibilities for every individual coming to the evaluation unit for services. With this in mind the utilization of the *DOT* allows an evaluator to gather more *relevant* data on which to make decisions regarding the client's work potential. Even though it is next to impossible to recreate identical aspects of actual work as far as dust, tolerance for noise and vibration and the inherent pressures associated with piece rate work are concerned, these are some of the variables with which the evaluator must contend. Perusing the *DOT* can provide information relative to these very factors as well as a host of others which will be investigated later in this chapter.

From research performed by this writer regarding occupational information and its use within an evaluation or training setting, it can be said that there is a paucity of material which evaluates or judges a client's skills according to the performance required by industry (Colvin, 1972). The *DOT*, if used correctly, can provide this information. Following along with this statement, the *DOT* used as a diagnostic tool will require the evaluator or counselor to keep abreast continuously with the local labor market where the client resides. All is for naught if a masterful evaluation report is composed which does not relate to actual areas of potential work—if not specific jobs themselves—as they exist in the client's geographical region.

Reflecting for a moment on what Crowe has said in his chapter, one might say that the *DOT* is best put to use at the data gathering stage of the evaluation process where we hope to accumulate as much relevant material as possible. And yet mere accumulation of vast amounts of data cannot assure you of making the proper decision. Therefore, a counselor's responsibility should center around not only data gathering but formulating some ideas as to the client's work potential in terms of such data previously derived. Following this logically should be where both the counselor or evaluator and the client have the opportunity to interpret the previous steps in an effort to arrive at some definite conclusions. In turn, decisions should be made reflecting the input of counselor and client toward the ultimate objective of meaningful activity, be it work or be it leisure time living.

UNDERSTANDING THE
DICTIONARY OF OCCUPATIONAL TITLES (DOT)

The *DOT* consists of several volumes of occupational information which have been revised several times since the original publication in 1939. The *DOT* provides a useful tool for the understanding of job content and the relationship of one job to another as well as providing a foundation for future work in occupational research. The third edition published in 1965 has become a standard source of occupational information in the broad area of manpower development and the world of work. The United States Department of Labor in conjunction with its State Employment Offices has developed a meaningful resource tool which has improved upon past classification systems in an effort to meet various demands. The basic responsibility was to reflect relationships among jobs not only in terms of the traditional work performed but also in terms of the requirements made on the workers.

Of the approximately 75,000 studies of individual job situations investigated by the United States Employment Service, more than 35,000 occupations have been defined in the *DOT*. Especially significant to the work evaluator who must predict client potential, the *DOT* has included eight classification components as significant factors to be considered in occupational selection. They are: training time, aptitudes, interests, temperaments, physical demands, working conditions, industry, and work performed. Further in this chapter each of these components will be described in detail and will key each component respectively to the responsibilities of work evaluators and counselors.

Data for the *DOT* was collected and developed using job analysis techniques established by the Department of Labor. In the majority of cases the same job was analyzed in two different establishments in one state and then in two different establishments in another state. The findings of the original studies were correlated and job definitions were prepared. Therefore, one will see that job definitions as given in the *DOT* are composite descriptions of jobs as they may *typically* occur rather than as they *actually* are performed in a particular establishment or in a given locality. With this in mind, one cannot overstress the importance of knowing and understanding the labor market from a firsthand basis. By this it is meant that to be effective at the evaluation process an individual cannot rely solely on the *DOT* to provide him with specific answers; the evaluator must personally investigate the labor market in his area as well as that found in other areas of the region in which he resides. Representative sampling must be undertaken to give the evaluation a flavor of various jobs found within different occupational settings. There is nothing which can replace the knowledge gleaned from an on-site visit with a local manufacturing concern. Such an approach as described above coupled with the vast amount of information found within the *DOT* definitely will enable the evaluator to approach his responsibilities more realistically than ever before imaginable (Cull & Colvin, 1972b).

The more than 35,000 occupations defined in the *DOT* have been incorporated into a classification structure in which the individual occupations are identified by a six digit code number. The structure consists of two arrangements of jobs—the Occupational Group Arrangement (OGA) and the Worker Trait Arrangement (WTA). These provide (1) a method of grouping jobs having the same basic occupational or worker trait characteristics so that the user can discern various relationships among occupations, and (2) a standard approach to classifying the abilities, vocational experiences, and/or potentials of workers. One can readily see that this structure can quite easily compliment the type of information an individual attempts to derive in the evaluation process.

VOLUME I OF THE *DOT*

Before continuing with further clarification of the OGA and WTA, it is important to examine the basic contents of Volume I of the *DOT*. Volume I provides the user with over 35,000 job titles listed in alphabetical order. Since there are many jobs similar in responsibility and worker requirements being performed under different job titles, the *DOT* has provided alternate titles which can aid the evaluator in locating respective work assignments. Basically the definition of each job contains information on what gets done, how it gets done, and why it gets done. These definitions also provide, indicate, or imply other types of information including (1) functions performed by the worker (greater detail will be provided for this and the following items), (2) significant aptitudes, interests, and temperments required by the job and (3) critical physical demands and working conditions (here physical demands are specific physical aspects required in job performance, and working conditions are physical surroundings in which specific occupational activities occur). In summary the complete job definition with information on the what, how and why of the job as well as indications of the knowledges and abilities required are designed to give a concise and concrete occupational picture which will convey some indication of the level of complexity involved.

INDUSTRY DESIGNATION

Found within each of the volumes of the *DOT* are 229 defined industries. Each is identified by a designation which is usually an

abbreviation of the name of industry. Each job definition is assigned one or more of these designations (which immediately follow the job title) for the purpose of indicating the type of economic activity with which the job is associated. Also they serve to
differentiate among identical titles in different types of activities.

Several bases have been used for determining what the various
industries will include: (1) the character of the services rendered,
as in amusement and recreation services; (2) the products manufactured, as in the rubber, tire and tube industry; (3) the primary
processes employed, as in the non-ferrous metal, smelting and refining industry; (4) the raw materials used, as in the stone work
industry. Usually a definition will receive the designation of the
industry in which the job is found; however, if the job is one of a
group that occurs in several industries because the work activities
involved are not peculiar to any single industry, it is given the
designation of the particular type of activity. Clerical jobs are
typical examples of this designation.

On the other hand a number of jobs occur in more than one
industry but do not fall within a type of work designation. Such
jobs bear the industry designation of the several industries in
which they are found, unless they occur in a number of industries
too large to be conveniently listed, in which case they are given
the designation *any ind.* (any industry) .

In compiling information for the *DOT* it is important to note
that not every job was observed in every industry in which it
existed. For this reason the assignment of an industry designation
does not necessarily limit a job to that industry. These designations are merely indicative of the possible areas of activity in
which the job may be found. Recalling what has been mentioned
earlier, the *DOT* should be used as a resource tool rather than
something which the evaluator thinks will answer all his problems
regarding vocational selection and client evaluation.

VOLUME II OF THE *DOT*

Whereas Volume I's responsibility was to list alphabetically
job titles with their definitions, Volume II serves as a method of
grouping jobs having the same basic occupational, industrial, or

worker characteristics in order to help the user discern relationships among occupations; also it is used as a standard approach to
classifying the abilities, vocational experiences and potentials of
workers. This writer considers Volume II the most important of
all *DOT* volumes thus far published. Within it the user can find
everything that may appear only in part in Volume I and the
supplements. It is in Volume II that explicit occupational and
worker trait information can be found along with other identifying information which can help the evaluator discern some implicit factors associated with job performance. In fact with Volume
II, a counselor can examine or describe any type of job within the
world of work without relying on any other source of occupational
material.

OCCUPATIONAL GROUP ARRANGEMENT (OGA)

Throughout this arrangement, jobs are grouped according to
a combination of work field, purpose, material, product, subject
matter, service, generic term, and/or industry, as reflected in the
first three digits of the *DOT* code number. All occupations are
grouped into nine broad categories, which in turn are divided
into divisions and then ultimately into groups.

The nine occupational categories of the OGA are identified by
the numbers 0 through 9, reflected in the first digit of the *DOT*
code number as follows:

0-1 Professional, Technical and Managerial Occupations
2   Clerical and Sales Occupations
3   Service Occupations
4   Farming, Fishery, Forestry and Related Occupations
5   Processing Occupations
6   Machine Trades Occupations
7   Bench Work Occupations
8   Structural Work Occupations
9   Miscellaneous Occupations

The categories (the second digit of the *DOT* code number) are
divided into eighty-four two-digit divisions, and the divisions in
turn are subdivided into 603 distinctive three-digit groups. Thus
far we have examined only the first three digits of the *DOT* code

number. As with all information found within the *DOT* the OGA's have been constructed in a hierarchical fashion going from the general to the specific; e.g., categories are broader definitions of occupations than are divisions and, in turn, divisions are broader definitions than groups.

With some practice most people can define the first three digits of a job title using the format described in the introduction to Volume II rather than relying solely on the alphabetical listing found in Volume I. After several attempts one probably will find that he can come up with the first three digits to a job title much faster than looking in the alphabetical listing.

WORKER TRAIT ARRANGEMENT (WTA)

The last three digits of the code number are based on the following findings of the United States Employment Service research:

1. Every job requires the worker to function in relation to data, people and things in varying degrees.
2. The relationships specific to data, people and things can be arranged in each case from the simple to complex in the form of a hierarchy so that, generally, each successive function can include the simpler ones and exclude the more complex functions. As noted in the introduction to Volume II as each relationship to people represents a wide range of complexity resulting in considerable overlap among relationships, this arrangement is somewhat arbitrary and can be considered a hierarchy only in the most general of terms.
3. It is possible to express a job's relationship to data, people and things by identifying the highest appropriate function in each hierarchy to which the job requires the worker to have a significant relationship.
4. Together, the last three digits of the code number can express the total level of complexity at which the job requires the worker to function. Immediately the evaluator can see the importance of considering the last three digits to the *DOT;* that is, a job's relationship to the data, people and things.

The following is a description of each of the last three digits, including the elements found within the hierarchy. The identifications attached to the relationships are referred to as worker functions, and provide standard terminology for use in summarizing exactly what a worker does on the job by means of one or more meaningful verbs.

DATA (4th Digit)	*PEOPLE* (5th Digit)	*THINGS* (6th Digit)
0 Synthesizing	0 Mentoring	0 Setting-Up
1 Coordinating	1 Negotiating	1 Precision Working
2 Analyzing	2 Instructing	2 Operating-Controlling
3 Compiling	3 Supervising	3 Driving-Operating
4 Computing	4 Diverting	4 Manipulating
5 Copying	5 Persuading	5 Tending
6 Comparing	6 Speaking-Signaling	6 Feeding-Offbearing
7 No significant	7 Serving	7 Handling
8 relationship	8 No significant relationship	8 No significant relationship

The following represents a breakdown of each term given above and should aid the evaluator in defining the broad worker functions:

DATA (4th digit): Information, knowledge, and conceptions, related to data, people, or things, obtained by observation, investigation, interpretation, visualization, mental creation; incapable of being touched; written data take the form of numbers, words, symbols; other data are ideas, concepts, oral verbalization.

0 *Synthesizing:* Integrating analyses of data to discover facts and/or develop concepts or interpretations.

1 *Coordinating:* Determining time, place, and sequence of operations or action to be taken on the basis of analysis of data; executing determinations and/or reporting on events.

2 *Analyzing:* Examining and evaluating data. Presenting alternative actions in relation to the evaluation is frequently involved.

3 *Compiling:* Gathering, collating, or classifying information about data, people, or things. Reporting and/or carrying out a prescribed action in relation to the information is frequently involved.

4 *Computing:* Performing arithmetic operations and reporting on and/or carrying out a prescribed action in relation to them. Does not include counting.

5 *Copying:* Transcribing, entering, or posting data.

6 *Comparing:* Judging the readily observable functional, structural, or compositional characteristics (whether similar to or divergent from obvious standards) of data, people, or things.

PEOPLE (5th digit) : Human beings; also animals dealt with on an individual basis as if they were human.

0 *Mentoring:* Dealing with individuals in terms of their total personality in order to advise, counsel, and/or guide them with regard to problems that may be resolved by legal, scientific, clinical, spiritual, and/or other professional principles.

1 *Negotiating:* Exchanging ideas, information, and opinions with others to formulate policies and programs and/or arrive jointly at decisions, conclusions, or solutions.

2 *Instructing:* Teaching subject matter to others, or training others (including animals) through explanation, demonstration, and supervised practice; or making recommendations on the basis of technical disciplines.

3 *Supervising:* Determining or interpreting work procedures for a group of workers, assigning specific duties to them, maintaining harmonious relations among them, and promoting efficiency.

4 *Diverting:* Amusing others.

5 *Persuading:* Influencing others in favor of a product, service, or point of view.

6 *Speaking-Signaling:* Talking with and/or signaling people to convey or exchange information. Includes giving assignments and/or directions to helpers or assistants.

7 *Serving:* Attending to the needs or requests of people or animals or the expressed or implicit wishes of people. Immediate response is involved.

THINGS (6th digit) : Inanimate objects as distinguished from human beings; substances or materials; machines, tools, equipment; products. A thing is tangible and has shape, form, and other physical characteristics.

0 *Setting Up:* Adjusting machines or equipment by replacing or altering tools, jigs, fixtures, and attachments to prepare them to perform their functions, change their performance, or restore their proper functioning if they break down. Workers who set up one or a number of machines for other workers or who set up and personally operate a variety of machines are included here.

1 *Precision Working:* Using body members and/or tools or work aids to work, move, guide, or place objects or materials in situations where ultimate responsibility for the attainment of standards occurs and selection of appropriate tools, objects, or materials, and the adjustment of the tool to the task require exercise of considerable judgment.

2 *Operating-Controlling:* Starting, stopping, controlling, and adjusting the progress of machines or equipment designed to fabricate and/or process objects or materials. Operating machines involves setting up the machine and adjusting the machine or material as the work progresses. Controlling equipment involves observing gauges, dials, etc., and turning valves and other devices to control such factors as temperature, pressure, flow of liquids, speed of pumps, and reactions of materials. Setup involves several variables and adjustment is more frequent than in tending.

3 *Driving-Operating:* Starting, stopping, and controlling the actions of machines or equipment for which a course must be steered, or which must be guided, order to fabricate, process, and/or move things or people. Involves such activities as observing gauges and dials estimating distances and determining speed and direction of other objects; turning cranks and wheels; pushing clutches or brakes; and pushing or pulling gear lifts or levers. Includes such machines as cranes, conveyor systems, tractors, furnace charging machines, paving machines and hoisting machines. Excludes manually powered machines, such as handtrucks and dollies, and power assisted machines, such as electric wheelbarrows and handtrucks.

4 *Manipulating:* Using body members, tools, or special devices to work, move, guide, or place objects or materials. Involves some

latitude for judgment with regard to precision attained and selecting appropriate tool, object, or material, although this is readily manifest.

5 *Tending:* Starting, stopping, and observing the functioning of machines and equipment; Involves adjusting materials or controls of the machine, such as changing guides, adjusting timers and temperature gauges, turning valves to allow flow of materials, and flipping switches in response to lights. Little judgment is involved in making these adjustments.

6 *Feeding-Offbearing:* Inserting, throwing, dumping, or placing materials in or removing them from machines or equipment which are automatic or tended or operated by other workers.

7 *Handling:* Using body members, handtools, and/or special devices to work, move, or carry objects or materials. Involves little or no latitude for judgment with regard to attainment of standards or in selecting appropriate tool, object, or material.

NOTE: Included in the concept of Feeding-Offbearing, Tending, Operating-Controlling, and Setting Up, is the situation in which the worker is actually part of the setup of the machine, either as the holder and guider of the material or holder and guider of the tool.

It becomes apparent that if the work evaluator considers the components described above in planning with his client toward a vocational objective or at least a training area, many of the variables previously considered insignificant will take on new meaning. In turn, it is reasonable to expect the evaluation process will become more than just a haphazard or poorly conceived plan of action regarding probable training selection. As stated several times there are too many variables that cannot be considered lightly in dealing with an individual and his future work situation. We must utilize every available opportunity to help us in this decision-making process.

Throughout the WTA section of Volume II, jobs are grouped according to some combination of (1) required general educational development, (2) specific vocational preparation, (3) aptitudes, (4) interests, (5) temperaments, and (6) physical demands. Each group contains narrative information identifying traits and abilities required of the worker, and a listing of occupations which requires these factors in common. Another category which is often overlooked in describing jobs is found in the appendix section of Volume II entitled working conditions. Basically this is the work-environment which surrounds a worker in a specific job. Actual working conditions are coded and provided the user in Supplement One to the *DOT*. (Further clarification will be given later regarding the various components in this volume). Using the data found within this publication together with that obtained in the evaluation unit will permit the user a better interpretation and evaluation of selected significant job characteristics for a wide range of occupations requiring similar traits and abilities. In turn, this will aid the evaluator to ascertain the relationships among jobs and transfer possibilities from one job to another.

There are 114 worker trait groups, organized within the following twenty-two broad areas of work:

Art	Law and Law Enforcement
Business Relations	Machine Work
Clerical Work	Managerial and Supervising
Counseling, Guidance and Social Work	Work
Crafts	Mathematics and Science
Education and Training	Medicine and Health
Elemental Work	Merchandising
Engineering	Music
Entertainment	Personal Service
Farming, Fishing and Forestry	Photography and Communications
Investigating, Inspecting and Testing	Transportation
	Writing

As an example of worker trait groups found within the area of work entitled Elemental Work one will find in *Volume II* Signaling and Related Work, Feeding-Offbearing and Handling. As designated in this volume the user is referred to specific page numbers where additional information can be found relevant to those particular worker trait groups.

Each worker trait group is defined by narrative information under four basic headings:

(1) Work Performed
(2) Worker Requirements
(3) Clues For Relating Applicants and Requirements
(4) Training And Methods Of Entry

This is followed by a section entitled Related Classifications (a list of other worker trait groups that have something in common with this group) , and a Qualifications Profile which specifies the general educational development, specific vocational preparation aptitudes, interests, temperaments, and physical demands required of the worker. Each of the items found within the Qualifications Profile will be elaborated upon later in this chapter.

Using as our example of worker trait groups, and specifically that of HANDLING, one is referred to page 360 of *Volume II*. In addition to the information previously described an additional page is included where jobs are listed and arranged numerically according to their complete code numbers. This listing is included so that the user has the opportunity to investigate the various jobs found within the world of work which have similar components to the worker trait group. If one would take the opportunity to peruse this list he will see that there is indeed some similarity between jobs even though they may be found within other industry designations and areas of work.

Using the example mentioned above—that of the worker trait termed HANDLING—let's examine indepth its components in relation to our responsibilities as an evaluator considering a client's potential job success. The following has been extracted from Volume II, page 360, to help identify and understand a particular worker trait.

HANDLING .887

Work Performed

Work activities in this group primarily involve performing routine, nonmachine tasks involving little or no latitude for judgment. Adherence to rigid standards or specifications is not involved.

Worker Requirements

An occupationally significant combination of: physical stamina; an inclination toward routine, repetitive activities; some dexterity with the fingers and hands; eye-hand coordination; form perception; and the ability and willingness to follow instructions.

Clues for Relating Applicants and Requirements

Good physical condition.
Undistinguished scholastic record.
Expressed preference for *outside* or factory work.

Training and Methods of Entry

The work is usually so elemental in nature that no previous training is required, and entry workers generally receive only a short demonstration or explanation of the tasks involved. The most important hiring factor is the ability of the applicant to meet the strength requirements which range from light to very heavy according to a specific job found within this work trait arrangement. Personal characteristics very often play a significant part. An employer usually will have much latitude in engaging people because of the nature of the work and the fact that many applicants can qualify for it. He frequently will be influenced by an applicant's record of reliability, honesty, and industry. These factors are also taken into consideration when it is decided who will receive training in more complex work and who will be promoted.

RELATED CLASSIFICATIONS	QUALIFICATIONS PROFILE

RELATED CLASSIFICATIONS

Manipulating (.844) p. 322
Tending (.885) p. 447
Feeding-Offbearing (.886) p. 356

QUALIFICATIONS PROFILE

GED: 1 2
SVP: 2 1 3
Apt: GVN SPQ KFM EC
      445 445 344 55
       4   534 433 44
Int: 3 1
Temp: 2 3
Phys. Dem: L M H V 4
[Work Cond: B 234567][2]

Further clarification will now be given for each of the components described above so that the evaluator, counselor or other members of the rehabilitation team can visualize how such material can be employed in his particular work setting. Those people responsible for client evaluation within facilities around the country can see the merits of standardized information as provided in the example chosen.[3] As an example, under the component—Work Performed—one readily will see that this is where the majority of people coming to rehabilitation for services have worked in the past. The key words in this component are "routine nonmachine tasks involving little or no latitude for judgment." Most mentally retarded and brain damaged as well as some clients with behavioral disorders probably fall within this category regarding their potential to successfully carry out work assignments.

Looking on to the Worker Requirements component an evaluator can see that again *routine repetitive activities* play a major role in performing HANDLING tasks. The description given for this component is general in nature. Therefore, it is imperative that one not reach a hasty decision regarding a client's ability to perform some job in this worker trait group.

The paragraph entitled Clues for Relating Applicants and

[2]Working Conditions does not appear as one of the factors within the Qualifications Profile; it has been included for illustrative purposes thereby representing all components as described in the Appendix section.

[3]Realizing that there is a total of 114 worker trait groups providing the user similar information in this section of *Volume II,* one can soon begin to appreciate its value in assisting a client evaluate his work potential.

Requirement is extremely important to consider when a client has come to you for services. The first requirement—good physical condition—is not always a requisite for good job performance at a specific task within the HANDLING worker trait group; yet, generally speaking it does require exactly what it asks for in many cases. Therefore, it is necessary for the evaluator to examine the specific job in question to see if it indeed requires a good physical condition in order to perform the work. The second factor, an undistinguished scholastic record, more often than not typifies many of those people going through the evaluation process. Taking this into consideration with the third factor, a preference for outside or factory work, substantiates the validity of using this resource tool in client evaluation since the majority of people coming to rehabilitation for services can only work in elemental work situations similar to assembly line (repetition) employment.

A key phrase in the Training and Methods of Entry section is "no previous training is required." This should allow the user to investigate opportunities where entry level positions usually are found. In turn, the rehabilitation counselor, case aide, or placement officer has the responsibility to investigate the labor market especially in terms of on-the-job training at entry level positions. This writer has thoroughly investigated the local labor market and with the larger companies the majority of the newly employed work force must enter at the bottom and work their way up. This includes not only those people with low educational backgrounds but the college graduates who eventually wind up in management positions! In these surveys it was surprising to find the number of businesses providing on-the-job training where seasoned company employees provide instruction as well as work evaluation (quite similar to that found in our workshops and comprehensive rehabilitation facilities) for potential of recently hired employees.

Continuing along this line, if the vocational evaluation units in our facilities were to have at hand and use occupational information as provided in the *DOT*, a definite edge would be afforded the client since this resource material has been keyed to ongoing jobs found in the labor market. There is nothing artificial nor has anything been fabricated in the *DOT;* all material was reported as it actually was observed in the industry investigated.

Related Classifications is included for just that reason: If an individual using this section of *Volume II* is having difficulty in locating some areas of work within the HANDLING worker trait group, the *DOT* provides several alternatives from which other appropriate selections may be made. In the example chosen for illustrative purposes, the researchers for the *DOT* have found that MANIPULATING, TENDING, and FEEDING-OFF-BEARING are quite similar to the worker trait components as evidenced in HANDLING.

QUALIFICATIONS PROFILE

If the justification for using the *DOT* had to be based on one particular section of one volume, this writer would have to say that the Qualifications Profile warrants its use. Within this one small area any professional working with people regarding vocational selection has the opportunity to investigate thoroughly the complex ramifications surrounding various jobs. As described earlier, coding has been done throughout the *DOT* for the sake of brevity; yet within the Appendix section a complete description of these code numbers is provided for easy reference. The following material has been extracted from the Appendix of *Volume II*.

GENERAL EDUCATIONAL DEVELOPMENT (GED)

Level	Reasoning Development	Mathematical Development	Language Development
6	Apply principles of logical or scientific thinking to a wide range of intellectual and practical problems. Deal with non-verbal symbolism (formulas, scientific equations, graphs, musical notes, etc.) in its most difficult phases. Deal with a variety of abstract and concrete variables. Apprehend the most abstruse classes of concepts.	Apply knowledge of advanced mathematical and statistical techniques such as differential and integral calculus, factor analysis, and probability determination, or work with a wide variety of theoretical mathematical concepts and make original applications of mathematical procedures, as in empirical and differential equations.	Comprehension and expression of a level to—Report, write, or edit articles for such publications as newspapers, magazines, and technical or scientific journals. Prepare and draw up deeds, leases, wills, mortgages, and contracts. —Prepare and deliver lectures on politics, economics, education, or science. —Interview, counsel, or advise such people as students, clients, or patients, in such matters as welfare eligibility, vocational rehabilitation, mental hygiene, or marital relations. —Evaluate engineering technical data to design buildings and bidges.
5	Apply principles of logical or scientific thinking to define problems, collect data, establish facts, and draw valid conclusions. Interpret an extensive variety of technical instructions, in books, manuals, and mathematical or diagrammatic form. Deal with several abstract and concrete variables.		
4	Apply principles of rational systems[1] to solve practical problems and deal with a variety of concrete variables in situations where only limited standardization exists. Interpret a variety of instructions furnished in written, oral, diagrammatic, or schedule form.	Perform ordinary arithmetic, algebraic, and geometric procedures in standard, practical applications.	Comprehension and expression of a level to—Transcribe dictation, make appointments for executive and handle his personal mail, interview and screen people wishing to speak to him, and write routine correspondence on own initiative. —Interview job applicants to determine work best suited for their abilities and experience, and contact employers to interest them in services of agency. —Interpret technical manuals as well as drawings and specifications, such as layouts, blueprints, and schematics.

	Reasoning	Mathematics	Language
3	Apply common sense understanding to carry out instructions furnished in written, oral, or diagrammatic form. Deal with problems involving several concrete variables in or from standardized situations.	Make arithmetic calculations involving fractions, decimals and percentages.	Comprehension and expression of a level to —File, post, and mail such material as forms, checks, receipts, and bills. —Copy data from one record to another, fill in report forms, and type all work from rough draft or corrected copy. —Interview members of household to obtain such information as age, occupation, and number of children, to be used as data for surveys, or economic studies. —Guide people on tours through historical or public buildings, describing such features as size, value, and points of interest.
2	Apply common sense understanding to carry out detailed but uninvolved written or oral instructions. Deal with problems involving a few concrete variables in or from standardized situations.	Use arithmetic to add, subtract, multiply, and divide whole numbers.	
1	Apply common sense understanding to carry out simple one- or two-step instructions. Deal with standardized situations with occasional or no variables in or from these situations encountered on the job.	Perform simple addition and subtraction, reading and copying of figures, or counting and recording.	Comprehension and expression of a level to —Learn job duties from oral instructions or demonstration. —Write identifying information, such as name and address of customer, weight, number, or type of product, on tags, or slips. —Request orally, or in writing, such supplies as linen, soap, or work materials.

¹Examples of "principles of rational systems" are: Bookkeeping, internal combustion engines, electric wiring systems, house building, nursing, farm management, ship sailing.

SPECIFIC VOCATIONAL PREPARATION (SVP): The amount of time required to learn the techniques, acquire information, and develop the facility needed for average performance in a specific job-worker situation. This training may be acquired in a school, work, military, instutitional, or avocational environment. It does not include orientation training required of even every fully qualified worker to become accustomed to the special conditions of any new job. Specific vocational training includes training given in any of the following circumstances:

a. Vocational education (such as high school commercial or shop training, technical school, art school, and that part of college training which is organized around a specific vocational objective) ;

b. Apprentice training (for apprenticeable jobs only) ;

c. In-plant training (given by an employer in the form of organized classroom study) ;

d. On-the-job training (serving as learner or trainee on the job under the instruction of a qualified worker) ;

e. Essential experience in other jobs (serving in less responsible jobs which lead to the higher grade job or serving in other jobs which qualify) .

The following is an explanation of the various levels of specific vocational preparation.

Level	Time	Level	Time
1	Short demonstration only.	5	Over 6 months up to and including 1 year.
2	Anything beyond short demonstration up and including 30 days.	6	Over 1 year up to and including 2 years.
3	Over 30 days up to and including 3 months.	7	Over 2 years up to and including 4 years.
4	Over 3 months up to and including 6 months.	8	Over 4 years up to and including 10 years.
		9	Over 10 years.

APTITUDES (Apt.)

Specific capacities and abilities required of an individual in order to learn or perform adequately a task or job duty.

G INTELLIGENCE: General learning ability. The ability to "catch on" or understand instructions and underlying principles. Ability to reason and make judgments. Closely related to doing well in school.

V VERBAL: Ability to understand meanings of words and ideas associated with them, and to use them effectively. To comprehend language, to understand relationships between words, and to understand meanings of whole sentences and paragraphs. To present information or ideas clearly.

N NUMERICAL: Ability to perform arithmetic operations quickly and accurately.

S SPATIAL: Ability to comprehend forms in space and understand relationships of plane and solid objects. May be used in such tasks as blueprint reading and in solving geometry problems. Frequently described as the ability to "visualize" objects of two or three dimensions, or to think visually of geometric forms.

P FORM PERCEPTION: Ability to perceive pertinent detail in objects or in pictorial or graphic material; To make visual comparisons and discriminations and see slight differences in shapes and shadings of figures and widths and lengths of lines.

Q CLERICAL PERCEPTION: Ability to perceive pertinent detail in verbal or tabular material. To observe differences in copy, to proofread words and numbers, and to avoid perceptual errors in arithmetic computation.

K MOTOR COORDINATION: Ability to coordinate eyes and hands or fingers rapidly and accurately in making precise movements with speed. Ability to make a movement response accurately and quickly.

F FINGER DEXTERITY: Ability to move the fingers and manipulate small objects with the fingers rapidly or accurately.

M MANUAL DEXTERITY: Ability to move the hands

easily and skillfully. To work with the hands in placing and turning motions.

E EYE-HAND-FOOT COORDINATION: Ability to move the hand and foot coordinately with each other in accordance with visual stimuli.

C COLOR DISCRIMINATION: Ability to perceive or recognize similarities or differences in colors, or inshades or other values of the same color; to identify a particular color, or to recognize harmonious or contrasting color combinations, or to match colors accurately.

Explanation of Levels

The digits indicate how much of each aptitude the job requires for satisfactory (average) performance. The average requirements, rather than maximum or minimum, are cited. The amount required is expressed in terms of equivalent amounts possessed by segments of the general working population.

The following scale is used:

1 The top 10 percent of the population. This segment of the population possesses an extremely high degree of the aptitude.

2 The highest third exclusive of the top 10 percent of the population. This segment of the population possesses an above average or high degree of the aptitude.

3 The middle third of the population. This segment of the population possesses a medium degree of the aptitude, ranging from slightly below to slightly above average.

4 The lowest third exclusive of the bottom 10 percent of the population. This segment of the population possesses a below average or low degree of the aptitude.

5 The lowest 10 percent of the population. This segment of the population possesses a negligible degree of the aptitude.

Significant Aptitudes

Certain aptitudes appear in boldface type on the qualifications profiles for the worker trait groups. These aptitudes are considered to be occupationally significant for the specific group; i.e., essential for average successful job performance. All boldface aptitudes are not necessarily required of a worker for each individual job within a worker trait group, but some combination of them is essential in every case.

INTERESTS (Int.)

Preferences for certain types of work activities or experiences, with accompanying rejection of contrary types of activities or experiences. Five pairs of interest factors are provided so that a positive preference for one factor of a pair also implies rejection of the other factor of that pair.

1 Situations involving a preference for activities dealing with things and objects.

vs. *6* Situations involving a preference for activities concerned with people and the communication of ideas.

2 Situations involving a preference for activities involving business contact with people.

vs. *7* Situations involving a preference for activities of a scientific and technical nature.

3 Situations involving a preference for activities of a routine, concrete, organized nature.

vs. *8* Situations involving a preference for activities of an abstract and creative nature.

4 Situations involving a preference for working for people for their presumed good, as in the social welfare sense, or for dealing with people and language in social situations.

vs. *9* Situations involving a preference for activities that are nonsocial in nature, and are carried on in relation to processes, machines, and techniques.

5 Situations involving a preference for activities resulting in prestige or the esteem of others.

vs. *0* Situations involving a preference for activities resulting in tangible, productive satisfaction.

TEMPERAMENTS (Temp.)

Different types of occupational situations to which workers must adjust.

1 Situations involving a variety of duties often characterized by frequent change.

2 Situations involving repetitive or short cycle operations carried out according to set procedures or sequences.

3 Situations involving doing things only under specific instruction, allowing little or no room for independent action or judgment in working out job problems.

4 Situations involving the direction, control, and planning of an entire activity or the activities of others.

5 Situations involving the necessity of dealing with people in actual job duties beyond giving and receiving instructions.

6 Situations involving working alone and apart in physical isolation from others, although the activity may be integrated with that of others.

7 Situations involving influencing people in their opinions, attitudes, or judgments about ideas or things.

8 Situations involving performing adequately under stress when confronted with the critical or unexpected or when taking risks.

9 Situations involving the evaluation (arriving at generalizations, judgments, or decisions) of information against sensory or judgmental criteria.

O Situations involving the evaluation (arriving at generalizations, judgments, or decisions) of information against measurable or verifiable criteria.

X Situations involving the interpretation of feelings, ideas, or facts in terms of personal viewpoint.

Y Situations involving the precise attainment of set limits, tolerances, or standards.

PHYSICAL DEMANDS (Phy. Dem.)

Physical demands are those physical activities required of a worker in a job.

The physical demands referred to in this Dictionary serve as a means of expressing both the physical requirements of the job and the physical capacities (specific physical traits) a worker must have to meet the requirements. For example, "seeing" is the name of a physical demand required by many jobs (perceiving by the sense of vision) , and also the name of a specific capacity possessed by many people (having the power of sight) . The worker must possess physical capacities at least in an amount equal to the physical demands made by the job.

The Factors

1 **Lifting, Carrying, Pushing, and/or Pulling (Strength).** These are the primary "strength" physical requirements, and generally speaking, a person who engages in one of these activities can engage in all.

Specifically, each of these activities can be described as:

(1) Lifting: Raising or lowering an object from one level to another (includes upward pulling) .

(2) Carrying: Transporting an object, usually holding it in the hands or arms or on the shoulder.

(3) Pushing: Exerting force upon an object so that the object moves away from the force (includes slapping, striking, kicking, and treadle actions) .

(4) Pulling: Exerting force upon an object so that the object moves toward the force (includes jerking) .

The five degrees of Physical Demands Factor No. 1 (Lifting, Carrying, Pushing, and/or Pulling) , are as follows:

S Sedentary Work

Lifting 10 lbs. maximum and occasionally lifting and/or carrying such articles as dockets, ledgers, and small tools. Although a sedentary job is defined as one which involves sitting, a certain amount of walking and standing is often necessary in carrying out job duties. Jobs are sedentary if walking and standing are required only occasionally and other sedentary criteria are met.

L Light Work

Lifting 20 lbs. maximum with frequent lifting and/or carrying of objects weighing up to 10 lbs. Even though the weight lifted may be only a negligible amount, a job is in this category when it requires walking or standing to a significant degree, or when it involves sitting most of the time with a degree of pushing and pulling of arm and/or leg controls.

M Medium Work

Lifting 50 lbs. maximum with frequent lifting and/or carrying of objects weighing up to 25 lbs.

H Heavy Work

Lifting 100 lbs. maximum with frequent lifting and/or carrying of objects weighing up to 50 lbs.

V Very Heavy Work

Lifting objects in excess of 100 lbs. with frequent lifting and/or carrying of objects weighing 50 lbs. or more.

2 **Climbing and/or Balancing:**
   (1) Climbing: Ascending or descending ladders, stairs, scaffolding, ramps, poles, ropes, and the like, using the feet and legs and/or hands and arms.
   (2) Balancing: Maintaining body equilibrium to prevent falling when walking, standing, crouching, or running on narrow, slippery, or erratically moving surfaces; or maintaining body equilibrium when performing gymnastic feats.

3 **Stooping, Kneeling, Crouching, and/or Crawling:**
   (1) Stooping: Bending the body downward and forward by bending the spine at the waist.
   (2) Kneeling: Bending the legs at the knees to come to rest on the knee or knees.
   (3) Crouching: Bending the body downward and forward by bending the legs and spine.
   (4) Crawling: Moving about on the hands and knees or hands and feet.

4 **Reaching, Handling, Fingering, and/or Feeling:**
   (1) Reaching: Extending the hands and arms in any direction.
   (2) Handling: Seizing, holding, grasping, turning, or otherwise working with the hand or hands (fingering not involved).
   (3) Fingering: Picking, pinching, or otherwise working with the fingers primarily (rather than with the whole hand or arm as in handling).
   (4) Feeling: Perceiving such attributes of objects and materials as size, shape, temperature, or texture, by means of receptors in the skin, particularly those of the finger tips.

5 Talking and/or Hearing:

(1) Talking: Expressing or exchanging ideas by means of the spoken word.

(2) Hearing: Perceiving the nature of sounds by the ear.

6 Seeing:

Obtaining impressions through the eyes of the shape, size, distance, motion, color, or other characteristics of objects. The major visual functions are: (1) acuity, far and near, (2) depth perception, (3) field of vision, (4) accommodation, (5) color vision. The functions are defined as follows:

(1) Acuity, far—clarity of vision at 20 feet or more.
Acuity, near—clarity of vision at 20 inches or less.

(2) Depth perception—three dimensional vision. The ability to judge distance and space relationships so as to see objects where and as they actually are.

(3) Field of vision—the area that can be seen up and down or to the right or left while the eyes are fixed on a given point.

(4) Accommodation—adjustment of the lens of the eye to bring an object into sharp focus. This item is especially important when doing near-point work at varying distances from the eye.

(5) Color vision—the ability to identify and distinguish colors.

WORKING CONDITIONS (Work Cond.)

Working conditions are the physical surroundings of a worker in a specific job.

1 Inside, Outside, or Both:

I Inside: Protection from weather conditions but not necessarily from temperature changes.

O Outside: No effective protection from weather.

B Both: Inside and outside.

A job is considered "inside" if the worker spends approximately 75 per cent or more of his time inside, and "outside" if he spends approximately 75 per cent or more of his time outside. A job is considered "both" if the activities occur inside or outside in approximately equal amounts.

2 Extremes of Cold Plus Temperature Changes:

(1) Extremes of Cold: Temperature sufficiently low to cause marked bodily discomfort unless the worker is provided with exceptional protection.

(2) Temperature Changes: Variations in temperature which are sufficiently marked and abrupt to cause noticeable bodily reactions.

3 Extremes of Heat Plus Temperature Changes:

(1) Extremes of Heat: Temperature sufficiently high to cause marked bodily discomfort unless the worker is provided with exceptional protection.

(2) Temperature Changes: Same as 2 (2) .

4 Wet and Humid:

(1) Wet: Contact with water or other liquids.

(2) Humid: Atmospheric condition with moisture content sufficiently high to cause marked bodily discomfort.

5 Noise and Vibration:

Sufficient noise, either constant or intermittent, to cause marked distraction or possible injury to the sense of hearing and/or sufficient vibration (production of an oscillating movement or strain on the body or its extremities from repeated motion or shock) to cause bodily harm if endured day after day.

6 Hazards:

Situations in which the individual is exposed to the definite risk of bodily injury.

7 Fumes, Odors, Toxic Conditions, Dust, and Poor Ventilation:

(1) Fumes: Smoky or vaporous exhalations, usually odorous, thrown off as the result of combustion or chemical reaction.

(2) Odors: Noxious smells, either toxic or nontoxic.

(3) Toxic Conditions: Exposure to toxic dust, fumes, gases, vapors, mists, or liquids which cause general or localized disabling conditions as a result of inhalation or action on the skin.

(4) Dust: Air filled with small particles of any kind, such as textile dust, flour, wood, leather, feathers, etc., and inorganic dust, including silica and asbestos, which make the

workplace unpleasant or are the source of occupational diseases.

(5) Poor Ventilation: Insufficient movement of air causing a feeling of suffocation; or exposure to drafts.

Utilizing the material found in the Appendix to *Volume II,* we can now interpret the Qualifications Profile in the example chosen. HANDLING, .887 is a worker trait characterized as a work situation not involving a great deal of latitude for judgment yet requiring common sense in order to carry out simple instructions; the individual also must perform simple arithmetic functions and he must be able to comprehend oral and sometimes written instructions. The above information merely reflects the information gleaned from the General Educational Development section of the Appendix at a level 1. Generally, the majority of jobs where HANDLING is a primary function of work a GED of 1 or 2 usually is sufficient to carry out an employee's specific responsibilities.

A Specific Vocational Preparation (SVP) of 2 indicates that in the HANDLING worker trait arrangement, an individual recently employed should require only a short demonstration up to and including thirty days to gain the necessary techniques necessary to carry out average performance within a specific job worker situation. The evaluator using this resource material should keep in mind at all times that the material provided in the Appendix section is general in nature and that in certain situations there may be occasions where actual vocational preparation may be extended within the elemental area of work.

The third section of the Qualifications Profile deserves special attention. One may recognize that the *Aptitudes* (G for intelligence; V for verbal; N for numerical; etc.) have been included and correlated with the General Aptitude Test Battery (GATB) compiled and administered by the U. S. Department of Labor. After glancing through the factors comprising this section, an evaluator can begin to see how much of each *Aptitude* a specific job requires for satisfactory performance. The numbers under each factor represent levels of ability or capacity for average performance. Therefore, in our HANDLING worker trait, the intelligence factor (G) of 4 usually includes the lowest third exclusive of the bottom 10 percent of the population. The same holds for verbal ability (V). Regarding numerical ability (N) people who fall within the lowest 10 percent of the population can still perform these tasks adequately. The format for interpretation is the same for the other eight factors within the *Aptitude* section. The second row of numbers has been included to provide flexibility for the professionals using this resource material; as an example, the 4 under numerical ability reflects that even though the lowest 10 percent of the population can perform numerical computations for the HANDLING occupations, there are some jobs which take in consideration only the lowest third exclusive of the bottom 10 percent of the population. Therefore, one can see this increases the latitude for flexibility in using such a resource in an evaluation unit.

As described in the *Interest* section of the Appendix, a 3 indicates that an individual prefers situations involving a preference for activities of a routine concrete organized nature rather than situations involving a preference for activities of an abstract and creative nature. As indicated in the brief introduction to the coded explanations, a preference for one factor also implies a rejection of the other factor across from it. In our HANDLING worker trait, a 1 also is included which means that a worker performing these functions has better success when his activities are concerned with things and objects rather than with people and the communication of ideas.

Continuing with the *Temperament* factor, a number 2 indicates there is a worker preference for situations involving repetitive or short cycle operations carried out according to set procedures or sequences. We can see that many of our clients, especially those at the lower IQ levels, fall within this Temperament range. It is often difficult for an evaluator or other members of the rehabilitation team to assess the types of occupational situations to which a worker must adjust *prior* to his actually working at this specific task; yet it is our responsibility to look at the individual in total perspective. With the aid of the *DOT* and its vital information we are in a much better position to reduce the probability of failure and, in turn, increase our success rates. Temperaments often are reflected in an individual's personality. This in itself supports the rationale of looking at the total person rather than focusing on the individual's immediate problem and his immediate job expectations.

The last factor given in the Qualifications Profile is entitled *Physical Demands.* In our example of HANDLING as a worker trait a wide range of physical demands exists, thereby supporting the rationale for including almost the entire gamut of strength requirements. As indicated in the Appendix section HANDLING occupations range usually from light work through medium, heavy and up to very heavy physical exertion levels where an individual may be called upon to lift objects weighing in excess of 100 pounds. The other predominate factor associated with HAN-DLING occupations is reaching, handling, fingering and/or feeling (4). The researchers who compiled the *DOT* have found that of those people performing HANDLING tasks climbing and/or balancing, stooping, kneeling, crouching and crawling, talking and/or hearing, or seeing are not necessary or vital requisites to carry out job responsibilities. They did feel and it was substantiated that using the arms and hands, and specifically the fingers, were necessary work ingredients to carry out activities successfully. As an evaluator this does not negate the fact that in certain work situations one of these other factors may be the predominate factor in work production.

The last factor is not included *per se* in the Qualifications Profile of *Volume II;* yet it is found in the supplement to the *DOT* under the column entitled *Work Conditions.* This writer has included *Work Conditions* as an additional factor of the Qualifications Profile since it ultimately is included within most job analysis made by placement specialists. Again using the descriptions found in the Appendix section we see that the majority of jobs in the HANDLING occupations are either inside or outside (there is really no preference for inside activity over outside activity). Additionally, people performing HANDLING tasks may be required to work in extremes of cold plus temperature changes as well as heat and its temperature changes; wet and humid conditions may be required to fulfill job responsibilities; noise and vibration along with hazardous duty may constitute a vital condition of employment within HANDLING positions; and finally fumes, odors, toxic conditions, dust and poor ventilation may be a work condition found within a specific HANDLING job. All of these variables must be evaluated in relation to a client's physical and/or mental problems *before* he has been placed in either training or on the job. Much time can be saved if some thought would go into analyzing the entire job spectrum through which the client ultimately will be employed.

A SUPPLEMENT TO THE *DOT*

A third volume to the *DOT* entitled a *Supplement to the Dictionary of Occupational Titles, Selected Characteristics of Occupations (Physical Demands, Working Conditions, Training Time)* was published in 1966 and has been overlooked by the majority of professionals working with people and their vocational selection. This supplement is merely an abbreviated version of Volume II including such items as the *DOT* code number, the WTA page number, the industry in which a *particular* job is found, the *DOT* title of a specific position, the physical demands of that position, its working condition, and finally training time including the GED and SVP. Everything within this volume has been coded thereby necessitating the user to refer back to the Appendix section until he becomes familiar with the particular code numbers.

Whereas the Qualifications Profile found in Volume II was general in nature in an effort to encompass a multitude of jobs found within various worker trait arrangements, the supplement contains selected characteristics which are identified enabling the evaluator to further define the specific work position in relation to his client's needs.

PUTTING IT ALL TOGETHER

The following material represents a client who has come to vocational rehabilitation for possible services. In order to gather as much relevant information as possible the rehabilitation counselor has asked for a vocational evaluation including a specific vocational report along with a complete psychological test battery with vocational implications as well as a physical capacities check list. The intention of this section of the chapter is to show how an evaluator or other members of the rehabilitation team can assemble relevant occupational information within the evaluation process and, in turn, relate it to general areas of work or, more specifically, actual jobs as they exist in the client's area of residence.

VOCATIONAL REPORT

John Doe   SSN: 267-70-3069
Box 99   DATE: February 16, 1973
Stuarts Draft, Virginia 24477

Mr. Doe is forty-nine years old and has a twelfth grade education. For the past two years Mr. Doe has worked at a textile mill as a cloth doffer and, more recently, as a utilities service man. This latter job, described in recent report of contact with employer, appears to have been janitorial service which also included cleaning the looms and machine parts. No other vocational history is available on Mr. Doe, who ceased all work in November 1969 due to back trouble, stomach trouble and nerves.

At the interview he stated his condition had worsened; i.e., his back hurt constantly, his legs swelled and ached, his nervousness had progressed, and he seemed to have no bowel control. At home he mostly sat around and apparently performed no household chores. Aside from nervousness, there were no visible signs of impairment other than his continual shifting from side to side and his rubbing the low back area.

As a cloth doffer, Mr. Doe described his job as involving lifting 150-200 pounds daily; carrying; pushing/pulling 150-1500 lbs; standing all day, walking throughout day; and stooping, bending and/or kneeling constantly. Cloth doffer, 689.886, is described according to the *DOT* as heavy work involving removing rolls of cloth from looms and trucking cloth to storage. A cloth doffer stops the machine when the roll has sufficient yardage, cuts cloth using scissors, and places the cloth roll on a hand-truck. He places an empty take-up beam on the back of the machine, attaches cloth, and restarts the machine. He writes identifying information, such as lot and style number on the ticket and attaches the ticket to the cloth roll. He trucks cloth to storage or inspection department.

As a utilities serviceman, Mr. Doe's job is best described in the *DOT* as a porter II (any industry) #381.887. A porter keeps working areas in production departments of industrial establishments in clean and orderly condition. He sweeps and mops floors using hand and power equipment. He cleans dust and dirt from ceiling, walls, and overhead pipes; he washes windows; he waxes and polishes the floor; he arranges boxes, material and hand-trucks in a neat and orderly manner; he cleans lint, dust, and oil from machines, using brushes or an air hose. This is considered light work according to the *DOT*, yet this examiner considers a porter's job in this type of establishment as being medium in physical demands. Both of Mr. Doe's jobs have been unskilled work in feeding-offbearing (.886) and handling (.887) respectively, both in the area of elemental work.

Current orthopedic surgical consultative evaluation revealed recent decompressive laminectomy at L-3, L-4, and L-5, and also partially at S-1 with intradural exploration. The findings revealed a very narrow canal and spondylotic changes at several levels. Mr. Doe continued to complain of pain, but walked with a normal gait without appreciable limp. There was minimal muscle spasm. Straight-leg raising and LeSegue signs were negative. Reflexes were hypoactive but present bilaterally. There was no evidence of atrophy or muscle weakness. X-rays showed operative defect of laminectomy and also previously noted marked narrowing of the L-5, S-1 interspace. Residual functional capacities were assessed as consistent with sedentary work. Mr. Doe was considered incapable of lifting more than 10-20 lbs and he was restricted from excessive standing, walking, stooping, bending, and kneeling, or climbing.

If Mr. Doe is restricted to sedentary work, he cannot return to either his job as a cloth doffer or as a porter. Before he can be considered a candidate for other work of a sedentary nature, the following factors must be considered:

1. As far as is known, he has never done sedentary work.
2. He is of advancing age.
3. As far as we know, he has never used his twelfth grade education in his work.
4. He would have to compete for sedentary unskilled work with younger, unimpaired men with probably more sophisticated level of education.

If Mr. Doe is restricted to sedentary work, he cannot return to his previous job as utilities service man in the textile industries. If development of vocational history should point to a variety of work experience including semiskilled jobs or if further medical assessment should reflect the capacity to stand for at least six hours per day, the following jobs might be suggested:

1. Clipperman, automatic (veneer and plywood) #663.885, sedentary work.
2. Color coater, (electronics), #652.885, sedentary.
3. Mounter or Assembler (electronics), #726.887, sedentary.
4. Poultry boner, (slaughter and meatpacking), #525.887, light work.

If Mr. Doe is, indeed, restricted to sedentary work only with no transferrable skills and/or work experience in nothing but heavy, unskilled jobs, his employment outlook is very dim. Also, a complete psychological should be administered to Mr. Doe in an effort to assess his intellectual powers as well as to assist the evaluator at the Woodrow Wilson Rehabilitation Center for possible retraining.

Vocational Specialist

PSYCHOLOGICAL REPORT

RE: DOE, John   AGE: 49   February 26, 1973
      Stuarts Draft, Virginia

This man was referred for a psychological battery prior to a vocational evaluation by the Supervisor of the Valley Sheltered Workshop. I had him in my office at the rehabilitation center on February 22, 1973, for a considerable battery of tests which I will describe below. John is a pleasant, agreeable person who seems to have had a fairly successful semiskilled vocational background based upon a good deal of potential ability; but due to a gradual development of physical problems and a nervous disorder coupled with advancing age, it is felt by many people who know him that he must make a new vocational selection somewhat less physically demanding. He is not certain in his own mind as to whether this is absolutely necessary and, if so, just what fields of vocational choice would hold the best opportunities for him. Most of his past experience has been as a laborer on construction jobs such as bridges and frames of buildings and most recently as a doffer and porter in a textile mill. While a youngster in school, he had a little bit of grocery store experience.

The problems which have developed across the years seem to have begun with a broken left leg, which after considerable period is fairly well healed. But secondary to it and now the major problem, he developed some arthritis in the spine and a nervous condition which have compounded his problems. He feels that because of age and this injury his equilibrium is not as good as it once was for walking on the concrete floors near the machinery. He has a little damage, apparently, in one of his eyes from a rust particle which scratched the cornea but just how great an interference this particular problem will be in the future seems to be at present uncertain; a consultation with an ophthalmologist is recommended.

Wechsler-Bellevue Scale for Adolescents and Adults: Record Form I. Verbal I.Q. 116, Efficiency Quotient 112. Performance I.Q. 93, Efficiency Quotient 73. Full Scale I.Q. 106, Efficiency Quotient 93. Upper average category. 65 percentile for the population as a whole.

Verbal Subtest Scores		*Performance Subtest Scores*	
Information	11	Picture Arrangement	5
Comprehension	14	Picture Completion	6

Digit Span	7	Block Design	7
Arithmetic	13	Object Assembly	9
Similarities	11	Digit Symbol	4
Vocabulary	12		

Bender-Gestalt Drawings: Fairly close to average. There does not appear to be any organic brain damage.

Wide Range Achievement Test:	*Score*	*Grade*	*Quotient*	*Ed. Age*
Reading	87	10.1	107	16-0
Spelling	58	6.9	83	12-5
Arithmetic	53	11.0	112	16-9
Average Educational Age	15.1			
I.Q. Equivalent	101			

Nelson Reading Test:	*Score*	*Grade*
Vocabulary	40	6.2
Paragraph	26	5.0
Total	66	5.7

Minnesota Spatial Relations Test: *A* and *B* boards administered. Raw Score—832. Estimated 15 percent on norms for men. One percentile on norms for eighteen-year-old boys.

Minnesota Clerical Test: Number Comparison—Four percentile on norms for adults gainfully occupied. Name Comparison—Seven percentile on norms for adults gainfully occupied.

Stenquist Mechanical Assembling Test (Series 1) : Individual raw score—86. Final T-score—75. Ninety-one percentile on norms for adult army men.

Bennett Mechanical Comprehension Test (Form AA) : Raw score —31. Twenty-eight percentile on norms for apprentice trainees.

I would like to make some interpretation of the psychological test score pattern as follows: We did a Wechsler Form I which shows that his verbal abstract ability has held up quite well across the years and at a significantly high level. Quantitative reasoning is still one of his best scores which I think has strong vocational implications. These verbal abstract scores placed him on I.Q. in the mid bright normal category; but taking his efficiency quotients at age forty-nine which may be at this age level a better indication of vocational potential, he declines only two points but still holds in the bright normal category. Going into the performance area of the test dealing with practical concrete materials, we would naturally expect more decline at his age and find it to be that way. Here by I.Q. he places at lower average in the I.Q., but the efficiency quotient reduces him to the borderline category. Taking all parts of the test together, he places upper average in I.Q. and lower average in efficiency quotient. I think, however, with as much divergence as we find here between verbal and performance abilities it is much better to take each separate score for what it respectively represents than to try to throw it altogether in a full scale score.

In the practical concrete part of the Wechsler, we find scores indicating form and pattern perception being the best in the range, but they are still at a mediocre level. How much of this is due to his original pattern and how much has come by way of advancing chronological age is difficult to tell; but it is my strong impression that this was always his pattern as, apparently, he has suffered no brain damage at any time as far as I am able to learn. Using the old deterioration formula of the Wechsler, he has only a two percent loss after the correction of sixteen which is applicable at his chronological age. I feel, therefore, that this man still has a good deal of potential ability for vocational functioning, but it certainly does run higher in verbal abstract than in the practical concrete areas as we can see in this pattern. I believe—after examining this pattern further—that is why he went into doffing rather than a more sophisticated area of work; i.e., he sought a lower level vocation because he was not too much mechanically inclined and perhaps he was never provided the motivation to accept the challenge of more difficult work.

Due to the fact that the Wechsler did not indicate too much mechanical ability, I checked further with three different types of mechanical tests. Using two boards of the Minnesota Spatial which indicates form and pattern perception, his score was low only at a 15 percentile for men. A part of this could have been due to the fact that his eyes are not functioning too well, and I feel that because of age he is considerably slowed in physical/mental re-action times. I also checked him with the very practical Stenquist Test where his score was considerably higher showing that he has a good deal of very practical mechanical insight. Taking the more technical Bennett Mechanical Comprehension Test, he only made a 28 percentile on norms for apprentice trainees. All of these, I think, support the Wechsler as indicating that he does not have and, in fact, probably never did have a high degree of mechanical ability. Being a high school graduate, I checked him using the Wide Range Achievement Test in the three basic educational skills. Here I found that reading by word calling he holds up fair-ly well at the tenth grade level, spells at the sixth, but his arith-metic has held up exceptionally well at grade eleven although this was an untimed score. He says he was always better in mathematics and has used his math to a considerable degree in his vocational work across the years. I checked him in reading employing the Nelson Reading Test for reading interpretation and find that he is several grades lower. I think again, we are dealing with a slowed reaction time. I was asked to give careful consideration to his clerical ability and used the old Minnesota Clerical Test on which he made a 4 percentile for adults gainfully occupied in number comparison and a seven percentile in name comparison. Again, I think reaction time and vision had something to do with the low scores.

Now thinking from a vocational point of view, we are dealing with a rather difficult situation. If John were age eighteen to twenty-four, I would know how to advise him entering vocational training; but with the accumulation of years, coupled with several interfering disabilities, it is rather difficult to tell just what is best for him to do. I would like to suggest three alternative possibili-ties. First, since he finds it very difficult to sever connection with his union in which he has developed a considerable amount of economic benefit, I feel that he should contact his union officials (he says he knows the shop steward) and see what the chances would be to continue employment in the same mill by dealing with materials considerably lighter than he previously had to handle. There might be bench work or possibly a supervisory position not requiring climbing, lifting, etc. that could be made available to him. If this can be arranged, I think he would be much happier to go along on this basis. If this is ruled out as a possibility, then he will have to accept the idea of making a new vocational adjustment. In that case, secondly, I would recommend the possibility of his taking a course here at the Center or perhaps suitable work in the workshop and prepare for general mechanics having his shop at home where he can continue his work and not have to surrender his own property which he prizes very highly. Thirdly, looking at the test score battery and disregarding chronological age, I feel that there is no question that the pattern indicates some supervisory skills; and since his quantitative reasoning holds up rather well, it would be possible to train him for a modified program of bookkeeping or accounting or some level of record keeping in spite of the fact that his reaction time has declined. I feel that this was unquestionably his pattern when he graduated from high school, but at his age of forty-nine, it is much more difficult to enter upon a training program of this type and make a good adjustment. I feel that he would be less interested in this than in the other two suggestions. Also, taking into consideration the doctor's request that the client seek work at the sedentary level, it is imperative the counselor in conjunction with other members of the rehabilitation team actively support Mr. Doe; i.e., he has been working at a much greater physical level in the past and he may overtly resist the so-called *easy job* in order to assert his masculine role. Even so he should be coaxed into seeing the practicality of a new vocational choice at the sedentary level. I hope this information supplies the essential data which is desired in the future vocational evaluation guidance of this case.

Psychologist

March 14, 1973

Evaluation Report—John Doe #267-70-3069

Mr. Doe entered the Workshop on 3-1-73 to begin his evaluation period. He was counseled on the routines of the workshop and on what he could expect from the workshop. He expressed a reluctance to start the evaluation period stating that he might have to forfeit some part-time work which might occur during the two week evaluation period.

Even though his motivation was questionable he proved to be cooperative in the workshop setting and therefore it is felt that the following report is a valid assessment of his employability.

Mr. Doe's first job assignment was assembling coin bag seals. The seals are constructed of a piece of string, a lead seal and a metal cap. The requirements for this job are as follows: hand-eye coordination, fine finger dexterity and bimanual dexterity. He demonstrated an ability to do simple, repetitive work while seated. The quantity of production on this task was consistently lower than would be expected in an industrial setting although there was no decline noted in production due to any physical discomfort.

His next job assignment was the placing of contacts into a contact board which is used in the manufacturing of electronic organs. This job requires the use of a simple hand tool to place the contacts into the board. The requirements are as follows: Use of a simple hand tool, grasping and fine manipulation, manual dexterity, hand-eye coordinations, reaching, handling and the ability to stand six to eight hours per day.

Mr. Doe demonstrated the necessary tolerance to stand on this job for only short periods of time and continued to work on this task for approximately two and a half days. There was no marked increase in complaints of pain or discomfort if he was allowed to sit. His quantity of production was consistent but rather low.

While performing this task Mr. Doe was observed on three

separate occasions to drop articles and proceed to bend to the floor to retrieve these items. In these instances he demonstrated some signs of pain and discomfort but not enough to warrant his stopping.

The third job assigned to the client was a string waxing job. Bundles of string were cut to specific lengths by one client. Mr. Doe was then responsible for dipping each end of the bundle of string into a vat containing heated wax. The excess wax is then removed by slapping the ends of the string against the inner lining of the vat. These strings are used in the manufacturing of the coin bag seals. The specific requirements for this job are as follows: gross hand dexterity, ability to reach and handle, slight bending and twisting, minor judgmental ability, and the ability to stand several hours a day.

His performance on this task was satisfactory. The rate of production on this task was higher than his production on prior tasks. He did occasionally voice physical complaints; however, no decrease in productivity was observed.

In summary of Mr. Doe's performance it is noted that on all jobs production ranged in the lower levels of what might be expected from an individual with extensive industrial experience. The rate of production did not fluctuate during the working day although he voiced occasional complaints of physical discomfort. He demonstrated an ability to stand for only one to three hours per day which according to the *Dictionary of Occupational Titles* *(DOT)* would classify him as being capable of doing some light work, but mostly activities considered sedentary in nature.

His clerical background was explored during interviews. The only clerical experience that he related was during the time following the leg fracture which is documented in his records. His duties were limited to checking incoming orders against the bills of lading at the grocery store. According to the client this was his only clerical experience and it lasted only for a period of a few weeks. (Note—refer to enclosed psychological report for further discussion of clerical ability.)

Based on experience with local industry and a knowledge of job requirements as outlined in the *DOT*, it is felt that he could draw from past experience and transferable skills to function in the following jobs:

1. Small electronic component assembler.
2. Production line solderer.
3. Deburrer and finisher.

The jobs were cited because of their presence in the local job market and also due to the fact that on-the-job training could be provided at no cost to the agency. After an extended training period there is a good chance Mr. Doe would be considered for full time employment.

We thank you for referring this client to us and if we can be of any further assistance please contact us.

Evaluator
_____

PHYSICAL CAPACITIES EVALUATION

Name of Client: John Doe   S/S No: 267-70-3069

To: Panel Medical Examiner or   Date: March 14, 1973
     Evaluation Staff

IMPORTANT: Please complete the following items *based on* findings only, not on patient's opinions or subjective complaints.

I. In an 8-hr work day, claimant can stand/walk
   [ ] None   [x] 1-4 hrs.   [ ] 4-6 hrs.   [ ] 6-8 hrs.

II. In an 8-hr work day claimant can sit:
   [ ] 1-3 hrs.   [ ] 3-5 hrs.   [x] 5-8 hrs.

III. Claimant can lift
   [ ] up to 10 lbs.   [x] 10-20 lbs.   [ ] 20-50 lbs.

IV. Lifting as indicated in item III can be performed during the work day.
   [x] occasionally   [ ] frequently   [ ] continuously

V. Claimant can use hands for repetitive:

A. simple grasping*   B. pushing and   C. fine manipulation
pulling

| x | yes | | | no | | x | yes | | | no | x | yes | | | no |

*only for light items weighing 10-20 lbs.

VI. Claimant can use feet for repetitive movements as in operating foot controls.

| | yes | x | no |

VII. Claimant is able to:

	Freq.	Occas.	Not at all
A. Bend		x	
B. Squat		x	
C. Crawl*			
D. Climb			x

*unable to assess

VIII. Claimant is able to reach above shoulder level:

| x | yes* | | | no |

*but not on a routine schedule throughout the day.

Signature of Evaluator

SUMMARY

In this chapter we have seen how the *DOT* can be used as a vital resource tool for not only the work evaluator but the rehabilitation counselor, job placement specialist, social worker, and all of the other members of the rehabilitation team. If a realistic appraisal of a client's work potential is to be made it is necessary we employ every available resource at our disposal. By the same token if we rely solely on occupational information such as the DOT its value will be lost. There must be an integration of this material with ongoing programs devised to meet the needs of not only the client but the community as well. There must be professional input where a conscientious evaluation has been performed taking into consideration an individual's problems in relation to his capability and future direction. This one to one ratio must be maintained; however, we will be in a much better position to make such an individual evaluation if we employ the resources of the *DOT* and similar occupational information.

REFERENCES

A Supplement to the Dictionary of Occupational Titles: Selected Characteristics of Occupations (Physical Demands, Working Conditions, Training Time), 3rd edition. Washington, U. S. Dept. of Labor, 1966.

Colvin, C. R.: The role of a vocational expert in the Social Security Administration's Bureau of Hearings and Appeals. In *Forensic Psychology and Disability Adjudication: A Decade of Experience*. U. S. DHEW, SSA, BHA, (SSA#72-10284), Washington, D. C. 1972.

Cull, J. G. and Colvin, C. R.: Dilemma diagnosed, *Journal of Rehabilitation*, vol. 38:28, 1972a.

Cull, J. G. and Colvin, C. R.: *Contemporary Field Work Practices in Rehabilitation*. Springfield, Thomas, 1972b.

Dictionary of Occupational Titles, Vol. 1, Definition of Titles, 3rd edition. Washington, U. S. Department of Labor, 1965.

Dictionary of Occupational Titles, Vol. II, Occupational Classification, 3rd edition, Washington, U. S. Department of Labor, 1965.

XI

PREVOCATIONAL EVALUATION

Richard R. Wolfe

Concerns of Prevocational Evaluation

Role of Prevocational Evaluation in Determining Eligibility

Areas of Prevocational Evaluation

Prevocational Planning and Counseling

Length of Prevocational Evaluation

Attitudes Relating to Prevocational Evaluation

Summary

References

CONCERNS OF PREVOCATIONAL EVALUATION

IN THE PRECEEDING CHAPTERS much time has been spent in discussing the vocational evaluation of the client. In subsequent chapters the reader will learn about specific evaluations in specialty areas. The role of prevocational evaluation tends to cut across many lines and disciplines, and it is often difficult to identify the point where prevocational evaluation ends and vocational evaluation begins.

In an unpublished paper distributed by the Materials Development Center, Stout State University, Menomenie, Wisconsin, the following concepts were presented as representing a general concensus of what is involved in prevocational activity (Materials Development Center, 1968).

1. Prevocational evaluation can be seen as a goal established through counseling.
2. Prevocational evaluation can be conceived of in terms of

guidance (that is, leading to work, specialized treatment, or nonemployment).

3. It can be conceived of as a three-step procedure: a general broad evaluation and exploration; more specific, expert evaluation; and vocational training. Often the prevocational activity in itself leads directly to placement.

4. In general: Exploration, evaluation, personal adjustment, and work adjustment constitute much of the process leading to placement. Here personal and work adjustment are not separable though when employment is the goal.

5. Prevocational evaluation can be described as including: exploration, evaluation, personal and work adjustment, and prevocational training.

No attempt will be made in the discussion that follows to respond directly to these concepts. Rather, it will be left to the reader to categorize and synthesize as he sees fit.

Rosenberg and Wellerson (1971) have stated that a prevocational program is concerned with such things as the client's work habits, work tolerance, and speed of production. They suggest that the prevocational evaluation program is medically oriented. They point out that the prevocational unit at the Institute for the Crippled and Disabled is operated by an occupational therapist who is, of course, under the supervision of the medical service. They further emphasized that the major objectives of a prevocational program are the development and the improvement of work habits, work tolerance, and productive speed. Here the term work habits was defined to include such traits as attendance, punctuality, neatness, grooming, attention span, industriousness, ability to follow oral orders, ability to follow written instructions, and the ability to work under supervision. Work tolerance was defined as the constitutional or acquired capacity to sustain work either standing and/or sitting. Productive speed was defined as the ratio of the amount of work produced to the amount of time taken to produce that quantity of work.

McGowan and Porter (1967) point out that prevocational units may be located in centers that are primarily medically oriented, or in centers that are vocationally oriented. In the former they are usually staffed by occupational therapists, in the latter, by industrial arts teachers, vocational counselors or persons with industrial experience. They further describe the services offered in prevocational evaluation programs as including such general areas as work experience, personal adjustment, work adjustment, counseling, physical conditioning, training in the basic academic skills of reading, arithmetic and writing, work training, evaluative procedures, and development of production speed sufficient to meet the demands of competitive industry.

ROLE OF PREVOCATIONAL EVALUATION IN DETERMINING ELIGIBILITY

Counselors have had the responsibility to determine the eligibility or non-eligibility for rehabilitation services of those disabled individuals who apply for such service. The counselor has traditionally made the very subjective determination of feasibility, that is, what is the prognosis that rehabilitation services would make the person fit to engage in a gainful occupation.

Many times the counselor has to make decisions regarding eligibility and feasibility for rehabilitation services on very limited information. This was especially true as more severely disabled and multidisabled clients were referred for rehabilitation service. Many clients were denied services because the counselor just did not have access to appropriate diagnostic services. The counselor could not assess by nonsituational techniques the work personality and skills of these clients.

With the passage of the 1965 and 1968 amendments to the Vocational Rehabilitation Act, an even greater emphasis was placed on the prevocational aspect of the rehabilitation process. The *extended evaluation* aspect of the Amendments permitted the counselor to provide rehabilitation services for the determination of rehabilitation potential.

Services that could be provided included: (1) evaluation, including diagnostic and related services; (2) counseling and guidance; (3) physical restoration services; (4) training, including personal and vocational adjustment; (5) books and training materials (including tools); (6) maintenance; (7) transportation; reader services for the blind; (8) interpreter services for the deaf;

(9) services to members of a handicapped individual's family when such services will contribute substantially to the rehabilitation of the handicapped individual; (10) such other goods and services as are necessary to render a handicapped individual fit to engage in a gainful occupation (Federal Register, 1969).

AREAS OF PREVOCATIONAL EVALUATION

Inherent in these regulations is the necessity to evaluate the client in many areas to determine if the client does have vocational potential, and perhaps even determine the vocation for which he is best suited. Comments will be made concerning areas that should be investigated in the prevocational evaluation. These would include medical, psychological, educational, vocational, socioeconomic, cultural and environmental. Some of these are discussed at length in other chapters, but not necessarily related to the topic of prevocational evaluation.

First, one has to consider the limitations imposed by the physical and/or mental disability. This might be learned through the general medical examination, or through specialist examinations. For example: the client may have a cardiac problem. It might well be in order to evaluate him at a rehabilitation cardiac unit to determine just what limitations are imposed due to the heart condition, and even more important, what is his capacity for work. The *blind* client might be fitted with special optical aids so that he can function in certain occupations which are the most appropriate for him.

The area of prosthetics is usually covered under the topical heading of medical services. It suffices here to say that proper fitting of the prosthetic device, and equally important, the training in the use of the prosthetic device are essential in considering the prevocational evaluation of clients. Even though the client has been fitted with and trained in the proper use of the prosthetic device, the counselor has no assurance that the client functionally uses the device in his day to day activity. How many prosthetic legs, hearing aids, braces, etc., are found stored in closets in the client's home rather than being utilized by the client. This suggests that in addition to being certain the client has been fitted with and trained in the use of the prosthesis, the counselor needs to counsel with the client if maximum results are to be obtained.

The client with psychiatric problems or those clients who might be classified as social deviants or behaviorally disordered present other problems to the counselor. Can the client's problems be controlled by appropriate medication? Will the client conscientiously follow the medication regime prescribed? Is the client able or does he even choose to modify his behavior? These may be both medical and counseling problems, the answers to which will determine if the client should be served.

In his contact with the client, the counselor needs to assess the psychological strengths and weaknesses of the client. For some clients this may mean a comprehensive workup by a competent clinical psychologist. For others, intensive study in a comprehensive rehabilitation facility may be indicated. Hopefully, in most cases the counselor's training will equip him to make this assessment.

The counselor needs to understand human dynamics and must be able to capitalize upon the client's psychological strengths and minimize the effects of the psychological deficits or weaknesses. How does the client react to success? How does he react to failure? Is the counselor able to modify the client's behavior? Can the client be helped with psychotherapy? What about motivation? Is the client motivation toward his own rehabilitation? Are the rewards far in the future while the client is functioning at the immediate gratification level? Can the counselor provide the incentive that will move the client in the positive direction? These are but a few of the psychological variants operating. Too often vocational planning fails because the counselor and client did not consider these variants.

Educational evaluation is discussed more fully in a later chapter, but it needs to be at least mentioned here. What is the academic skill level of the client? This becomes especially important as we look at the older worker. What possibilities exist for the older laborer who becomes disabled and is no longer able to function in his occupation? If his academic skill level is low, the counselor tends to reject him. The counselor needs to be able to find other occupational possibilities for this worker, yet he has to be realistic concerning the length of time it might take in order to raise academic skills to the level where retraining might be feasible.

This is equally true for the severely disabled client. Rehabilitation services have proved to be successful with the quadriplegic who happens to be of high intellectual level. Rehabilitation services thus far have failed to make much impact on the vocational rehabilitation of the marginal worker who later became a quadriplegic.

Does the client have any special abilities? Frequently the counselor can learn about these abilities as he looks at the interests and hobbies of the client. A well phrased question by the counselor might well get the client to discuss many things he has done or can do.

To take the educational aspect one step further, what is the client's ability to learn? The counselor should be very zealous in guarding against the waste of the client's time by permitting him to pursue training programs for which he does not have the capacity to compete. Clients may suggest possible areas of training based upon very poor concepts of what is involved. It is the responsibility of the counselor to evaluate the client's potential for any training program. Clients may have the right to fail, but the counselor should not encourage the client to enter programs for which failure is certain.

Too frequently the counselor looks at the academic achievement and the intellectual functioning level of the client, and if sufficiently high, counsels the client into a college program. It is important that the counselor be more aware of the world of work. If the counselor were more aware of the labor market and the client's interest, and if he were more imaginative, there would probably be less college training plans and happier, better work-adjusted clients. Newspaper, radio and television reports now suggest that the U. S. Labor Department projections are that the need for college-trained workers will be less than 20 percent of the labor market.

PREVOCATIONAL PLANNING AND COUNSELING

Vocational evaluation at the prevocational level is critical to effective planning with the client. If the client has had work experience, the counselor needs to learn the extent of this experience, level of functioning of the client on the job prior to disablement, and whether or not the client can still function in that job subsequent to disablement. If the person can return to his former occupation or a related occupation, the counselor's problems are much reduced. If as a result of the disability the client can no longer function in the job, the counselor's role becomes more complex. If the client is young and has no work experience, a different set of problems becomes apparent.

In counseling with the client who has worked but can no longer perform on that job, the counselor should look at what potential does remain. Are there related jobs that the client could perform? What about interests or hobbies and other jobs in which the client has worked. As suggested earlier, the client might be able to return to employment by the provision of various adaptive devices. Restructuring, or reengineering, of the job might provide the answer to the question, can he return to his old job? In more severe cases, it might be important to utilize various vocational diagnostic tests to determine interest and/or aptitude.

The young client without work experience is confronted with a different set of problems. In some instances, the solution to his problem might well be similar to that of the older, severely disabled client. Frequently this individual is referred to a psychologist for a battery of vocationally oriented tests. More often, however, the counselor will refer him to the state employment service, requesting that the employment service administer the General Aptitude Test Battery (GATB) to him. This approach may be at least minimally satisfactory for some clients, and coupled with effective counseling may be sufficient.

For the more severely disabled and for those clients with limited communication skills, this minimal approach is totally unsatisfactory and when utilized by the naive counselor, too often results in the determination that the client cannot profit from rehabilitation services, and his case is closed. Some simple illustrations will hopefully bring into focus the need for more complete prevocational evaluation. Probably the most important prevocational evaluation is that of the personal adjustment of the client.

The newly blinded adult who has had a good employment history and is motivated to return to work often finds this impossible due to problems resulting from his disability. His job may require visual inspection; how the client might get to work; mobility in general; how can he communicate; even such simple things as the activities for daily living become a major problem. For this individual, comprehensive personal adjustment training in a rehabilitation center for the blind might be the most appropriate answer. Once adjusted to the problems presented by his disability, the client can then begin to focus his attention toward vocational goals. Even at this point, counseling is critical if the client is going to function at or near his level of ability.

The worker who has suffered a cerebral vascular accident which has left him partially paralyzed has a different set of problems. Again, total evaluation is necessary. Medically, what problems persist? What psychological problems have surfaced as a result of the disability? What mental deficits remain? What is his work tolerance? The individual may have been treated through a comprehensive rehabilitation center. He may have been fitted with prosthetic devices and trained in their use. Hopefully, he has been taught how to cope with the various activities for daily living, including mobility. If not, before he can be considered for vocational training or placement, he will have to learn how to adjust to the problems created by his disability. To add to his problems, what is his work tolerance? How many hours a day can he work? What other vocational limitations have been imposed by the disability?

Most of the vocational information needed at this point can probably best be obtained through an effective workshop evaluation program. The various techniques and programs available through the workshop are discussed in other chapters. It should be pointed out here, however, that the uniqueness of the workshop allows for the evaluation of present potential of the client. It also provides the vehicle through which the client can work with minimal pressure to build work confidences, work tolerance, work habits, and also learn ways to maximally utilize those physical and mental systems still intact.

Although many might feel that the workshop program would create the best evaluative environment for the client so severely disabled, there are situations where such a program is not feasible. A workshop is not available in every community. The client is not always willing to relocate, even temporarily, to a community that supports a workshop. In these situations some counselors have utilized on-the-job training sites to evaluate the work potential or job readiness of the client. On-the-job training has the desirability of placing the client in the environment where he would be expected to function if employed. The job situation is real, not simulated. A major problem with utilizing on-the-job training as an evaluative technique, especially with the more severely disabled client, is finding employers who are willing to take the time to evaluate the client. Unless adequate remuneration is forthcoming to the employer, the cost in supervisory time, loss of production, space allocation, etc., making it prohibitive for the employer to consider evaluating the client who needs it most.

Realistically, a combination of evaluation and work adjustment in a workshop, with progression to on-the-job training, would give the counselor a better insight as to the work potential of the client. Too often this does not occur because of the time and expense involved.

LENGTH OF PREVOCATIONAL EVALUATION

One point to be considered in the prevocational evaluation of the client is the length of time for the evaluation. If the state-federal program of rehabilitation is reviewed, it is evident that for certain enumerated severe disability areas, a maximum of eighteen months extended evaluation is permitted. In all other disability groups, a maximum of six months extended evaluation is permitted. One should note, however, that this extended evaluation is for the purpose of determining rehabilitation potential (establishing eligibility). Once the client is made eligible for rehabilitation service, there is no legal limit as to how long the prevocational evaluation might be. Each counselor must determine this for each individual case, and he must be realistic in terms of both the costs of the evaluation and the potential of the client. The cost for the prevocational evaluation is important, of course, but it must be recognized that through an excellent prevocational evaluation, money as well as counselor and client time can be saved.

Much time has been spent on the vocational aspect of the prevocational evaluation. This is not to imply that the other areas to be evaluated are less important. The medical, psychological, and educational aspects are adequately covered elsewhere in this text. The area of socioeconomic, cultural, and environmental evaluations are less clearly defined and depend much on the subjective interpretation of the counselor.

ATTITUDES RELATING TO PREVOCATIONAL EVALUATION

In reviewing the socioeconomic aspect of prevocational evaluation, the counselor is frequently caught between the idealism of rehabilitation and the pragmatic realities facing the client. It is well to believe that everyone should work, that is, make his contribution to society. *Welfare,* however, is no longer the negative term it used to be. Society has recognized that it has an obligation to provide for at least minimal needs. Social security benefits are made available to many disabled persons. Either welfare or social security benefits may be substantially less than the client earned before he became disabled. These same benefits may be greater than the individual's earning capacity even after the maximum rehabilitation services that might be provided. If this is the case, what is the potential for vocational rehabilitation? It becomes obvious that the disabled client cannot afford to risk certain financial benefits available through these programs. One could argue that this becomes a case for counseling. Yet, placed in the position of the client, the counselor would undoubtedly make the same kinds of decision the client has made. If the proposed welfare reform measure, including the guaranteed annual income, becomes a reality, the counselor might find the client more positively *motivated* toward his own vocational rehabilitation, especially if he can improve his standard of living. Until, or unless the client can improve his socioeconomic position, vocational rehabilitation will be difficult, if not impossible to effect.

In some cases also mitigating against any possible vocational rehabilitation for the client is the client's family. How does the disability affect the family members? The counselor must become aware of the power structure within the family constellation. What is the attitude of the client's family concerning his returning to the world of work? Those family members closest to the client may actually prefer he not return to work. This reaction may be a result of fear of what may happen to the client should he return to work. The fear of the loss of what little security remains may surface much irrational behavior. It suffices to say here that the counselor must evaluate the total family situation and be willing and able to counsel with the family members. In evaluating the strengths and weaknesses of the family situation, the counselor can enlist all positive aids in support of the rehabilitation of the client.

The counselor should also become aware of the community attitude toward the rehabilitation of the client. The community in question is that social community known to the client. Here again, the counselor can solicit support if he is aware of the meaning of disability to that community.

The cultural aspects related to prevocational evaluation, likewise, create problems for the counselor. To the predominant culture, the eight hour work day, getting to the job on time, minimal absenteeism, etc., are accepted. With some of the minority cultures, these things are not important. It is important that the counselor be aware of cultural differences and recognize deviations from the predominant culture that are attributable to those cultural differences. It may mean a total reorganization of counselor thoughts and perceptions if rehabilitation is to be even a remote possibility. Counseling toward what is acceptable may be the proper recourse for the counselor. In other cases, it may be more feasible to modify the vocational situation. The counselor too frequently expects the client to change, and if the change does not come quickly, declares the client nonfeasible for service. Then too, the counselor needs to know what disability really means within the client's culture. With a clearer understanding of cultural differences, the counselor has a better chance of guiding the client into the path that may lead to vocational rehabilitation.

Just as cultural differences are important in assessing the vocational potential of a client, so must environmental conditions be considered. The person who lives in the ghetto may experience the worst that poverty has to offer, yet he may feel even more threatened outside that environment. Even transportation via a public transit system may pose hurdles with which he cannot cope. The prejudices, the knowledge that he is different, the fear of the unknown—all are threatening to him. Does the counselor work with the client to solve these problems, or does he reject the client as being unmotivated?

Included also in the environmental study, the counselor must consider the client who has a prison record. The problems presented by this history may cause the lesser informed counselor to reject the client because he does not see any potential for employment. The counselor must always be cognizant of his own biases and prejudices. The client who has been a drug abuser or an alcoholic presents yet another set of problems. The fact that a person is a member of a disadvantaged group, or has a long history of unemployment or underemployment should enter into the prevocational evaluation. Any environmental condition, then, that deviates from the norm may have significant bearing concerning the vocational potential of the client.

SUMMARY

An attempt has been made to focus on all aspects of evaluation and to relate each to the prevocational evaluation. They are intertwined in practice and cannot be neatly segmented. No attempt was made here to be comprehensive in each type evaluation. In other chapters, these various areas are discussed in greater detail. The prevocational evaluation aspect may be inferred, but the discussions are more global.

There is no attempt made to suggest that the various evaluations related to prevocational evaluation end when the purpose for prevocational evaluation ends. Rather, each of these should be considered as ongoing evaluations, the results of which might alter the rehabilitation plan minimally, or radically. It is only as the counselor continuously reviews and evaluates new data, and is willing to modify plans according to any new input that the counselor can be reasonably assured that the client is being rehabilitated according to his best potential.

Prevocational evaluation results in facilitating the client's entry into the labor market. If the process is not facilitating, it has failed.

For the counselor who is dynamic, innovative, imaginative, it is the prevocational evaluation phase that allows him to function at his best. It is during this phase that he is trying things and doing things that are unconventional. Supervisors could do well to evaluate their counselors on the basis of what the counselor does in the prevocational evaluation of the client. Once a vocational goal has been determined, the rehabilitation process tends to become routine.

As vocational rehabilitation serves more and more disabled, disadvantaged clients, prevocational evaluation will become even more important. The effective counselor knows that through his prevocational evaluation efforts come his successful rehabilitations.

REFERENCES

Federal Register, 34(200):16804, 1969.

Institute for Vocational Rehabilitation, Materials Development Center, Stout State University, Menomenie, Wisconsin. "Prevocational Evaluation, Unit 3-002," Mimeographed paper. Oct. 17, 1968.

McGowan, J. F. and Porter, T. L.: *An Introduction to the Vocational Rehabilitation Process.* Washington, U. S. Department of Health, Education and Welfare, Social and Rehabilitation Service, Rehabilitation Services Administration, 1967.

Rosenberg, Bernard and Wellerson, Thelma: A Structured Prevocational Program. In Moses, H. A. and Patterson, C. H.: *Readings In Rehabilitation Counseling.* Champaign, Stipes, 1971.

XII

SCIENTIFIC OBSERVATION IN WORK EVALUATION

ROBERT P. OVERS[1]

Goals

Scope

Event Sampling

Time Sampling

Position Sampling

Observed Behavior Versus Inferred Attitudes

Reliability

Client Information Synthesis

Writing Work Evaluation Reports

References

A MAJOR SKILL of the work evaluator is insightful observation. In contrast to the vocational counselor, social worker, psychologist or psychometrist, the vocational evaluator who is often an occupational therapist observes the client for a long period of time and can expose the client to stimuli which will test his reactions. In comparison with the parents and spouses of the clients who observe the client for longer times and watch the client respond to a wider range of stimuli, the work evaluator usually has more objectivity and insight.

Most evaluators quickly become astute observers with exper-

[1]*The American Journal of Occupational Therapy,* Volume 22, No. 6, 1968 pp. 530-533.

ience. However, many work evaluators are unaware of the methodology of scientific observation which has been developed in other fields (Festinger and Katz, 1953; Medley and Mitzel, 1963; Wright, 1960). It may be beneficial to review how scientific observation may be applied to the field of work evaluation.

Herbert F. Wright (1960) discusses the open and closed methods. in the open method the observer is sensitive to the total situation: this is characteristic of most of the observations currently made by work evaluators. In the closed method, the evaluator focuses on only one dimension of client behavior and temporarily disregards other dimensions.

Goals

(1) The idiographic goal of studying one particular client for the purpose of understanding his behavior better is the most familiar.

(2) The normative goal is to observe a number of individuals to estimate average behavior of a group of clients.

(3) The systematic goal is to observe clients in terms of a psychological or sociological theory of behavior.

It is necessary to distinguish carefully in all observation between the literal description of the behavior itself and the interpretation of the behavior by the observer. Observers will vary, however, in even their literal descriptions of behavior because of the psychological set which they bring to the situation.

Scope

The scope of the behavioral event being observed influences the interpretation of the content. An aggressive act may be understood as occurring: (1) because of the internal hostile thoughts of the paranoid schizophrenic, without outside stimulus, (2) as a normal reaction to being shoved through a subway doorway, or (3) as one event in the long feud of the Hatfield and the McCoys.

A scope limit must be established. This can be a time limit or an event limit. Since most behavioral events are influenced by a preceding event and influence a subsequent event, arbitray dividing lines must be drawn to determine scope boundaries. For instance, if a client is observed to be laughing by himself his contact with reality may be questioned by the evaluator. However, if the observation includes a longer scope limit, in the case both a longer time limit and an expanded event limit, it will be observed that the laughter is a normal reaction to the fact that another client just finished telling him a joke. The meaning of the observed behavior is completely altered merely by expanding the scope limit.

Any part of behavior may be analyzed on at least four levels of abstraction: (1) behavior unique to the individual, (2) behavior as an interaction process between individuals, (3) behavior of the group (if any) to which the subject belongs, and (4) behavior accounted for by the values, norms, and expectations derived from the larger society which both clients and evaluators bring to the situation.

Of primary interest is the degree to which the client's behavior is effective, sometimes called adaptive or adjustive. But effective for what? One client's behavior may be highly effective for securing the attention and recognition he craves from other clients but highly ineffective in preparing him for placement. Since the evaluator ordinarily attaches greater value to the placement goal we may expect a biased observation of the attention-getting incident.

Event Sampling

It is impossible for the evaluator to keep track of all of the interesting behavioral events to be observed in a work evaluation program. He may wish to select certain behavioral events upon which to concentrate his attention. For instance, in appraising a withdrawn client, he may wish to maintain an event diary of the number of interpersonal contacts. He may note the quality of the interactions: Who initiated the interaction? Was the other person of the same or opposite sex?

Time Sampling

Work evaluators are rarely consciously aware of the representativeness of their observations. Client behavior may vary from hour to hour and from day to day. It may improve or become less satisfactory during the course of the evaluation. While only in research is a formal plan used, nevertheless, some item sampling plan is desirable.

For instance, if the client has a systematic disorder and is fatigued at the end of the work day, there will be a patterned behavior difference between early morning and the late afternoon. If he is observed only in the morning, a report will not represent his total behavior. Neither will the Monday morning behavior of a weekend alcoholic be representative. Evaluators should be sure that their informal sampling covers all of the different time periods of the client's work week. Also, the signficance of the rare, dramatic episode must be judged in comparison with a long period of routine behavior. This is termed the *Critical Incident Method.*

The use of very simple hardware can supplement the evaluator's memory and enhance his effectiveness as a recording instrument. A baseball umpire's ball and strike indicator or a golf stroke counter are cheap and effective. These may be used to tally the number of times a disturbed client puts his head down on the table or stares off into space. By systematic sampling, a record may be made as to whether he is improving or regressing in the relation to work. This is more accurate than using merely the unsubstantiated impression of the evaluator.

Position Sampling

The physical position of the observer affects what he observes. If the evaluator only observes from his desk, some actions may be missed. A representative sample of observations from all the possible observational points is likely to reveal different aspects of a client's behavior.

Observed Behavior Versus Inferred Attitudes

In work evaluation reports it is important to differentiate between the behavior actually observed and the inferences attributed to it. When one client yells at another does this represent hostility or horseplay? The observer's own attitudes toward the incident will influence his interpretation of the behavior. Normal lower-class behavior frequently appears aggressive to middle-class people. Plausible inferences based on observed behavior are extremely important in understanding the client. The clinical psychologist (Klopfer, 1960) breaks down information about the client into what he calls three levels of communication:

(1) Level of public communication, as, for instance, what the parents will tell the evaluator about the client.

(2) Level of conscious perception, such as, what the client will admit about himself, as in a counseling interview or in filling out a personality inventory.

(3) Level of private symbolization, which may be described as material which the client does not care to admit or which is not within his level of awareness, but which may be inferred by his response to projective tests. Something of the private symbolization level may be inferred from careful observation.

The way observed behavior is interpreted is influenced by the professional training of the observer and by the psychological and sociological theories of human behavior in terms of which he customarily interprets human behavior. This is not bad. Behavior is much more meaningful if interpreted in terms of a plausible theory. It is well, however, for the evaluator to be consciously aware of the theory of his choice, or if he is eclectic, to have a rationale for his position.

Reliability

Medley and Mitzel (1963) cite three types of reliability measures;

(1) Stability coefficient: This is the correlation between observations made by the same evaluator at different times. If there is a high correlation the inference is that both the client and the evaluator are behaving consistently. This is the most common form of comparison and is used informally in the evaluation of nearly every client. If there is a low correlation, several possibilities are considered: (a) the behavior of the client is variable, (b) the perception of the behavior by the evaluator is variable, (c) the

interpretation of the behavior by the evaluator is variable, (d) some combination of variance.

(2) Reliability coefficient: This is the relationship between observations made by different evaluators at different times. If a high correlation exists, it may be assumed that both client and observers are behaving consistently and that as measuring instruments the evaluators resemble each other.

On the other hand, if a low correlation occurs some of the following interpretations are possible: (a) the client behaves differently at different times, (b) the client behaves differently when observed by different evaluators, (c) the observers are perceiving the same behavior in different ways, (d) the observers are interpreting the same behavior in different ways.

(3) Coefficient of evaluator agreement: This is the correlation between scores based on observations made by different evaluators at the same time although this is less common among work evaluators. If a high correlation is achieved consider that: (a) both observers perceive the behavior in the same way, (b) both observers interpret the behavior in the same way. If there is low correlation we infer that: (a) the observers are perceiving the behavior differently, (b) the observers are interpreting the behavior differently.

Assumptions about the consistency of client behavior are uncertain if the realiability of the evaluator has not been measured. The calibration of the evaluator as a measuring instrument may change. What he may classify as extreme client aggressive behavior at one time may at a later date appear only moderately aggressive.

Client Information Synthesis

The greatest understanding about a client comes from a synthesis of the material from all three sources of data: an examination of the life history data, psychological testing, and work evaluation. A synthesis is not merely the summing together of the information. It is an endeavor to weave together the three. If two or more of the separate appraisals find the same trends in the client, we may accept this trend with considerable assurance.

Many times, however, findings are in disagreement. Two possible reasons are:

(1) The client is in fact responding differently at different times, in different situations or differently at different levels. This is a most significant fact to know about the client.

(2) The findings may reflect disagreement because the appraisors have different values, different norms, are looking for different things, have a different vocabulary or have semantic differences in using the same vocabularly. To understand and reconcile these differences is an important step in professional growth for all of the staff involved.

There are alternate ways of achieving a synthesis: (1) informal conferences between the two or three separate people involved before they write their reports, (2) passing around preliminary reports to the staff of other departments for review and critique before final reports are written. The sheer mechanical problem of assembling the data from all three approaches in pursuit of synthesis is a difficult one. A staffing conference presents orally the highlights of the findings from each approach. This is helpful but frequently in the interest of preserving harmony among the staff, there is a tendency to gloss over differences.

The magnitude of the coordination problem varies according to the size of the agency. In a small agency, where most of the appraisal is done by the work evaluator, there is less of a coordination problem. On the other hand, unless the work evaluator is a multiskilled individual, he is not able to combine with his own skills those of a psychologist, social worker, and vocational counselor.

Since the client is normally seen by each separate department in turn, one solution in a large agency is to have the first person who works with the client set forth his perception of the client as an hypothesis. It is then up to the next staff member to accept, reject or amend this hypothesis. The work evaluator will consider the client's behavior as he observes it in the light of the hypothesis that has been advanced and either accept, reject or amend this hypothesis. When it is time to make a decision concerning the client's outcome a report will be available which will undoubtedly have disagreements but which, at least, will be discussing the same appraisal dimension.

As each staff member finds out what other staff members are accepting or rejecting in the hypothesis, it will sharpen his perception of what he is doing and reveal biases of which he was unaware. This will help to establish appropriate boundary lines between different types of appraisals.

Writing Work Evaluation Reports

Since the work evaluation report is heavily leaned upon in decision-making about the client's outcome, it is wasteful to evaluate clients and then fail to properly present the findings. There are also semantic problems to be resolved. Different professions use a shared vocabulary about human behavior in a slightly different way.

In summary, work evaluation should apply the methods and techniques of scientific observation to observing clients. The synthesis of information derived from an analysis of the life history date, psychological test data and work evaluation data is required to achieve a basis for understanding client behavior.

REFERENCES

Festinger, L. and Katz, D.: *Research Methods in the Behavioral Sciences,* New York, The Dryden Press, 1953.

Klopfer, W. G.: *The Psychological Report,* New York, Grune & Stratton, 1960.

Medley, D. M. and Mitzel, H. E.: Measuring classroom behavior by systematic observation. In N. L. Gage, (Ed.): *Handbook of Research on Teaching.* The American Educational Research Association, Chicago, Rand McNally, 1963.

Selltiz, C., Jahoda, M., Deutsch, M., and Cook, S.: *Research Methods in Social Relations,* New York, Holt, Rinehart, Winston, 1965.

Travers, R.: *An Introduction to Education Research,* New York, MacMillan Company, 1964.

Webb, E. J., Campbell, D., Schwartz, R. and Sechrest, L.: *Unobtrusive Measures,* Chicago, Rand McNally, 1966.

Wright, H. F.: Observational child study. In Paul H. Mussen, (Ed.): *Handbook of Research Methods in Child Development.* New York, Wiley, 1960.

PART FOUR

EVALUATIONS IN SPECIALTY AREAS

Purpose of Psychological Testing in Work Evaluation

Purposes and Approaches of Educational Evaluation

A Model for Vocational Evaluation of the Disadvantaged

The Rehabilitation Facility's Role in Evaluating the Welfare Recipient

XIII

PURPOSE OF PSYCHOLOGICAL TESTING IN WORK EVALUATION

David D. Clark

><><><><><><><><><><><><><><><><><><><><><><><><><><><><><><><><

Introduction
Review of the Literature
Personal Functioning Importance
Coping With Stress
Information From The Psychological Evaluation
Evaluating Procedures
Suggestions for the Evaluator
References

><><><><><><><><><><><><><><><><><><><><><><><><><><><><><><><><

INTRODUCTION

WITH CONSIDERABLE INTEREST I listened as my high school counselor interpreted vocational and aptitude test scores to me. I found I was destined to be a forest ranger, as I scored very high on the Kuder *outdoor*. Unabashed, I did not heed the good advice and went on to college to obtain a B.A. in Psychology. After presenting my credentials to the State Employment Commission, I was again subjected to vocational testing (I had a useless degree). To my growing concern I was again advised to be a forest ranger. As a compromise, since a high score was also obtained in spatial relations, I was advised to start over in landscape engineering. They actually talked me into taking a course in mechanical drawing, which I flunked. Undaunted, I went on to gain my doctorate and began teaching evaluation in a university counseling center. One day with some free time I took some of those tests I was so busy administering. It was with more than casual concern that I again found myself atop a lookout tower and without even a score in the area of psychology. Something had to be wrong. At that point I thought it best to interview the client (which had not been previously done) to try to relate test scores to the person (which was a reverse).

REVIEW OF THE LITERATURE

This personal experience led me to an evaluation of the literature from a practical standpoint. It is one thing to describe job characteristics and another to accurately match and interpret those characteristics in such a way as will result in successful placement. Perhaps there are some psychological characteristics common to both forest rangers and independent psychologists. Psychological testing must certainly take into consideration the significant psychological variables of both the job and the individual. The purpose of psychological testing is to gain knowledge of the significant, related variables of both the worker and the work.

A review of the literature shows evaluation and research seeking out any and all possible relationships which might exist so that job success may be more accurately predicted, but I do not find that there is a one to one correlation of strength in any area. Certainly any variable can be either a *satisfier* or *dissatifier* (Waters and Waters, 1969) for that individual.

There appears to be limited suport for a personality type for any specific occupation. Because a person is highly qualified or identified with some occupational group does not presume to exclude him from success in other groups. Personality variables are related to job characteristics, but job characteristics may be common to many jobs (Borg, Bratfisch, and Dornic, 1970 and Doll and Gunderson, 1969). Matching personal and social characteristics of the client to the social and personal characteristics of a vocation often makes more sense in the long run than being only concerned with the physical characteristics of the job. The evaluation of personality and self-concept hold very vague and tenous relationships with any particular occupation. Even if some personality variables are highly related to some occupational category this is not to say that this person might not be just as successful in many other occupations.

PERSONAL FUNCTIONING IMPORTANCE

It is becoming increasingly clear in the literature of the past ten years that the personal functioning of the client, no matter what the handicap is, is of major importance in helping him to personal success through vocational training and placement. We are becoming more concerned not with just whether he can become a capable employee but whether he can become a more effective person through being an employee. We know that just because the person has the ability to perform a task does not mean that he will perform it or that he will enjoy it.

Most people can do many jobs well, but if the job does not fit a need for that person he will not last. At some level personal satisfactory is necessary with some aspect of any job. How to evaluate or work with a client who has a totally inadequate self-concept and no vocational or personal interest is certainly a challenge. Persons come in with no idea of what they want and are seldom pleased when we list off a number of occupations. Some persons are restricted from a vocation that they liked well, others cannot find themselves and it is difficult, if not impossible, to become involved in an occupation when one is having difficulty being involved in himself. Gonyea (1962) at the University of Texas brought out the most interesting point that those persons who came in for vocational help were those who would least benefit from it. This is certainly one of the prime problems in vocational evaluation. Not only do many clients come in for help, much of the time we go out and get them.

Vocational evaluation and training and placement that are truly client centered are time consuming, expensive, and usually successful. When the evaluation and the program do a personal and continuing job with the client, prior to and in conjunction with training, things seem to work out better than if the client is simply fitted into this or that slot. Successful programs are concerned not only with the physical characteristics of the job, but with the psychological and social successes. I feel that these are the most important, assuming a basic level of competency, and will determine whether or not the client stays on the job. The difficult factor is to find the type of vocation which more or less fits the individual's personal characteristics and that he can, in his present condition, both perform and obtain satisfaction from. This personal functioning can be partially evaluated through objective test results. These tests, and more importantly, the structured personal interview, are what is truly important in a more clear evaluation of that person's functioning.

An evaluation of the factors of success, intellegence, education, and experience is important and a part of any test battery. The evaluator should always realize that the tests, or test batteries, are no more than structured interviews. Objective test scores are to confirm what one obtains in interview. To report only test scores, or to make all judgments dependent on tests, is to miss the point. I had a professor at one time who said if we were not able to get out of thirty minutes of interview what we would get out of three hours of testing, then we needed to start over. The interview that accompanies tests need not be prolonged. It should be simple and direct, with a view of obtaining information that will enable the psychologist to more accurately evaluate and interpret formal test data. If the patient's thinking is unrealistic, or unsure, or non-existent, evaluation can still obtain useful data for future planning.

I attempt to obtain information on the personality correlates of what I call contact, stress, and drive. These characteristics of the job are more important than the job itself. One of the most important characteristics of all occupations is the nature of contact that the individual has with others. Although all occupations involve some degree of contact, I ask clients whether or not they would prefer to be more involved with people, or with things. If things, we go on to whether they be large or small, simple or complicated, prestigious or common. If people, we go on to ask whether they would prefer to be with large groups, several persons, or just a few. From there, we ask whether or not the individual would prefer impersonal, informal, or close personal contact with others. We would also ask whether they would prefer aggressive, dependent, or a helping relationship type contact.

Once we determine the basically important characteristics of the job then we can be concerned with other things such as; intelligence, manual dexterity, manipulative skills, experience, etc. Personal skills are usually as important as performance skills, if not more so.

Personality correlates are important in predicting job success from a number of areas. Every job maintains a level of stress, whether from threat or boredom. The individual's ability to cope with the kind of stress involved is important.

COPING WITH STRESS

How stable is the individual on the job? Can he stay with it when it no longer offers a challenge? Can he deal with aggressive persons? Can he stand or sit for prolonged periods? The individual's ability to cope with job stress factors is a significant variable at any occupational level. Not only is actual stress important, but *perceived stress* as well. We have all seen *chronic students* those who were able but could not face graduation could not stand the stress of the position that they would occupy when qualified (Borg, Bratfisch, and Dornic, 1970; Froberg, *et. al.,* 1969; and Froberg, *et. al.,* 1970) .

Most persons constantly need more stress or challenge while others can stand very little or practically none. These factors are psychological. We also see a large group that are culturally acclimated to what I call nonstress. We have seen how difficult it is to motivate the hard core unemployed. How difficult it is to motivate welfare recipients to work (Antebi, 1970 and Scott and Phelan, 1969) . The ability to withstand the stress of a job is a most significant variable. The actual and perceived stress of an occupation and the individual's ability to cope with it are prime criteria. Some persons are only satisfied with a high level of stress challenge, while others fold at any involvement or threat from others. The information relating to these factors should be obtained in interview.

Stress is related to motivation, as the individual's response can certainly be rewarding. The criterion for motivation varies, though, and has much to do with job satisfaction. Although significant objective factors such as intelligence, education, experience, and the individual's qualifications in each, are important to a psychological evaluation (Doll and Gunderson, 1969; Fogli, Hublin, and Blood, 1971; Gay and Weiss, 1970; Mayo, 1969; Rosenfield and Zdep, 1971; Soloff and Bolton, 1969; and Summers, Burke, Saltiel, and Clark, 1971), intelligence and education are more directly related to the extrinsic and intrinsic variables of motivation. Personal satisfaction, prestige, sense of accomplishment, etc. are important variables for more highly educated and intelligent persons, but not so important to others. For some, job security, retirement, sick pay, and fringe benefits are much more important; for others frequency of pay periods and physical demands of work are primary. It is pointless to discuss job satisfaction with a person capable of unskilled, manual labor. Likewise, many persons engage in relatively unrewarding jobs with high prestige. We need to know the level of motivation of an individual to relate it to a job.

INFORMATION FROM THE PSYCHOLOGICAL EVALUATION

The type of information obtained in a psychological evaluation is somewhat difficult to communicate. Things would go much easier, though, if we were obligated to read our own reports. We spend a great deal of time writing reports, but we do not spend an equal amount of time reading the reports that are sent to us. We should be able to criticize the reports that are sent, as well as the ones that are received. The professional evaluator can save himself and his colleagues a tremendous amount of time, if he will pause to evaluate his own verbage.

The psychologists' attempt to relate the variables and data of interview, as well as objective test data, together into a brief report about *that* person is what is essential. It is easy to maintain the established procedure. We learn how to write a report in graduate school and twenty years later we are still following the same format. In the academic world volume is most highly prized.

When one is in practice and supports one's self in an hourly fashion, efficiency becomes more highly prized. It is possible that efficiency may improve quality.

I was once a member of a diagnostic team which cranked out beautiful reports of four to six pages of single spaced material on some poor child who was flunking the second grade and happened to be in the middle of his family. At our center we did not have time to read each others reports because everybody's report was so long and we had to depend on a verbal abstract to save time. We would all come into the staff meeting with volumes of material on the child and then someone would say "What do you think?" and two or three persons would say in two or three sentences what the whole problem was. The volume of material would then be shuttled through the secretary to be typed up without the benefit of the verbal abstract. Some unlucky soul was usually responsible for writing recommendations and summarizing the thing. This was usually done from notes made from our verbal interchange. We assumed that someone out there was going to read the whole thing carefully. When the report was delivered to its final source would say "What is the problem?" and a brief verbal report would indicate it. Then the volume of material would quietly go to its file there to remain undisturbed for the remainder of that child's education.

EVALUATING PROCEDURES

We need to continually evaluate our own procedures. This is very difficult to do but it is facilitated by inviting our colleagues' criticism. In an attempt to evaluate one's own procedures, some introspective questions are in order. First, will it be read? A tremendous amount of data is accumulated for the purpose of accumulating data and does no more than stuff someone's file. It should not be necessary to have to scan a report to try to find the purpose for which the evaluation was written and for something which has meaning in terms of that client. So we ask, will it be read? Will all of it be read and what will not be read? If it will not be read then why write it? Who has enough time to read a fraction of the reports that are written? Who has time to read the literature? I have taken a cue from the journals and abstract reports which of necessity have some detail. It is much easier to read an abstract than to scan the entire report. An abstracted evaluation prior to the full text is not sacreligious and can be very efficient and an objective time saver.

Finding time to engage in full time evaluation and keeping up with the literature in the field is a herculean task reserved only for the most intelligent and superior readers and limits the less gifted to surveying the abstract. Having lived in the world of *publish or perish* I am aware that one good piece of research can be expanded into several articles and with a little professional co-operation can be expanded indefinitely. Thus, to find information useful to one's occupation is a challenge and time consuming job. What all of this means is that there is really no point in making a psychological evaluation longer than it needs to be because that uses up my time as well as my readers. The longer I am in practice the less I write and the less elaborate I become. This is because time is short and I am talking to real people in the reports. Again, quality need not be sacrificed for quantity.

Secondly, who is going to read the report? Many reports are addressed to the file cabinets which will house them. They are not directed to a real person and are usually written in the third person "The examiner determined," "The patient was observed to, etc." Reports are about people who have names and are written by people. A report that states "It is my opinion that" and if the report is signed, I am being communicated with by a real person. If I read something that says "The examiner's impression was that," then I know I have someone who was fearful to enter into the evaluation.

SUGGESTIONS FOR THE EVALUATOR

Finally, I would suggest a few points for the evaluator's report. First, write only what is relevant to that patient and to that reader. That is to say, if all test findings on a particular patient fall within the normal expected ranges and there are no deviations in any area and when both parties are familiar with what we mean by normal, then there is not much point in taking up two pages to describe how he functions normally. Likewise, if evaluations are written regularly on say, deaf students, to counselors for the deaf, some material becomes assumed which would not be mentioned, but would perhaps be included when writing to some outside party. It is pointless to include a complete breakdown of normal developmental history. I have seen reports where all developmental milestones from birth to the sixth grade were individually listed even though all were in the normal range. I get tired of searching for a clue as to what is wrong and why all this data is being reported.

Second, involve the personality of the patient in some way as to make that person unique. We need to provide some cues as to the recall of this person in some way. A physical description, a quote, some event, etc. to tie the report to the patient. There is something unique about everyone, even though some person's uniqueness is that he may be just plain vanilla. Try to find something in the way of a physical description, a comment, a happening, or something about the patient so that whoever is reading the report can get a visual image and recall the experience that they have had with the patient, or will have. If possible in a report, I always like to quote a patient as that makes them more human.

Third, provide test data objectively and interpret it in simple terms with which the reader is familiar. A simple term is always preferable to a demonstration of one's own vocabulary. I find that very few persons are insulted by simple, common terms. Technical terms of one's own profession are common only to the user. Fourth, and finally, say only what needs to be said and then stop.

REFERENCES

Antebi, R. N.: State benefits as a cause for unwillingness to work. *British Journal of Psychiatry, 117*(537):205-206, 1970.

Borg, G., Bratfisch, O. and Dornic, S.: On perceived difficulty. *Reports from the Institute of Applied Psychology,* University of Stockholm, 1970, No. 19, p. 13.

Clark, D. D.: Evaluation: A psychologists view. *Vocational Evaluation and Work Adjustment Bulletin, 2*(2):3-6, 1969.

Doll, R. E., and Gunderson, E. K.: Occupational group as a moderator of the job satisfaction-job performance relationship. *Journal of Applied Psychology.* 53(5):359-361, 1969.

Fogli, L., Hulin, C. L., and Blood, M. R.: Development of first level behavioral job criteria. *Journal of Applied Psychology.* 55(1):3-8, 1971.

Froberg, J., *et. al.*: Conditions of work and their influence on psychological and endocrine stress reactions. *Reports from the Laboratory for Clinical Stress Research,* Karolinska, Sjukuset, 1969 No. 8, p. 18.

Froberg, J., *et. al.*: Conditions of work: Psychological and endocrine stress reactions. *Archives of Environmental Health, 21*:780-797, 1970.

Gay, E. G. and Weiss, D. J.: Relationship of work experience and measured vocational needs. Proceedings of the annual convention of the American Psychological Association, 5 (Pt. 2):663-664, 1970.

Gonyea, G. G.: Appropriateness of vocational choice as a criterion of counseling outcome. *Journal of Counseling Psychology, 9*(2):213, 1962.

Mayo, C. C.: A method for determining job types for low aptitude airman. *USAF AFHRL Technical Report,* 1969 (Nov.), No. 69-35.

Rosenfield, M. and Zdep, S. M.: Intrinsic extrinsic aspects of work and their demographic correlates. *Psychological Reports. 28*(2):359-362, 1971.

Scott, J. D. and Phelan, J. G.: Expectancies of unemployable males regarding source of control of reinforcement. *Psychological Reports, 25*(3): 911-913, 1969.

Soloff, A. and Bolton, B. F.: The validity of the vocational adjustment workshop. *Educational and Psychological Measurement, 29*(4):993-998, 1969.

Summers, G. F., Burke, M., Saltiel, S. and Clark, J. P.: Stability of the structure of work orientations among high school students. *Multivariate Behavioral Research, 6*(1):35-50, 1971.

Waters, L. K. and Waters, C. W.: Correlates of job satisfaction and job dissatisfaction among female clerical workers. *Journal of Applied Psychology, 53*(5):388-391, 1969.

XIV

PURPOSES AND APPROACHES OF EDUCATIONAL EVALUATION

GORDAN KRANTZ

Introduction
Vocational Evaluation in School Settings
Vocational Evaluation in Relation to Vocational Education
Vocational Evaluation in Relation to Special Education
Vocational Evaluation in Relation to the Disadvantaged
Classification of Vocational Evaluation in Educational Settings
St. Paul System
Minneapolis System
An Interdistrict System
The Duluth System
The Robbinsdale System
Vocational Evaluation in Rural Education Settings
Services of Serve
Issues in Evaluation in Educational Settings
References

INTRODUCTION

VOCATIONAL EVALUATION is not merely *an art practiced in re-habilitation centers*. It is essentially a technology, a practical art based upon a body of science. As such, it is most helpfully defined by its procedures and theories and by the needs to which it speaks. With the definition of vocational evaluation as a technology in mind, it becomes possible to consider its use in a number of settings including in the public schools.

The professional literature, because information is seldom labeled and indexed in those terms, does not readily lend itself to a survey of vocational evaluation of the *individual* in school settings. Information retrieval gets confused with *program* evaluation, which is an entirely different thing. Educational literature seldom indexes vocational evaluation as a term, and the literature of rehabilitation has concentrated mainly upon rehabilitation facilities which serve the state/federal rehabilitation program. This situation is changing, however. Journals devoted to education are beginning to take note of vocational evaluation and work adjustment while rehabilitation literature is increasingly reflecting the interaction between traditional rehabilitation and public education.

Vocational evaluation is no stranger to the school setting. It has been used in one form or another for a long time. In fact, some of the technological development of vocational evaluation was carried out in the schools, as exemplified by research and development projects focused upon technological development. There has unquestionably been a good deal of unpublished vocational evaluation activity conducted under local initiative within various school systems.

VOCATIONAL EVALUATION IN SCHOOL SETTINGS

Vocational evaluation techniques in school settings are such a commonsense idea that they are an international practice. In Sweden, for example, all eighth grade pupils spend three weeks working in industry as part of their guidance program, thus utilizing real work as a guidance tool and as a contributor to the educational-vocational diagnosis.

In the United States, vocational evaluation and other uses of real work in connection with education have a long, informal history. A good deal of this history is associated with vocational education, though quite a bit of it in recent decades has been associated with special education. Within the last decade there has been an almost explosive growth of cooperative arrangements between special education and the various state rehabilitation agencies; in these arrangements vocational evaluation is often given, inside or outside the school setting, as a part of the coopera-tive arrangement. Some of this kind of arrangement is of very long standing. For example, there has been such a cooperative contract in St. Paul and Minneapolis, Minnesota since 1930.

The field is difficult to survey for another reason besides the lack of a good literature index. This other reason is the wide variety of practices, so that it is very nearly impossible to categor-ize the use of vocational evaluation in the public schools according to any single rational scheme. The spottiness of what follows is substantially due to that difficulty.

Before going into the actual practices and their varieties, it may be helpful to locate vocational evaluation and its related technologies with respect to the educational process. In order to do that, a simplified and idealized chart of the relationship is given here. It is simplified in that the many back-loops and al-ternatives have been cut down, and it is idealized in that real life matters seldom go in such a logical manner. The chart is entitled *Vocational Service Flow of the Severely Disabled and Marginal Rehabilitation Client.*

The chart is given here so that some points can be made about the relationship of vocational evaluation to the total educational process. It was originally prepared for the orientation of special educators whose interest had traditionally terminated near the top of the chart. Their interest no longer terminates there, and they need to have a grasp of what is available either in the community or within resources that they themselves can build. The reader may as well know that there are some ulterior motives to the chart as well: one is an attempt to get some standardization of terms in the geographic area for which the chart was intended; another intent was to try to get the use of resources ordered into a more efficient sequence; and finally but not at all least, the in-tent of the chart was to show that there is a valued outcome possi-bility for every student. Unlike other agencies the public schools cannot turn down a student because he lacks potential for a few selected occupational outcomes, and the schools must learn to value that which is optimum for the student.

A warning should be given here for fear that it will be other-

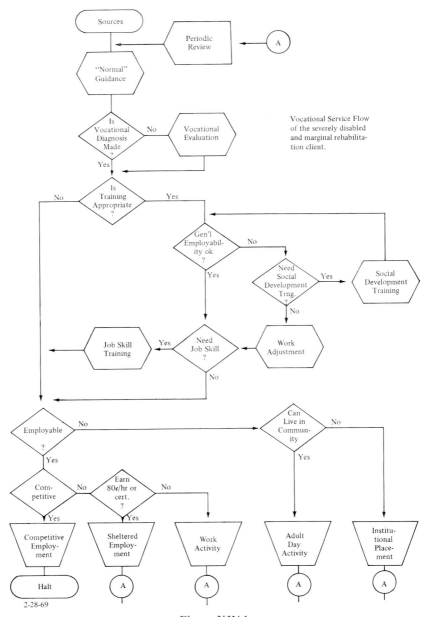

Figure XIV-1.

wise overlooked. The symbols on the chart do not refer to agencies. A six-sided symbol represents an operation that is carried out regardless of where it is done. To use vocational evaluation as an illustration and referring back to the opening paragraph of this chapter, the reader should understand that vocational evaluation is the same body of technology whether it is practiced in a rehabilitation center, a workshop, a mobile van, or a room in a school building.

The whole chart has a characteristic which brings us to the application of these ideas to education. The thinking of educators used to stop at *normal* guidance, the process of giving counseling over the desk and with the use of tests, if tests are indicated. As far as the bottom row of the chart goes, education used to concern itself only with the out-bucket labeled competitive employment. Times have changed. Educators now find themselves concerned either with securing or providing almost all of the operations shown within the six-sided figures and coming to grips with all of the possible occupational outcomes in the bottom out-buckets. Thus, education is no longer simply a source of cases and thus, education is concerned with vocational evaluation.

In many places, vocational evaluation is being used as a contributor to the educational diagnosis as well as to the more traditional vocational diagnosis. This is because, as noted, education has broadened its outlook. We may quarrel with the breadth of the existing vision, but there is no doubt that the vision has expanded very substantially in recent years.

Three major elements of education have become involved with this technology. In the order in which they entered the field formally, they are special education, educational programs for disadvantaged youth, and vocational education. The first is still the largest portion of public education involved in this, but the last has the potential for the most massive importation of such rehabilitation technologies as vocational evaluation.

Before attempting to describe some of the variations in the practice of vocational evaluation by education, it may be well to look at each of these three of the involved arms of public education.

VOCATIONAL EVALUATION IN RELATION TO VOCATIONAL EDUCATION

The vocational evaluation activities in connection with vocational education are still not easily listed. They are among the least visible except in terms of individual programs known by word of mouth or by direct contact. Until very recently vocational education has been charged with providing an educational service to a select clientele. Its essential and legitimate purpose was to serve the labor market. This mandate was changed somewhat in 1963, but the impact of the changed mandate was minor until the summer of 1968. At that time the laws regarding vocational education were changed (PL 88-210, Vocational Education Act of 1963, Amendments of 1968) so as to make clear the mandate of serving the occupational needs of the handicapped, the disadvantaged, and others who were formerly screened out of technically oriented programs. The results of this clearly stated addition to the mandate of vocational education is not yet visible, and there has not been sufficient time for much experimentation to be conducted and reported. However, we may reasonably expect that vocational evaluation will emerge as one of the useful technologies for generating an educational-vocational diagnosis when vocational education attempts to deal with a student body which it could previously screen out. Some of the difficulties that may arise will be touched upon later.

VOCATIONAL EVALUATION IN RELATION TO SPECIAL EDUCATION

The status of vocational evaluation in relation to special education is more visible. One reason is that Research and Demonstration projects have been funded by the federal rehabilitation agency in special education settings throughout the country, and the grant status of these projects makes their activities visible through their public reports. Another reason for visibility is the reporting of cooperative agreements between the schools and the state rehabilitation agencies. It should be borne in mind that the cooperative agreements are standardized in the form of the contract, but they are actually quite diverse and responsive to local circumstances in the nature of the program which is implemented through the cooperative agreement. The reports of these agreements and their operation tend to dwell upon the contract itself and its rationale, upon caseflow (though seldom with any mention of individuals not served under the agreement), and upon the opinion of the participants regarding how effective the agreement is. The contents of the program and especially the technical specifications of the vocational evaluation are detailed in only a few of the reports. However, most reports at least imply the use of vocational evaluation procedures.

VOCATIONAL EVALUATION IN RELATION TO THE DISADVANTAGED

Regarding vocational evaluation of disadvantaged youth, most of whom are involved in or have dropped out of school programs, the situation is more diverse and less uniformly scattered over the country than is true of the other two interest groups. Fortunately, some of this material has been pulled together (Gordon, 1969).

Thirty-five experimental and demonstration manpower development and training projects were reviewed. Disadvantaged youth and their problems are such that the conventional testing approach has seldom been very effective. Gordon (1969) reports that:

> If vocational tests have little or no useful validity as predictors of job success of disadvantaged youth, some projects have been able to show a very bright ray of light: MFY (Mobilization for Youth in New York) reports that those who successfully completed training in the skills recommended for them on the basis of work sample testing was 87 percent. . .thus, work sample testing may be far more effective than traditional vocational assessment.

The work sample procedures used by MFY were adapted from the TOWER system, one of the widely used vocational evaluation packages. Gordon reports:

> Many projects employ work experience stations for their youth, either in-house or in workcrews; by farming the youths

out to work stations in public agencies; or in regular on-the-job training. However, no project report gives any particular form for evaluation of youths' performance in work experience stations. Most assessments seem to have been done informally ("JT is working along nicely now") without detailed or complete evaluation.

This state of affairs is strikingly similar to what is true of the utilization of vocational evaluation in most public school settings. Gordon incidentally makes a comment regarding the programs for disadvantaged youth which could profitably be studied by those who design programs more definitely allied with education.

> The most important general feature of the program is that it locates the problem of youth unemployment within the unemployed youths themselves and tries to produce change in the youth by direct intervention in their behavior and experience . . .rather than through direct structural or social action. It must be clearly stated then that the orientation of the E & D program has rested on an assumption which is of questionable validity.

This comment was prompted by Gordon's observation that project reports typically cite great improvements in the personal characteristics of their clients but an inability of the manpower system to provide employment for this large volume of improved individuals. He proposes direct intervention in the manpower structure to make a place for these people.

CLASSIFICATION OF VOCATIONAL EVALUATION IN EDUCATIONAL SETTINGS

Although the diversity of practice almost defies categorization, some kind of classification is almost essential in order to discuss the field. The issue is not one of whether education will interact with vocational evaluation. The issues have to do with the purposes to which the evaluations will be put, with the choice of procedures to be carried out, with the understanding of what constitutes employability that underlies the procedures, with the location in which the evaluation is done, and with the administrative structure or structure of responsibility under which the evaluation is carried out. These things tend to be interwoven, and the illustrations given will show that fact.

The writer's home state will be used to illustrate some of the diversity in this field. Other states are probably not very different from Minnesota except that an occasional state may have such a unified system of interaction between education and rehabilitation that a single major system prevails. The hoped-for major impact of these illustrations is: "There is more than one right way to do things, and there is still no only way to fly."

Minnesota has both urban and rural characteristics. In the era of modern transportation there really need be no such thing a completely isolated rural region, but transportation is not always used effectively and some practical isolation remains. The metropolitan area centered upon Minneapolis and St. Paul is singularly rich in rehabilitation resources, and there is a statewide use of these resources. There is also a tradition of local initiative and ingenuity in the more rural portions of the state. Impetus to development has been given by the 1957 law making mandatory the public education of the *educable* mentally retarded and the 1971 law extending this coverage to the *trainable*. In some of the larger school districts the techniques of rehabilitation are considered to be part of the proper content of the secondary special education. In at least one of the multidistrict vocational education complexes, the technology is considered to be part of the proper content of vocational education for atypical students. Some school districts operate rehabilitation activities on their own responsibility and under educational direction while others secure the service under a cooperative agreement with the state rehabilitation agency.

Even for a single state, not all of the illustrations can be given. Please bear in mind that the illustrations themselves cannot be reduced to a single scheme of classification but that the classification schemes mentioned above (purposes of evaluation, choice of procedures, theory of employability, setting or location, and administrative or responsibility structure) can be detected in the illustrations.

ST. PAUL SYSTEM

St. Paul structures its school rehabilitation program around the cooperative agreement between the school district and the state rehabilitation agency. This is in addition to the city's participation in the SERVE program to be mentioned later. There are some three hundred mentally retarded students in the St. Paul school system at the senior high level. Each of these tenth, eleventh, and twelfth graders spends some of his time in a self-contained special education program and some of his time in a rehabilitation center or workshop or in job experience, arranged for and purchased by the vocational rehabilitation personnel of the cooperative program. The eight-week vocational evaluation program used at one of the major facilities is focused largely upon the work sample approach and upon the utilization of workshop stations. The program in the other major facility is focused upon the use of real work obtained competitively and operated under workshop circumstances. In the case of either facility, the vocational evaluation comes early in the student's senior high career, and the vocational adjustment coordinator (the vocational rehabilitation counselor employed in the cooperative program) serves as liaison between the vocation evaluation and the student's classroom experience. The classroom teacher receives a copy of the evaluation report. The evaluation program within the community rehabilitation facility is thus employed as a tool of educational diagnosis, and the findings are influential upon the classroom half of the student's subsequent program. The theoretical basis for the evaluation technology and the nature of the practice which derives from theory in the first mentioned facility is eclectic but of the general kind familiar to traditional rehabilitation facilities. It is concerned with such factors as interpersonal relationship, maturity, dependability, and the acceptance of supervision. In the second facility, now the one used most commonly, the theoretical formulation is that of Gunzburg (1964), a hierarchial scheme of skills which starts with very basic development in motor, social, occupational, and self-care spheres and builds to several levels. The focus in both facilities at this stage in the student's career is upon general employability rather than upon vocational choice. This focus reflects both the early stage in the student's career at which it is applied and the generalized nature of retardation as a disability.

St. Paul also has a somewhat specialized program that is an extension of the one just described. In the second mentioned rehabilitation facility, but with the evaluation setting limited to that portion which is licensed as a *work activity center,* a program has been built upon resources contributed by vocational education, special education, vocational rehabilitation, and the state department of welfare. It was in this program that the Gunzburg scheme was definitively adopted.

MINNEAPOLIS SYSTEM

Minneapolis has two somewhat parallel school rehabilitation programs. One is operated under the cooperative agreement with the state rehabilitation agency and has its primary impact after the schools have completed the work with the student. Rehabilitation counselors are stationed in the school offices under a cooperative contract, and they extend the normal services of the state rehabilitation agency to those students who are referred by the schools. The student who functions adequately in the special education program is referred near the end of his school career to the vocational rehabilitation office, and a wide range of community resources are used. The theory and practice of vocational evaluation in this part of the program is thus dependent upon the orientation of the community facility which is called into play. It seldom contributes to the educational diagnosis of the student since he is usually picked up at the termination of his school program. Changes in this are taking place, however, as an additional program is phased in. This new program is funded under vocational education monies and enables the attachment of a work coordinator to each of the senior high schools special education programs. Both in-school and community real work stations are used in addition to the services that can be purchased by vocational rehabilitation, and the work coordinator carries out the same liaison role as does the vocational adjustment coordinator in St.

Paul. Consequently, the work does impact upon the student's remaining in-school program.

Minneapolis also has a School Rehabilitation Center operated entirely with public school resources and under public school direction. Its essential nature is that of being a special education resource of last resort. Students are referred because their problems are residual to what the major special education or regular education program can meet rather than on the basis of their having a specified disability. During the current year, most of the students entering this program had been school drop-outs or had been institutionalized. The vocational evaluation conducted in the school rehabilitation center and the educational vocational diagnosis to which it contributes are fluid and ongoing rather than point-in-time. The student may remain in the program for a considerable period of time during which evaluation is continuous. The theoretical basis for the evaluation is quite eclectic. It may be significant that the job placement specialist is the person who administers work evaluation procedures. The case manager, a kind of rehabilitation counselor operating under school responsibility, also uses work samples and other tasks as the basis for his clinical observation.

A Work Opportunity Center is operated by the Minneapolis schools under the auspices of vocational education. It is designed to serve youth who have dropped out or cannot function in the culture of the standard high school. It offers technical training in job placement, a facilitation of return to high school for those who want it, high school graduation, preparation for general educational development testing, and vocational exploration. One of its reports states that, "Students who participate in center programs have not usually been successful in their efforts with standardized tests and inventories. The staff feels that the use of such instruments, except when adapted for specific purposes, will not yield valid results." In keeping with the center's philosophy of student exploration and self discovery, the technology of vocational evaluation is not highly developed nor is it adapted to a vocational diagnosis of the directive type. Try-out in trade areas and the use of community work placement themselves are used as evaluation tools. Subjective reports and observations oriented toward student self-evaluation are the predominant vocational evaluation tools.

AN INTERDISTRICT SYSTEM

The Cooperative School-Rehabilitation Center constitutes a public special education facility formerly operated by some forty-seven school districts in the Minneapolis-St. Paul metropolitan area. It is now a subsidiary of an interdistrict vocational education complex. It serves some three hundred *less able* mentally retarded adolescents whose handicap is too severe for them to be served in the special education programs of their home school districts. It provides the equivalent in life preparation of a secondary education and one of its major emphases is upon occupational competence. Vocational evaluation is by work samples, by real work on the workshop model, and by part-time job placement. As a regular part of the curriculum a work laboratory is operated within the Center. The work samples and the real work in the laboratory are mainly manipulative in nature. The theory of employability which underlies the vocational evaluation in the Center is eclectic though it is part of a larger theory of total life competence which is recently formalized and peculiar to this one program. Since the students may be in the program for periods of several years and since vocational evaluation procedures are part of the student's program from the beginning, the vocational evaluation and the educational vocational diagnosis to which it contributes are ongoing. The student's function in vocational evaluation is one of the factors which enter into the design of his individual curriculum schedule. Placement in semi-sheltered jobs, usually in the large geriatric nursing home which is located on the same campus, often occurs early enough in the student's career so as to permit the experiences to serve as part of the evaluation process. Placement on competitive jobs in the community is typically more of a device for transition to employment than for vocational evaluation.

THE DULUTH SYSTEM

Duluth is an area in transition of vocational evaluation procedure. Its school rehabilitation program incorporates the cooperative vocational rehabilitation counselor position as well as a center designed on the rehabilitation center model and operated by the school system. Increasingly, the school-operated center seems to be focusing upon its contribution to the educational diagnosis of students who will have additional time in the public schools for the enhancement of their employability. Life competence, in the theoretical orientation of the center, is visualized under such broad headings as intellectual factors, work personality, work habits, and physical capacities. Each of these broad areas is broken down into subconcepts; work habits subsume the behavioral aspects of speed of work, accuracy of work, completion of task, ability to follow rules, and grooming and manners. Since the same formulation of life competence underlies the in-classroom aspects of the Duluth program and since contact is maintained with the home school, the evaluation findings of the center are an integral part of the student's total senior high school programming. Some of the evaluation tasks include the use of real work. The transition referred to above comes about because Duluth has recently established a community workship, and it is being used increasingly in conjunction with the education program. The fact that the community facility is staffed by personnel who formerly worked with the schools tends to make this transition an orderly one.

Anoka is a relatively independent population center within the Minneapolis-St. Paul metropolitan area. Its school district is fairly large, having over 30,000 pupils. In its area vocational technical school Anoka operates a *Work Adjustment Center*. Both special education and vocational education are involved in programming there, and a cooperative agreement is in effect with the state vocational rehabilitation agency. Both youth and adults are served, but the median age is within the youth range. Admission to the center is based upon the state vocational rehabilitation agency standards for eligibility, and that agency usually pays the tuition fee. The theoretical basis which underlies the vocational evaluation of the center is drawn from trait and aptitude psychology (curriculum demands are typically described in categories similar to those of the General Aptitude Test Battery) and from the trade area concepts of vocational education. In addition to an extensive battery of standardized tests, the incoming student is evaluated with the aid of work samples. From that point on vocational evaluation shifts predominantly to a job exploration approach with the student trying out from one to three trade areas. Other work samples and vocational evaluation techniques are presented during the course of trade area exploration. Following evaluation the student is trained in a job skill in one of the trade areas available through the Work Adjustment Center itself or through the technical school in which the center is located. Since the center accepts referrals from outside the Anoka school district, the rehabilitation counselors who makes these referrals have found the evaluation program to be an entree into the technical school's trade training.

THE ROBBINSDALE SYSTEM

Robbinsdale, a suburb which immediately adjoins Minneapolis, illustrates a school rehabilitation program in which the school operates no rehabilitation facility but in which the facilities of a highly developed urban community are available. The Robbinsdale school district serves a student body of over 25,000. It has a cooperative agreement with state rehabilitation agency whereby two vocational adjustment coordinators make the services of the state agency available within the district. For student evaluation going beyond its own guidance program, the Robbinsdale school rehabilitation program makes use of the Anoka Work Adjustment Center, a large and sophisticated rehabilitation center in Minneapolis, and some of the services of the regional Vocational Rehabilitation Project located in the Industrial Relations Center of the University of Minnesota. Each of these three major resources has a distinctive theory of employability. The Anoka facility has, as has been noted, been oriented on trait psychology and trade areas. The rehabilitation center in Minneapolis is fairly eclectic but organizes some of its evaluation procedures around of a theory of critical vocational behaviors; in this theory, employability consists of emitting behaviors which are dealt with directly rather than being attributed to such internal constructs as attitude, emotional syndromes, or even aptitude. The Industrial Relations Center has a well developed theory of work adjustment (Dawis, Loftquist, and Weiss; 1968). The paper and pencil instrumentation of the theory essentially rules out the direct use of work sample techniques. When the Robbinsdale school rehabilitation program needs to have vocational evaluations conducted in any of the community facilities, these evaluations are purchased by the state rehabilitation agency. Their most usual purpose is to delineate training potential or job placement possibility. By their senior year almost all of the mentally retarded students served in the Robbinsdale school district are in a work-study program. The evaluation aspects of these job placements are relatively minor since they come too late in the students career to impact substantially upon his educational diagnosis, and the observation and report methods are largely informal.

VOCATIONAL EVALUATION IN RURAL EDUCATIONAL SETTINGS

Rural Minnesota is served variously. Many of the areas in the state are satelite to the urban centers in the matter of vocational evaluation. Generally speaking, vocational evaluation in the rural areas is obtained by the state vocational rehabilitation counselor who serves the area or who is associated with the school district on a cooperative basis. The evaluation is generally purchased from the rehabilitation facilities and is usually obtained after or near the end of the student's school career, too late to make substantial impact upon curriculum assignment. Actual work placements are often used in the home communities, sometimes within the school facilities themselves. The community job placement are typically made in the twelfth grade or near the time of the student's earlier departure from school with the major focus upon transition to employment rather than upon vocational evaluation.

Interdistrict cooperatives in special education and in vocational education have come to cover pretty much the entire state of Minnesota. As these cooperatives assemble need and resource over a larger area, they tend to become more sophisticated in the use of many technologies. The technology of vocational evaluation is prominent among these.

SERVICES OF *SERVE*

SERVE is a mechanism that appears to have unusual vitality and growth potential in Minnesota. The acronym stands for Special Education-Rehabilitation-Vocational Education and is so named because it combines the resources of these three kinds of program. SERVE is not exactly a program itself but rather is the administrative vehicle whereby a program is provided. At the time of this writing, it exists in the eastern portion of the Twin Cities metropolitan area, including St. Paul and its surrounding suburbs. A SERVE publication may be quoted to show the strong relationship between the administrative structure and the topic of this chapter: What does the youngster get? A set of general learnings at the secondary level in concert with his abilities, interests, and aptitudes, all of which are geared to life adjustment and the world of work; introduction to work experience at the pre-vocational level; access to specialized and community services such as job sampling, OJT, community laboratory experiences, work adjustment, evaluation and training in rehabilitation facilities; access to post-school community services such as trade schools, business colleges; and induction into employment with ongoing follow-up. The three major resources designated in the SERVE acronym are assembled primarily in terms of regulation and funding with the administration of the program coming to a head in a special education council drawn from its thirteen-member school districts. As is indicated by the quotation, SERVE draws upon a variety of settings in which to offer the vocational evaluation and initially was quite eclectic in its theoretical approach. More recently it has adopted a formal orientation focussing upon vocational behaviors and is conducting inservice training of its staff along that line. The front-line staff, in addition to the traditional school and community facility personnel, are work-study coordinators.

Vocational education in the State of Minnesota illustrates the interweaving among the many influences described so far. The vocational behaviors scheme, being adopted by SERVE, is drawn from a recently completed experimental instrument designed for the State Vocational Education Division. The instrument is a vocational behaviors scale in some twenty-five dimensions of behavior, each of which is scored at one of three levels (inadequate, adequate for sheltered employment, adequate for competitive employment). The manual of the scale calls attention to the resources of vocational evaluation and work adjustment and contains such statements as, "The behavior (of accepting supervision) centers upon that role relationship. If your training program offers no setting in which this supervisor-subordinate role is carried out, then you might question how completely it can prepare people for work," and "Another possibility that you should not overlook is that maybe you have not observed the student in this dimension of behavior and should take steps to do so." Training institutes in the use of this scale are scheduled to be carried out throughout the state during the coming year with the corresponding implication that vocational education of handicapped students has some relationship to vocational evaluation.

ISSUES IN EVALUATION IN EDUCATIONAL SETTINGS

That lengthy recitation of Minnesota programs is not exhaustive. There are even more patterns of service in existence than are described here. Other states may have more diversity, or less. The point is that a great deal of diversity exists even within a single state. The activity relating to vocational evaluation in the public schools touches upon enough issues so that some of them should be discussed. At the least the following considerations are brought to mind by the illustrations.

One of the issues is the extent to which vocational evaluation as a technology can contribute to an educational diagnosis. This issue strikes at the heart of one's conceptualization of the proper role of the schools. If the role of the schools is to carry out the procedures which they have traditionally performed, then vocational evaluation cannot contribute to an educational diagnosis. On the other hand, one may define education as being whatever learning program is required to prepare the individual for participation in life. Then the vocational diagnosis, with the technology of vocational evaluation which serves as a tool of that diagnosis, is also an educational matter. To the extent that vocational preparation is the business of the public schools and to the extent that there are students not adequately served by a guidance program built around the college preparatory model, vocational evaluation can be a tool of educational diagnosis.

Another issue has to do with the validity and effectiveness of the evaluation technology as it is practiced. Vocational evaluation in the public schools is too often characterized by a great deal of face validity and very little other formal validation. The evaluation procedures look valid. On the other hand, formal predictive, construct, or even concurrent validity studies are exceptional rather than the rule. Public schools are primarily service organizations. Their place in the social structure is relatively secure, and their caseloads are obtained by fiat rather than by competition. In such a circumstance and in the absence of specific allocation of R & D funds and personnel, research into the validation of internal procedures seldom gets carried out. (This is not only a problem in public schools, of course.)

Some reference to a theory of employability has surfaced in many of the illustrations. This may well be the basic issue. Some programs look for the employment traits of the individual, others look for the ability to learn specific trades, others assess internal adjustment or need structures, still others look for certain critical vocational behaviors. Procedural issues such as whether to use actual work or abstract work sample are much less fundamental than is the issue of theory. The diversity of the theories of employability is really what lies behind diversity of program procedures. It is too early to settle the issue of a theory of employability because, to put it bluntly, no single theory has yet proved itself to be clearly the best. Yet, there certainly should be some identifiable circumstances in which one theory or another is more useful. More tangibly, each program should have enough of a grasp of its own theory so that it can say what it looks for in evaluation, what it proposes to treat in its service program, and what goals it hopes to help its students to reach; this is a theory of employability.

The illustrations have shown that administrative allegiance, nature of caseload, degree of sophistication, and degree of coordination with community resources all are matters that somehow get settled in a particular way in each location. Perhaps these matters are not issues, perhaps they are merely options whose selection can be arbitrary without damage to the program. Perhaps, on the other hand, they constitute a whole complex of options that together make up an issue. If so, the issue can be stated in some such terms as, "Which of society's agents—the schools themselves or other existing agencies or perhaps agencies that do not now exist—should carry this responsibility?" If that issue is resolved, then the other elements in the complex can be approached from at least a secure base of responsibility.

Other issues have not surfaced with quite the same visibility as those just mentioned. They are likely to become issues in the future, however.

The limits of the utility of vocational evaluation are likely to become an issue. The schools are increasingly being called upon to deal with the kind of student who could previously be discarded, and this brings into the school guidance systems the students who are poorly testable by paper and pencil methods. Vocational evaluation shows promise of being able to test the untestable person, but the question remains as to the utility of doing assessment at all on the vocational diagnostic model for these new kinds of persons. The retarded and the distinctly disabled, those who by reason of disability face a vocational problem in which the choice of occupation is critical, may well be served by a prescriptive vocational diagnosis which points to a highly specific rehabilitation plan. On the other hand, the schools are increasingly coming to grips with students whose problem is not that of a sharply restricted set of vocational options. Does the technology of vocational evaluation have utility in the life of this kind of students? Are its resources best devoted to evaluation or (if there is a distinction) to exploration? These are empirical questions, the answers to which must be given on the basis of systematic observation and program research.

If substantial expansion in this activity takes place, another issue will arise. It will be the issue of whether a vocational evaluation focused upon problems within the individual is the most helpful approach as caseloads expand and thereby make an impact upon the total manpower economy. As long as vocational evaluation is applied to an insignificant percentage of the labor force, it is possible for the evaluator to concern himself with the characteristics of the individual and with maximizing the individual in relation to a fixed manpower system. When the percentage increases greatly, however, the impact of the sheer volume of clients served makes it impossible for the manpower economy to remain constant. Such a significant expansion seems likely to come about if the schools find vocational evaluation to be a helpful technique in dealing with the guidance of a substantial proportion of the student body, since the schools cannot limit their concern to the relatively few people who carry neat disability labels. Should the schools turn out students maximally adapted to function in a manpower structure which has no numerical room for them? Will vocational evaluation only generate courses of action which serve as equalizers of student characteristics and thereby change the identification but not the absolute number of those who cannot find a place in the manpower economy? These questions must also be faced by practitioners of more conventional assessment methods, of course, and the answers are of urgent interest to all Americans.

It may be in the schools that this next issue will be joined most conclusively. This is the issue of the scope of outcome against which the evaluation questions are addressed. In the past and in settings other than the public schools, vocational evaluation often had the option of saying something like, "This client is not feasible." In the schools, no such option exists. Every person is going to have some kind of life outcome, and the question posed to the evaluator is more like, "What is the optimum kind of outcome to which we can address our service program to this person?" This forces the evaluator to think in broader occupational terms. For example, the evaluator will need to know what are the demands placed upon a person and the capability he must show in order for him to function in a work activity setting. The evaluator will also need to know how to describe a course of educational-vocational action that will enable a severely limited person to function optimally in constructive home occupation. It is in the schools that the vocational evaluator must have a broad vision, because he has neither the moral sanction nor the societal mandate to discard clients who lack potential for the few outcomes valued by some other kinds of agencies.

Finally, issue or not, there is the matter of the identity and visability of vocational evaluation programs in the public schools. Many of the practitioners and program designers are only incidentally identified with the technology and are out of its main stream. Some of them are not aware that it can be both technically difficult and powerful and that, although vocational evaluation is not completely mature, neither is it completely primitive. The practitioner and program designer in the public schools can too easily be by-passed by technological progress and can end up reinventing the wheel. More aggressive professional communications and much less parochialism regarding setting is needed. The responsibility lies with those professional people who have already identified themselves as the scientists and the practitioners in the technology of vocational evaluation.

REFERENCES

Dawis, R., Loftquist, L., Weiss, D.: *A Theory of Work Adjustment* (a revision). Work Adjustment Project, Industrial Relations Center. Minneapolis, University of Minnesota, 1968.

Gordon, J.: *Testing, Counseling and Supportive Services for Disadvantaged Youth*. Institute of Labor and Industrial Relations. Ann Arbor, Michigan University and Wayne State University, 1969.

Gunzburg, H. C.: *The Social Education First Aid Teaching Set*. London, SEFA Publications, 1964.

XV

A MODEL FOR VOCATIONAL EVALUATION OF THE DISADVANTAGED

Julian M. Nadolsky

>>

Introduction
Development of a Model For the Vocational of the Disadvantaged
Discussion
Summary
Conclusions
References

>>

INTRODUCTION

A LTHOUGH VOCATIONAL EVALUATION can assist effectively in the vocational planning for any individual (handicapped or nonhandicapped), such programs have been confined primarily to the rehabilitation scene. However, during recent years, and especially since the passage of the 1968 amendments to the Vocational Rehabilitation Act, many agencies outside of rehabilitation have incorporated practical vocational evaluation methods into their programs for the culturally disadvantaged. Most of these programs are supported by the Manpower Administration, United States Deaprtment of Labor, and include the many Concentrated Employment Programs (CEP), Work Incentive Now (WIN), Job Corps, and Neighborhood Youth Corps programs located in both rural and urban areas throughout the country. In working with the culturally disadvantaged, the Manpower Administration has maintained an active interest in the practical, realistic approach to vocational evaluation as employed in rehabilitation. It has sponsored the development and validation of a work sample battery (Jewish Employment and Vocational Service, 1968) for use with the culturally disadvantaged and is currently under contract with the Jewish Employment and Vocational Service (J.E.V.S.) to provide training to manpower personnel in the use of the J.E.V.S. Work Sample System. Although the J.E.V.S. Work Sample System is a recent innovation in vocational evaluation, it is extensively used to evaluate the vocational suitability of the culturally disadvantaged in programs supported by the Manpower Administration. This system has not yet become an integral part of vocational evaluation programs in rehabilitation since the distribution of the J.E.V.S. system is limited to those individuals who have had specific training in its use. Due to contract obligations and staff limitations, training in the use of the J.E.V.S. Work Sample System is primarily confined to those indiivduals who are responsible for its operation and application in WIN, CEP, and Job Corps programs.

Although vocational evaluation programs have been in existence for several decades in this country, to date, it remains undetermined whether such programs are governed by a shared and cohesive   body of knowledge. Separate summarizations of the vocational evaluation process by Moed (1960) and Neff (1968) revealed that five different approaches are employed by vocational evaluators in rehabilitation. These five approaches include:

(1) the mental or psychological testing approach,
(2) the job analysis approach,
(3) the work sample approach,
(4) the situational approach, and
(5) the job tryout approach.

Although these five approaches are not distinct, self-limiting entities, their existence suggests that vocational evaluators have emphasized the use of differential methodology and criteria to perform their daily work.

Most of the vocational evaluation programs in rehabilitation

were designed for individuals who were vocationally handicapped or disadvantaged as a result of physical, emotional, or mental
impairment. On the other hand, the majority of individuals evaluated under the various manpower programs are vocationally
handicapped or disadvantaged in the absence of physical, emotional, or mental impairment. Such individuals are vocationally
handicapped or disadvantaged as a consequence of a general inability to understand the meaning and nature of the social structure and a lack of those educational and social experiences which
are pertinent and essential to full participation within society.
Unlike the physically, emotionally, and mentally handicapped,
most of the relevant life experiences of the socially and culturally
disadavantaged have occurred outside the social mainstream.
Consequently, it is questionable whether vocational evaluation
programs designed for a disabled, but culturally consistent, population can be readily and successfully employed with a population of non-disabled individuals who are handicapped as a consequence of inadequate social integration.

At this point in time, vocational evaluation is primarily confined to rehabilitation and manpower programs since such programs are designed to assist disabled and disadvantaged individuals in their pursuit of an appropriate and meaningful vocation.
Altough five approaches have been identified as being basic to the
field of vocational evaluation, no single approach maintains a
regulatory effect over the entire field. Since there is little evidence to support the effectiveness of one approach over the other,
consideration must be given to all of the basic approaches in the
development of a vocational evaluation model. Due to differences
in the degree of social integration among the disabled and the
disadvantaged, it remains undetermined whether existing programs, methods, and techniques of vocational evaluation can
readily and effectively meet the assessment demands of the disadvantaged. The manner in which these methods and techniques
can be integrated into a unified, pertinent model for vocational
evaluation also remains to be determined.

The purpose of this study was to develop a model for the vocational evaluation of the disadvantaged. In order to maintain

consistency with current practices and to assure program continuity, the development of a vocational evaluation model for the disadvantaged should encompass all of the relevant methodology which is considered to be appropriate and effective for the target population. Consequently, it was imperative to focus upon the assets and limitations of current vocational evaluation methodology, both within and outside the domain of rehabilitation. By so doing, an attempt was made to review all aspects of the vocational evaluation process and the content, purpose, and sequential application of its related techniques and procedures within various rehabilitation and manpower programs throughout the country.

In order to gather descriptive data on the four basic approaches that were common to vocational evaluation, the workshop participants were assigned to one of four subgroups based upon the vocational evaluation approach utilized by their facility. Each subgroup was assigned a group leader and provided with a list of suggested topics for discussion. The responses of each subgroup, to the various discussion topics were recorded and were analyzed separately. The results of these analyses are reported below.

Psychological Testing Approach. The subgroup which utilized a psychological testing approach to vocational evaluation reported that the goals or objectives of any vocational evaluation program were to assess the intellectual, social, medical, and emotional assets and limitations of an individual and to relate those findings to a suitable vocational objective. The same basic goals should be followed for any population, whether that population is physically disabled or culturally disadvantaged. Psychological tests can assist in fulfilling these goals by providing objective measures of the degree to which an individual possesses various traits and skills, such as intellectual ability, aptitude, interests, personality or temperament, dexterity, level of emotional and social adjustment, and academic skills.

It was reported that psychological tests were not appropriate for use with the disadvantaged, although many tests were widely used in the vocational evaluation process with this population.

The psychological tests most commonly used included:

1. *Intelligence Tests:* the Wechsler Adult Intelligence Scale (WAIS), the Wechsler Intelligence Scale for Children (WISC), the Peabody Picture Vocabulary Test, the Revised Beta Examination, and the Army General Classification Test (AGCT).

2. *Aptitude Tests:* The General Aptitude Test Battery (GATB), the Differential Aptitude Test (DAT), the Minnesota Clerical Test, and the Bennett Test of Mechanical Comprehension.

3. *Achievement Tests:* the Wide Range Achievement Test (WRAT) and the Gates-MacGinitie Reading Test.

4. *Interest Tests:* the California Picture Interest Inventory and the Kuder Preference Record.

5. *Personality Tests:* the Edwards Personal Preference Schedule, the Minnesota Multiphasic Personality Inventory (MMPI), and the Taylor-Johnson Temperament Analysis.

6. *Dexterity Tests:* the Purdue Pegboard, the Minnesota Rate of Manipulation Test, the Crawford Small Parts Dexterity Test, the O'Connor Finger Dexterity Test, and the Bennett Hand-Tool Dexterity Test.

7. *Projective Techniques:* the Rorschach, the Thematic Apperception Test (TAT), the House-Tree-Person Projective Technique (HTP), and the Rotter Incomplete Sentences Blank.

8. *Other Tests:* the Bender-Gestalt Test, the Memory For Designs Test, the Vineland Social Maturity Scale, and the McDonald Vocational Capacity Scale.

Most psychological tests are designed for a *middle class* or *average* population. When used with a disadvantaged population, psychological tests often induce an unrealistic, unfamiliar, and artificial atmosphere which creates a barrier to successful performance on the tests. In addition, the abstract nature of most psychological tests may provoke anxiety and inhibit motivation to the extent that a client may either terminate his vocational evaluation program or markedly restrict his functioning within that program.

In order to lessen the undesirable effects of phychological

tests with a disadvantaged population, the following procedures should be employed:

1. Prior to administering psychological tests, provide the client with an orientation to the entire vocational evaluation process. The role of psychological testing (as only one of many procedures used during this process) must be clearly explained during this orientation.

2. Administer the easiest or less involved tests first so that anxiety is minimized.

3. In order to lessen fatigue and frustration, limit the testing periods to approximately three hours.

4. If possible, tests should be administered individually. This allows for individual adaptation and observation while increasing the opportunity for a client to understand the tests.

5. When necessary, test instructions must be altered, varied or clarified so that the client understands the test that follows. However, once the client has begun working on the actural test further instructions should be avoided unless specified in the test manual.

6. Psychological tests may be readministered only if alternate forms are available or if a similar (but not the same) instrument is used for the second administration. The scores obtained on readministration would probably be a more accurate estimate of the client's measured trait(s) since he will have had the opportunity to become familiar with test procedures. Rather than relying upon tests readministration procedures, it would be advisable to use an instrument such as the Test Orientation Procedure (published by the Psychological Corporation) to familiarize disadvantaged clients with the format of psychological tests. Although it is possible to plot the results of several test readministrations on a learning curve, most tests do not possess sufficient length or breadth to demonstrate meaningful trends on a learning curve.

7. In interpreting test results to disadvantaged clients, emphasis should be placed upon the positive aspects of the client's performance. The relationship between specific test scores and general occupational requirements should be stressed. It is imperative to interpret the results of psycho-

logical tests in nontechnical language so that the client understands the rationale behind the selection and use of specific in-depth evaluation techniques and procedures. The vocational evaluation process becomes meaningful to the client only if he understands what he is doing and why it is being done.

Psychological tests are a primary and basic technique in the vocational evaluation process within rehabilitation. Due to their inherent advantages psychological tests will continue to receive widespread application among vocational evaluators. Conversely, as a result of the limitations or disadvantages of psychological tests other techniques and procedures are also essential to the vocational evaluation of the culturally disadvantaged. The major advantages of using psychological tests in vocational evaluation of the culturally disadvantaged include:

1. Their ability to provide relatively quick, inexpensive, and objective measures of a client's general abilities and limitations.

2. Their ability to diagnose specific problem areas (i.e., brain damage, reading deficit, hypomania, and other characteristics) so that appropriate treatment or remedial programs can be established.

3. Psychological test results can assist the evaluator in the decision-making process by lending objective support to personal observations and to the reports obtained from other staff. They can also negate observational and report data and lead to a more thorough understanding of the individual.

4. The use of psychological tests in vocational evaluation provides a direct orientation to our *test laden* world.

The major disadvantages of using psychological tests in the vocational evaluation of the culturally disadvantaged include:

1. The unfair, *middle class* content and context of most tests.

2. The anxiety-provoking nature of most test situations.

3. The irrelevance of most test instruments to the actual job situation.

4. Their questionable validity and reliability for a disadvantaged population.

It was reported that psychological tests were capable of providing certain types of information that could not be obtained from other evaluative techniques and procedures. They could assist in defining the area and level of disadvantagement, and could determine the underlying emotional factors which must be considered in vocational planning. They could also determine the actual level of previous achievement and provide clues relative to the degree and direction of client motivation.

If properly used, psychological tests can assist the vocational evaluator in his understanding of each client as an individual. Such an understanding enables the evaluator to establish and maintain an appropriate and meaningful program of vocational evaluation for each individual client. A program based upon understanding reduces the chance of voluntary, premature termination on the part of the client and increases the probability of success in evaluation and in a subsequent job.

Work Sample Approach. The subgroup which utilized a work sample approach to vocational evaluation reported that the goals or objectives of any vocational evaluation program were to determine the specific assets and limitations of each client as an individual (including medical, psychological, social, educational, and other assets and limitations) and to relate these findings to appropriate vocational objectives. A subsequent goal of vocational evaluation was to outline the specific services that must be provided in order for the client to attain the recommended vocational objective. Vocational evaluation programs should maintain the same basic goals or objectives for any population, although the specific methods and procedures employed will vary with the individual. Work samples can assist in fulfilling these goals by determining an individual's ability to function within a variety of vocational areas while providing the evaluee with direct feedback relative to his performance in these vocational areas. Consequently, work samples can provide both the evaluator and the evaluee with first-hand information about the evaluee's ability to function within a variety of controlled occupational settings.

Since work samples are in-depth evaluation techniques designed around specific areas of work, they should not be used until the evaluator has acquired a general understanding of the vocational assets and limitations of his client. The selection of specific work samples should be based upon this understanding and should be relevant to the client's vocational interest and ability. Although work samples should be differentially selected for each client, all work samples are used to assess the client's ability to function within specific areas of work.

It was felt that many commercially distributed work samples were appropriate for use with disadvantaged clients. The most popular and well-known work samples were those encompassed within the TOWER system and the Jewish Employment and Vocational Service (JEVS) System of vocational evaluation. Although all of the work samples within either of these systems are not appropriate for use with all disadvantaged clients, many of them are directly applicable to this population. It was felt that many of the existing work samples could be effectively used with the disadvantaged if their instructional formats were altered from a *reading* format to an audio-visual format. In adidtion, this sub-group reported that a variety of *homemade* work samples and simulated tasks (which present practical work situations to the client) are currently used by most vocational evaluators.

Work samples are designed to assess the global behavior of an individual as he relates to the basic duties, equipment, and tools of a particular occupational area within a controlled environment. The work sample instructions must provide a clear and detailed explanation of the work environment structure, of the tools and equipment to be used, and of the specific tasks to be performed. If the occupational area under consideration normally requires reading ability or the ability to follow diagrams, such procedures should be incorporated into the work sample instructions. On the other hand, if the occupational area does not require reading ability, the work sample instructions should be presented orally. Instructions for existing work samples may be altered for the disadvantaged if such alteration is consistent with the normal demands of the occupational area.

Work samples should be selected for each client on the basis of previously obtained information derived from psychological tests, biographical data, and the evaluation interview. For this reason, the type and number of work samples that should be administered to a given client will depend upon the specific assessment needs of that client. Needless to say, the number of days that a client should be involved in work sample assessment will vary.

Prior to administering a work sample, the evaluator should provide a brief orientation to the work sample so that the client understands its purpose, structure, and limitations. He must be certain that the client understands the procedures involved in performing the work sample tasks and that all of the necessary equipment, tools, and materials are readily available to the client. Although it is imperative for the evaluator to observe the client's performance throughout the work sample, he should not provide direct supervision on each operation. Rather, the evaluator must give the client an opportunity to express himself (his vocational assets and limitations) in action as he performs the work sample. The evaluator must provide the client with the freedom to perform the work sample in his own personal way.

Both the process and the product should be considered in work sample scoring. Primary emphasis should be placed upon process scoring since such scoring enables the evaluator to understand the manner in which an individual relates to the work sample tools and equipment, to its duties, and do its instructions. Product scoring lends itself to objectivity, but does not take into consideration such factors as individual initiative, adaptability, or creativity. The goal of work sample assessment is not to create a final product, but to gain an understanding of an individual's potential for employment within various occupational areas. Since the process, rather than the product, should be emphasized in work sample scoring it is usually unnecessary to readminister work samples.

Due to the practical, realistic design of most work samples, a client is provided with immediate and direct feedback as he responds to the work sample tasks. Consequently, in the ongoing performance of a work sample most clients gain some insight into their ability to function within particular occupational areas. Although the acquisition of direct insight reduces the amount of interpretation required of the vocational evaluator, interpretation of work sample results is necessary to clarify misconceptions and to pinpoint specific client assets and liabilities within each occupational area. Work sample interpretation is also necessary in order for the evaluator to communicate to the client his understanding of the client's performance.

The interpretation of work sample results to disadvantaged clients can be effectively accomplished by emphasizing the positive aspects of a client's performance and by comparing his performance on work samples within different occupational areas. For many clients, the results obtained on work samples provides the evaluator with sufficient information to enable him to make appropriate and meaningful vocational recommendations. With other clients, the results of work samples do not provide conclusive evidence upon which to base vocational recommendations, although these results usually demonstrate the existence of certain strengths and weaknesses within specific occupational areas. If properly used, the information obtained from work samples can establish a basis for continued in-depth evaluation within specific occupations. These results can pinpoint the specific job tryouts and situational tasks that would be most appropriate and meaningful for further in-depth evaluation.

It was reported that the major advantages of using work samples in a program of vocational evaluation for the culturally disadvantaged include:

(1) the practical, realistic nature of such instruments and
(2) the immediate, direct feedback offered to the client throughout the duration of the work sample task. A work sample heightens the opportunity for self-understanding since it enables the client to gage his own performance as he responds to the task.

Two major limitations of work samples with the culturally disadvantaged were reported. These include:

(1) the possible difficulty that a client may encounter in relating the work sample to an actual job and

(2) the inability of most work samples to submit to a comparative study of their results. In other words, it is virtually impossible for vocation evaluators to meaningfully compare the performance of several clients who have been exposed to the same work sample. This latter limitation relates directly to the global nature of a work sample and to the *subjective* methods employed in process scoring.

In summary, it was felt that work samples can provide certain types of information that cannot be obtained from other sources. They can give an indication of an individual's ability to work within the limits of a structured situation. They can also provide information on a client's ability to follow instructions and to use the basic tools required in a particular occupational area. It is through the media of work samples that many disadvantaged clients encounter their first experience with occupational requirements and with the tools, equipment, and duties encompassed within relevant occupations.

Situation Approach. The subgroup which utilized a situational approach to vocational evaluation reported that the goals or objectives of any vocational evaluation program were to determine the feasibility of employment for each client and to enable the client to become aware of the vocational world as it relates to his physical and mental capabilities. In addition, vocational evaluation should result in specific recommendations for treatment, training, or direct entry into a suitable vocation. Although the goals of vocational evaluation are the same for any population, this subgroup felt that a disadvantaged population may require initial and ongoing orientation procedures in order to establish and maintain a program which is relevant to the stated objectives. Situational tasks can assist in the achievement of the above-mentioned objectives by confronting the individual with the physical and mental demands of actual, rather than simulated, work. Through the use of situational tasks the evaluator is able to test tentative hypotheses about the client's vocational behavior by observing this behavior as the client performs in an actual work situation.

When working with the culturally disadvantaged, it may be

appropriate to utilize situational tasks fairly early in the evaluation process in order to provide a realistic orientation to vocational evaluation and to establish relevancy for the vocational evaluation process. However, situational tasks should be used primarily to test tentative hypotheses formulated from previously acquired information. For this reason, their major application would follow, and be based upon, the results of psychological tests, biographical data, the evaluation interview, and work samples. The major goal or objective of situational tasks in vocational evaluation is to provide the evaluator with supplemental information about the client's actual vocational behavior within a controlled, but completely realistic, work setting. Information obtained on realistic situational tasks would be compared with his performance on the more abstract psychological tests and the simulated, but less realistic, work samples. Consequently, the results of situational tasks would be used mainly to confirm, reject, or alter tentative hypotheses about a client's vocational behavior.

It was felt that most situational tasks would be appropriate for use with a disadvantaged population, but that the most appropriate tasks would be those which provide monetary reward for the work performed. In order to be appropriate and meaningful for most clients, situational tasks must include not only traditional assembly operations, but also a variety of machine tending, clerical, maintenance, and service tasks.

The goal of situational assessment in vocational evaluation is to observe work behavior. For this reason, primary emphasis should be placed upon the process employed by a client in performing the job task, rather than upon the level of production attained. However, it is important to obtain a measure of the client's production capability (both in terms of quantity and quality) so that vocational recommendations will be appropriate. When necessary, situational tasks may be readministered several times and the level of production attained on each administration can be plotted on a learning curve. By using such procedure, the evaluator can gain an understanding of a client's production capabilities, his frustration tolerance, and the effects of fatigue upon work performance.

Prior to administering situational tasks, the purpose of the task should be carefully explained to the client so that he understands its relationship to the remainder of the vocational evaluation process. Consequently, the introduction of each situational task should be preceded by an explanation of the relationship between that task's purpose and the client's performance on particular psychological tests and work samples. Likewise, the interpretation of the results of situational tasks should be related to the client's demonstrated abilities on psychological tests and work samples. These results should also be interpreted in terms of their relationship to job criteria and to the client's potential for success in similar competitive occupations.

The major advantages of situational assessment include the realistic nature of its work tasks and the one-to-one relationship of these tasks to community occupations. Situational tasks are highly appropriate in vocational evaluation programs for the disadvantaged since they enable the client to express himself vocationally within a realistic, but sheltered, environment. The major limitations or disadvantages of situational assessment include the vast amount of time, effort, and space required to locate and set up an adequate number of appropriate, ongoing tasks within a particular facility. In addition, most of the data derived from situational tasks are based upon subjective observations of work behavior which are often difficult to quantify.

Situational tasks are often the only vocational evaluation technique to offer an opportunity for behavior observation within an environment where many variables operate simultaneously. The element of combined and uncontrolled variables may elicit work behavior responses which have not been previously observed. Thus, the uniqueness of situational assessment lies in its capacity to create work behavior observations in a realistic, semistructured, contolled work environment.

Job Tryout Approach. The subgroup which utilized a job tryout approach to vocational evaluation reported that the goals or objectives of any vocational evaluation program were to assess the client's current level of functioning and his potential to achieve maximum self-fulfillment in life through the attainment of a meaningful vocational goal. The vocational evaluation process encompasses an assessment of the client's personality, attitudes, aptitudes, work traits, work skills, and physical capacities. The same basic goals or objectives are applicable to any population. Job tryouts can assist in the fulfillment of these goals or objectives by providing an assessment of the client's capacity, as a total personality, to function in a real work situation that is consistent with a previously determined vocational objective.

Job tryouts should be employed during the latter stages of the vocational evaluation process, after the evaluator has gained a clear understanding of the client's level of functioning and has established some tentative vocational objectives which are consistent with this level of functioning. Consequently, the primary goal of job tryouts in vocational evaluation is to verify the tentative vocational objectives or hypotheses established by the vocational evaluator. Job tryout results are used to confirm, reject, or alter tentative vocational objectives and to lend further support to the decision-making process.

Although any type of job tryout within existing vocational training programs or community occupations are appropriate for use with the culturally disadvantaged, the selection and use of specific job tryouts will be highly dependent upon their availability, their suitability for particular clients, and the evaluator's need for further specific information. In order to effectively use job tryouts within the vocational evaluation process, the evaluator must function as a coordinator between the client and the job tryout supervisor. He must communicate to both the supervisor and the client his rationale for selecting and using specific job tryouts. In order to minimize the effects of supervisor biases, the evaluator must explain each variable that is to be observed and reported on by the job tryout supervisor. For maximum benefit, the evaluator should provide the supervisor with a check list or rating scale form through which observations may be structured and recorded. Prior to placing the client on a job tryout, the evaluator should explain his reason for selecting that particular job tryout and inform him of the basic demands of that job.

Since the technique of job tryout is used to verify hypotheses formulated by the vocational evaluator, the number of different job tryouts used will vary with the client. For most clients, job tryouts will be unnecessary since the vocational evaluator should be able to base vocational recommendation upon the results of psychological tests, work samples, biographical data, observations, and the evaluation interview. The length of a specific job tryout will vary with the client and with the complexity of the job. However, if properly structured, most job tryouts should not exceed a one week period of time.

Job tryouts are employed to assess global behavior in an actual job situation. For this reason, primary emphasis should be placed upon evaluating global client behavior in that work situation. Emphasis is placed upon an evaluation of the process that the client goes through, rather than upon the completion of a final product. Since the emphasis is on process evaluation, it is unnecessary to readminister the same job tryout. The results of job tryouts should be interpreted to the client by integrating these findings with the results of psychological tests and work samples. Through the integration and synthesis of all pertinent information, the client is able to understand the rationale behind the experiences encountered during the entire vocational evaluation process and the reasons for success or failure in particular vocational areas.

This subgroup reported that the major advantages of a job tryout approach to vocational evaluation include the realistic nature of the work situation and the direct relationship of the job tryout to a specific occupation. In addition to providing the evaluator with valid information about a client's ability to function within a specific occupation, the job tryout enables the client to experience the job as it actually exists in the competitive labor market. When properly used, job tryouts can effectively assist disadvantaged clients in understanding the realities of work and the particular demands of those specific occupations under consideration.

The major disadvantages of job tryouts in vocational evaluation include the limited availability of job tryout sites, the amount of coordination required to effectively establish and utilize job tryouts, and the time consuming natue of the job tryout technique. This latter observation is especially true when several job tryouts are employed with a particular client. In addition, the results obtained from job tryouts are dependent upon the competency of the job tryout supervisor and the demands of a given job tryout site. Since the specific requirements of the same occupation will vary from one establishment to another, the results obtained on job tryouts may not have universal application. The widespread use of job tryouts in vocational evaluation may result in a duplication of effort and a repetitious review of capacities and skills which were previously assessed. Consequently, vocational evaluation programs designed for the culturally disadvantaged should employ job tryouts on a selective basis so that motivation and interest will be maintained and enhanced throughout the entire vocational evaluation process.

By focusing upon the content and methodology of vocational evaluation, the results of this study reflect the present nature and scope of the vocational evaluation process as applied in rehabilitation and manpower programs. Through the analysis, synthesis, and logical ordering of these results, a model for vocational evaluation can be developed to clarify and explain the relationship between the various observed phenomena.

DEVELOPMENT OF A MODEL FOR THE VOCATIONAL EVALUATION OF THE DISADVANTAGED

The results of this study revealed that the primary objective of most vocational evaluation programs was to determine the vocational potential of each client evaluated and to establish vocational goals that were consistent with this potential. In other words most vocational evaluation programs surveyed were designed to evaluate each client as an individual and to relate their findings to the world of work. They did not confine their programs to a few specific vocational areas, nor limit client involvement to a few predetermined areas of vocational choice. Rather, the initial emphasis was upon uncovering the specific assets and limitations of each individual and relating these results to possible areas of vocational involvement. On the basis of the initial findings, each client was provided with appropriate practical tasks and activities through which he could gain a better understanding of the vocational areas under consideration and portray, in action, his ability to function within these areas. Consequently, each client was provided with an opportunity for self-evaluation, rather than being vocationally categorized by a second party.

The same general types of vocational evaluation techniques and procedures provided the core content for most programs surveyed. Furthermore, it was felt that these same general techniques and procedures were applicable to any population, regardless of whether disabled or disadvantaged. A systematic program of vocational evaluation would employ the ten techniques in the following sequence:

1. Biographical Data
2. The Evaluation Interview
3. Psychological Tests
4. Work Samples
5. Occupational Information
6. Situational or Workshop Tasks
7. Informal Conferences with Other Staff
8. Job Tryouts
9. The Formal Staff Conference
10. Vocational Counseling.

By combining the results of all vocational evaluation programs surveyed, a structural model can be developed for vocational evaluation which is essentially isomorphic with those critical aspects of observed reality. The model presented in Figure 1 is based upon a logical ordering of ten techniques and procedures which encompass the core content of vocational evaluation and which provide the structure for a systematic program of vocational evaluation.

Analysis of Figure 1 shows that the scope of vocational evaluation is broad and diverse since it encompasses the entire world of work. Consequently, vocational evaluation programs are, or should be, limited only by the types or varieties of occupations currently in existence within a given society. For maximum effec-

MODEL FOR VOCATIONAL EVALUATION
OF THE DISADVANTAGED

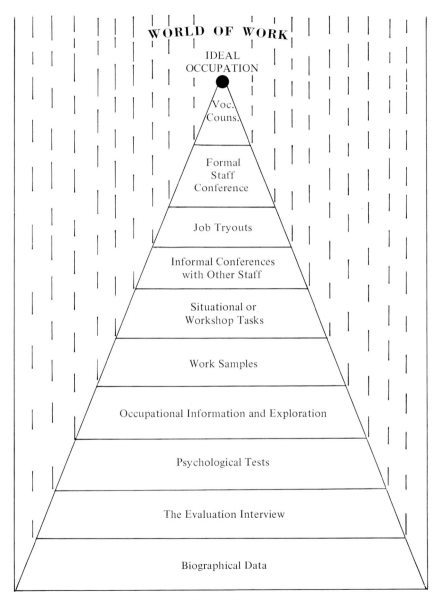

Figure XV-1.

tiveness, occupations within the world of work should be classified according to the similarity of their duties and their requirements for entry. The Occupational Group and the Worker Trait Classification System presented in Volume II of *The Dictionary of Occupational Titles,* Third Edition (1965) provides a meaningful structure for the classification of occupations within the United States. A similar publication is currently being prepared by the Canadian government.

Figure 1 indicates that the goal of vocational evaluation is to determine the most feasible or ideal occupation for each client evaluated. This occupation is one in which the client can comfortably achieve vocational success and through which he can realize his vocational potential. Due to individual differences in physical and mental ability, aptitude, interest, temperament, educational attainment, work experience, and vocational skill, the ideal occupation will be different for most clients evaluated.

The Model for Vocational Evaluation is based upon a logical narowing of vocational choice by and for each client through the elimination of occupations which are outside the realm of possible attainment. When a client is referred to vocational evaluation it must be assumed that he possesses the potential to succeed in any occupation within the world of work. This assumption must be made since the evaluator does not know the client and is unaware of his specific vocational assets and limitations. Thus, at the base of the figurative pyramid the client is viewed as an individual with unlimited capacity for involvement in the world of work. As the client moves through the vocational evaluation process, or upward on the pyramid, a logical narrowing of vocational choice occurs as a result of an increased awareness of his actual capacity to participate in the world of work.

The evaluator's task is to assist the client in determining those occupations or occupational groups that are appropriate for entry and the specific occupation in which optimum success can be anticipated. In order to systematically make this determination, the evaluator must first gain a general understanding of the client in his present situation. This initial understanding is attained through the collection and use of biographical data. The various types of biographical data are designed to identify the individual in his present situation by discovering the events and experinces in his past history that have served to create and mold his individuality. Based upon this initial identification, the evaluator is able to realistically eliminate certain occupations from consideration before the client is even encountered in a face-to-face relationship.

Once the client enters a vocational evaluation program, the evaluator must meet with him on some common ground in order to orient him to the program and to gain a better understanding of the client as an individual and as a potential worker. In addition to communicating the purpose and goals of vocational evaluation to the client, the evaluation interview is used to enhance the evaluator's understanding of the client through the verification of biographical data, the clarification of biographical data, or the acquisition of supplementary information. It is through the evaluation interview that biographical data becomes alive and meaningful. As a result of a more thorough understanding of the client's past history, present situation, and future aspirations it is possible to eliminate additional occupations from consideration.

The third step in vocational evaluation is designed to provide the evaluator with information about the degree to which the client possesses certain traits or abilities which are abstract in nature, but considered to be normally distributed among the general population. Psychological tests are used in vocational evaluation to heighten the evaluator's understanding of the client's general vocational assets and limitations. They provide objective data on the client's level of intelligence, aptitude, and educational attainment in relation to a normative group, and supply data on the specific interests and personality or temperament factors which underlie and motivate his overt behavior. Although most psychological tests do not relate directly to vocational criteria, they do assist the evaluator in logically eliminating those occupations from consideration whose general requirements are highly inconsistent with the obtained test results.

The same techniques and procedures that are employed during the initial stages of vocational evaluation (i.e., biographical data, the evaluation interview, and psychological tests) are basic to any traditional program of vocational assessment. Although these techniques and procedures constitute the core content of traditional vocational assessment programs, they are used by vocational evaluators merely to orient the client to the vocational evaluation process and to gain a general understanding of the client's vocational assets and limitations. The evaluator then utilizes this understanding to structure a program of vocational evaluation which is appropriate for, and meaningful to, each client.

Although the information obtained during the initial stages of vocational evaluation can best be characterized as being relevant primarily to the evaluator, a marked change in emphasis occurs during the fourth step of vocational evaluation. With the provision of occupational information and the utilization of occupational exploration procedures, emphasis is placed upon the client gaining an understanding of that portion of the world of work which is within, the realm of possible attainment. The client is confronted with the realities of appropriate occupations and is provided with the opportunity to explore these occupations and gain first-hand knowledge of their specific nature and demands.

During the past few years several well-designed, practical occupational exploration programs have become available to vocational evaluators through commercial firms such as Singer/Graflex, Mind Incorporated, and Science Research Associates. Although these programs provide excellent media for occupational exploration, similar benefits can occur through client exposure to the realities of specific occupations during planned site visits to appropriate industries. Regardless of the media used for occupational exploration, emphasis is placed upon the development of vocational awareness within the client. As the client gains first-hand knowledge of relevant occupations he adopts a decision-making role and personally narrows down the field of vocational choice.

Once a client is equipped with an awareness of that portion of the world of work which is meaningful to him and has made some tentative personal decisions about the areas of work that are of direct interest and concern, the vocational evaluation process moves into a stage of in-depth assessment on related practical tasks and activities. During this stage the client is confronted with his own vocational assets and limitations on job tasks that he puts into operation and maintains or performs in his own personal way. The most highly structured technique that provides the vehicle for confrontation is the work sample. The work sample is a structured evaluation technique which allows the client to participate fully in the evaluation process as an active partner. Throughout the duration of the work sample, the client's work behavior and his potential for success with specific occupational areas are portrayed in action.

In order to be of maximum benefit and to avoid duplication and redundancy, work samples should be structured around areas of work or occupational groups, rather than individual occupations. The two well-known work sample systems (the TOWER System and the JEVS Work Sample System) are based upon an occupational group concept. The TOWER System contains over 110 work samples which are organized within fourteen broad occupational groups; while the twenty-eight work samples incorporated into the JEVS System cover twenty different areas of work within ten worker trait groups.

Regardless of which work samples or work sample systems are employed, the emphasis is upon *confrontation:* a personal encounter with one's own vocational assets and limitations. As the client responds to each work sample task or activity he is required to activate his abilities in a manner that is meaningful to him and enables him to complete the task in his own personal way. In so doing, the client comes face-to-face with the realities of the occupational areas under consideration and with his own vocational abilities and deficiencies. It is through active confrontation that the opportunity for self-discovery and self-evaluation emerges.

As a result of an expanded self-awareness the client may make the decision to terminate his performance on the work sample, to use a different method of attack, or to continue his performance on the work sample with increased effort. If the evaluator understands the work sample and is a skilled observer he should readily detect the nature of the client's decision and its underlying reasons. Thus, in the ongoing performance of a work sample the subjective experiences of the client and the *objectives* observations of the evaluator should coincide with each other. The dual nature of this experiential encounter results in a logical elimination of certain occupational groups by both the client and the evaluator. It also enables the evaluator to formulate tentative hypotheses about the client's work behavior and vocational potential which may be tested through exposure to appropriate work situations or job tryouts.

Although situational tasks and job tryouts are both designed to test tentative hypotheses, these two evaluation techniques maintain markedly different specific goals or objectives. Situational tasks are used in vocational evaluation primarily to observe client work behavior in a realistic, semistructured, controlled work environment; while job tryouts are employed to assess the level of skill that a client possesses and expresses in an actual and specific job situation.

Situational tasks are usually provided through the media of subcontract operations in a semisheltered work environment. Although the client is placed on real work tasks and activities which closely resemble an industrial occupation, most of the tasks performed do not relate directly to a single occupation within the competitive labor market. Rather, the situational tasks derived from sub-contracts usually encompass a variety of routine, repetitive operations which are basic to the performance of several related occupations. In this respect, situational tasks resemble the occupational group orientation of work samples.

On the other hand, the job tryout is designed to confront the client with the realities of a specific occupation. The job tryout is usually accomplished through the placement of the client in a specific occupation within the community or in a specific vocational training program for a brief trial period. Thus, as the client moves upward on the figurative pyramid from the work sample, to the situational task, to the job tryout there is a logical movement toward specificity within the vocational evaluation process.

Situational tasks and job tryouts are an essential part of vocational evaluation when the evaluator does not feel sufficiently comfortable to make vocational recommendations that are based upon the established tentative hypotheses. In other words, they are used when the evaluator is uncertain of the client's actual work behavior and vocational potential and feels the need for specific supplemental information in order to confirm, reject, or alter his tentative hypotheses.

Situational tasks and job tryouts are not necessary for all vocational evaluation clients, but when they are employed it is essential for the evaluation to determine the exact reasons for their use and to communicate these reasons to the appropriate ancillary staff (i.e., the workshop director or the job tryout supervisor). Since other staff members usually supervise the client on situational tasks and job tryouts it is imperative that the evaluator establish and maintain effective lines of communication with these staff. He must establish tentative objectives for each client placed on situational tasks or job tryouts, communicate these objectives to both the client and the ancillary staff members, and receive appropriate feedback from all concerned. Consequently, it is necessary for the evaluator to confer with each staff member on an informal basis in order to obtain information which can lead to the confirmation, rejection, or alteration of his tentative hypotheses.

When the tentative hypotheses indicate the need for client exposure to both situational tasks and job tryouts, the client should be placed on appropriate situational tasks prior to arranging for job tryouts. The work behavior uncovered during situational assessment may have a significant bearing upon the evaluator's ability to structure appropriate job tryouts. Furthermore, the general work behavior information derived from situational assessment enables the evaluator to gain a more complete understanding of the job tryout results. As the evaluator acquires appropriate feedback from the ancillary supervisory staff he is able to confirm, reject, or alter his tentative hypotheses and logically narrow down the field of vocational choice.

When both the client and the evaluator have gained a clear understanding of the client's work behavior and vocational potential this information should be discussed with other professionals who have worked with the client and who will be involved in the implementation of vocational recommendations. The most common vehicle for the discussion of vocational evaluation results and for the planning of service implementation is the formal staff conference.

The vocational evaluator must assume a leadership role during the formal staff conference. He must not only present his findings on each client, but also ask pertinent questions and solicit relevant comments and suggestions from other staff. During the formal staff conference the vocational evaluator must determine whether there are any medical, social, or psychological contraindications which could have a significantly harmful effect upon the client's ability to function within the proposed occupational areas. He must also determine the extent to which his proposed or tentative vocational recommendations can be implemented. In short, the formal staff conference is designed to provide the evaluator with conclusive evidence about the overall feasibility of his tentative recommendations. By using the information gained during the formal staff conference the evaluator is able to eliminate certain occupations from consideration and formulate his final vocational recommendations.

Prior to terminating a client from vocational evaluation it is necessary for the evaluator to communicate the results of vocational evaluation to the client and to explain the vocational alternatives which are derived from these results. In order to avoid misinterpretation and to enhance the client's understanding of the entire vocational evaluation process, it is imperative that the evaluator integrate all relevant information and explain each tentative hypothesis in a manner that will clearly disclose the feasibility and contra-indications for each hypothesis. The evaluator must also discuss these findings and hypotheses with the client and allow him to express his feelings about the vocational evaluation process and its results. He must enter into a vocational counseling relationship with the client in order to effect a mutual understanding of the vocational evaluation process as it applies to the client's vocational future.

Vocational counseling is designed to assist the client in deciding upon realistic vocational goals. It also enables the client to arrive at an understanding of the processes which may be followed for goal attainment. It is through vocational counseling that the client acquires a functional understanding of his vocational potential and of the methods that can lead to its fulfillment. Vocational counseling also provides the evaluator with an opportunity to understand his results as they relate to the client's future aspirations. The mutual understanding achieved during vocational counseling enables both the client and the evaluator to agree upon an ideal occupation and to establish meaningful vocational alternatives and priorities. Through the vocational evaluation report this same information is communicated to a third party for implementation.

The ultimate goal of vocational evaluation is to determine the ideal occupation for each client evaluated. This goal may rarely be attained since no one can know and understand the exact nature of ultimate or ideal things in life. Furthermore, the results of any evaluation, whether it be medical, social, psychological, or vocational evaluation, if incorporated into the self-system and successfully implemented or attained are no longer valid. For example, suppose the results of a medical evaluation indicate that a given patient is in need of surgery to correct a herniated lumbar disc. Once the patient incorporates these results into his self-system and undergoes a successful operation these results are no longer valid—the patient no longer needs lumbar surgery. Likewise, if an ideal occupation is recommended and attained as a result of vocational evaluation, this recommendation is no longer applicable to, or valid for, that client. The occupation, once attained, does not remain ideal for that client since a completely different set of circumstances prevail.

Although vocational evaluation programs should strive to attain an ideal objective, the amorphous and unstable nature of the *ideal* concept must be recognized. Researchers who create designs to study the effectiveness of vocational evaluation must particularly understand and accept the shortcomings and limitations imposed by the changing nature of this concept. Consequently, the measure of success in vocational evaluation entails more than a cursory follow-up to determine the degree of consistency between vocational recommendations and vocational outcomes. Rather, it must consider the extent to which vocational evaluation has enabled the client to grow, emerge, and attain satisfaction within an ever changing environment as a result of ongoing self-evaluation.

DISCUSSION

The model presented in Figure 1 is based upon data obtained from forty different vocational evaluation programs. Due to the nationwide distribution of this sample, the model should have relevance to the establishment and operation of vocational evaluation programs within a broad geographical area. Since the model is structural in nature, it should be relevant to any population, regardless of whether that population is disabled or disadvantaged. However, it must be emphasized that this model is a simplified version of reality designed to delineate the structure of the vocational evaluation process by attending to its central variables (i.e., the ten evaluation techniques and procedures) .

The model, in itself, merely provides a structural framework for the vocational evaluation process. It does not offer an explanation of the specific nature and function of each variable, nor does it account for the various relationships among the variables. Furthermore, the model does not demonstrate the exact process by which a given client moves through the structure.

By commenting upon the ten variables, an attempt was made to explain the underlying rationale for each variable and to describe the general process through which the variables operate within the structure. However, these comments failed to depict the operating changes that occur within the structure through the interaction of the variables with each other and with the environment.

Since vocational evaluation is an individual-oriented service, the operation and interaction of the variables and the specific process through which a client is evaluated must vary with the needs of each individual. In other words, if vocational evaluation is to be appropriate for, and meaningful to, each individual the specific techniques and procedures must be selected and employed on the basis of a vocational evaluation process that meets the assessment needs of the individual. Due to the individualized nature of the vocational evaluation process, a functional model would have to be constructed for each individual in order to assure complete isomorphism and to accurately represent reality. However, the physical characteristics of each functional model would essentially remain unchanged.

The physical structure of the vocational evaluation process, as encompassed within the model presented, is a relatively stable entity. It does not vary significantly for each individual. Regardless of the specific assessment needs of an individual client, the techniques and procedures should be employed in the same logical sequence. However, when employed in an individualized program of vocational evaluation, each technique or procedure will provide the evaluator with varying degrees of information and will enable him to differentially narrow down the field of vocational choice with each client evaluated.

For example, suppose biographical data reveals that a particular client is paraplegic and confined to a wheelchair. On the basis of biographical data alone, the vocational evaluator is able to eliminate all occupations from consideration which require the ability to stand. This information enables the evaluator to narrow down the field of vocational choice to a much greater extent than would be feasible for another client whose major employment handicap is of a social or cultural nature. Consequently, the width of each variable will be different for most clients evaluated, but the physical position of these variables will remain the same within the structural model. Although each variable within the model presented maintains an identical width, this notion was incorporated into the model merely to achieve consistency and to enhance the structural properties of the model. It does not have any interpretive significance, nor does it impose structural or functional limitations upon the vocational evaluation process.

The critical variables (i.e., the ten evaluation techniques and procedures) encompassed within the model are arranged in a sequential order based upon the point at which they receive *major emphasis* during the vocational evaluation process. However, with some clients, many of these techniques and procedures are also employed at different stages of the evaluation process. For example, since psychological tests are used in vocational evaluation primarily to provide the evaluator with an understanding of the client's general assets and limitations, they are *emphasized* relatively early in the vocational evaluation process. This does not mean that all psychological tests must be administered early in the vocational evaluation process, but rather that they receive *major emphasis* after the evaluation interview.

Many psychological tests are designed to provide the evaluator with information about a client's ability to perform specific types of work. The Bennett Mechanical Comprehension Test, the Stenographic Aptitude Test, and the Graves Design Judgment Test are examples of such instruments. Tests of this type would not be used with every client, but only with those clients who are being considered for specific areas of work. Consequently, they would be employed at a later stage of the vocational evaluation process, when the evaluator is basically concerned with determining a client's potential for entry into specific occupational areas.

Likewise, vocational counseling is *emphasized* during the final stage of the vocational evaluation process since it is at this point that the evaluator and the client must arrive at mutually agreeable and feasible vocational alternatives. However, many clients may also require vocational counseling earlier in the vocational evaluation process in order to assist in the selection of meaningful occupational exploration procedures, work samples, situational tasks, or job tryouts. Since vocational counseling is appropriate and necessary for all clients as a last step in the evaluation process, it receives *major emphasis* during the final stage of vocational evaluation. Although several of the remaining techniques and procedures may be selectively employed at different stages during the vocational evaluation process, they are *emphasized* in the sequence shown on the figurative model.

The Model of Vocational Evaluation depicts the structure of the vocational evaluation process from the referral of a client through his termination from the program. This model indicates that a client is terminated from vocational evaluation equipped with a mutually agreed upon ideal vocational objective and a set of appropriate vocational alternatives and priorities. However, if problems arise that require immediate attention or correction, a given client may be terminated from vocational evaluation prior to the completion of his program.

For example, at different stages of the vocational evaluation process, the evaluator may discover that other services are essential in order for a client to satisfactorily complete his program. When necessary, such a client may be prematurely terminated from vocational evaluation with recommendation for appropriate treatment. Such recommendations may include medical consultations for corrective surgery, eyeglasses, hearing aids, or related services; or various psychosocial recommendations such as family therapy, psychotherapy, or work adjustment training. When a client is prematurely terminated from vocational evaluation there should be a recommendation for re-evaluation after the necessary treatment has been received.

The Vocational Evaluation Model does not encompass follow-up services since such services are not a routine part of the vocational evaluation process. Rather, follow-up is undertaken after a client has completed vocational evaluation and after sufficient time has elapsed for the recommendations to be implemented. Although follow-up is not essential to the vocational evaluation process, such services are necessary in order to determine the effectiveness of a vocational evaluation program and to incorporate appropriate and meaningful changes into the program. Through follow-up there is an opportunity for the evaluator to engage in meaningful self-evaluation and program evaluation.

The changes that occur as a result of follow-up will probably not have an immediate effect upon the structure of the vocational evaluation process, but these changes will affect the specific functional procedures employed by vocational evaluators. Structural changes in the vocational evaluation process and in the model presented will occur only through marked and significant changes in function. Thus, the Model for Vocational Evaluation, as presented in Figure 1, is a relatively stable entity.

SUMMARY

Several decades ago, vocational rehabilitation personnel recognized the inherent limitations of traditional vocational assessment methodology for evaluating the work behavior and vocational potential of many handicapped individuals. As a result of this awareness, there was a gradual incorporation of realism into the vocational assessment process within rehabilitation. This practical, realistic approach to vocational assessment became known as vocational evaluation and developed into a major and essential diagnostic service in the rehabilitation process.

For many decades, vocational evaluation programs were primarily confined to rehabilitation. However, during recent years an increasing emphasis has been placed upon the development and expansion of vocational evaluation services within both rehabilitation and manpower programs. This emphasis has been demonstrated by the growing commitment of the Rehabilitation Services Administration and the Manpower Administration toward improvement in the quantity and quality of vocational evaluation services. In an attempt to meet the growing demand for improved vocational evaluation services, the federal government has provided financial support to a few agencies and universities that offer training programs for vocational evaluators and that are involved in the development of materials for vocational evaluation (Nadolsky, 1971a). To date, no attempt has been made to define the concept of vocational evaluation or to develop a consistent body of knowledge for the field—a body of knowledge which could be disseminated to vocational evaluators during the training process.

This study was designed to identify the present nature and

scope of the vocational evaluation process by attending to the content and methodology of vocational evaluation is applied in rehabilitation and in manpower programs. The results of this investigation led to the development of a model for vocational evaluation which could be applied with any population, regardless of whether disabled or disadvantaged.

Through a review of related literature an understanding of the scope, nature, content, and methodology of vocational evaluation was acquired. This understanding was used to establish a basis for appropriate data collection. The literature review revealed that many techniques and procedures were routinely employed by vocational evaluators and that five different approaches were common to vocational evaluation programs in rehabilitation. The five approaches included:

(1) the psychological testing approach,
(2) the work sample approach,
(3) the situational approach,
(4) the job tryout approach, and
(5) the job analysis approach.

Vocational evaluation services have become a definite and distinct entity within facilities operated or supported by rehabilitation and manpower programs. These two agencies have also been charged with the primary responsibility for providing various vocational-related services to the socially and culturally disadvantaged. Consequently, the subjects selected for participation in this study were essentially derived from vocational evaluation programs within the rehabilitation and the manpower domain.

The results of this study indicated that most programs of vocational evaluation, regardless of whether they were rehabilitation or manpower-oriented, maintained a similar set of goals or objectives and utilized the same general types of techniques and procedures. With respect to the specific techniques and procedures used, a few basic differences were noted between rehabilitation and manpower-oriented programs of vocational evaluation. These basic differences were as follows:

1. Manpower-related vocational evaluation programs utilized the Adult Basic Learning Examination (ABLE series) as a

basic achievement test; while this instrument was not used by vocational evaluators in rehabilitation.

2. The TOWER system was used to a greater extent by rehabilitation-oriented vocational evaluators; while the manpower-oriented evaluators placed emphasis upon the use of the J.E.V.S. system.

3. When job tryouts were used by rehabilitation-oriented vocational evaluators, the job tryout site was usually located in a vocational training area within the rehabilitation facility; while manpower-related vocational evaluators frequently utilized community employment situations as sites for the job tryout.

4. Vocational evaluation programs located in manpower related facilities placed emphasis upon an orientation to the world of work, the provision of occupational information, and the use of occupational exploration procedures; while rehabilitation-oriented programs rarely utilized such procedures. Furthermore, it was observed that a few fell-developed, programmed occupational exploration procedures were utilized by cerain manpower-oriented vocational evaluation programs in order to familiarize the client with the realities of various occupational areas prior to assessing his ability to function within these areas.

5. Rehabilitation-oriented vocational evaluation programs sought more extensive medical data on their clients than did the manpower-oriented programs.

This investigation was not undertaken to discover differences which existed between vocational evaluation programs supported by, or affiliated with, rehabilitation or the Manpower Administration, but to determine the present nature and scope of the vocational evaluation process and its related content and methodology. With the exception of the few basic differences noted, most of the programs surveyed were similar in nature and scope and employed essentially the same categories of techniques and procedures.

By combining the results of all vocational evaluation programs surveyed, a structural model was developed for vocational evaluation which was essentially isomorphic with the critical aspects of observed reality. The model was based upon a logical ordering of ten techniques and procedures which encompassed the core content of vocational evaluation and which provided the structure for the development of a systematic program of vocational evaluation.

The model depicted the vocational evaluation process as a figurative pyramid inserted within a square that was open at the top. The vertical ends of the square represented the boundaries of the entire world of work. The base of the pyramid represented the vocational evaluators complete lack of understanding of a client's vocational potential upon referral; while its apex depicted the ideal occupation within the world of work for each client evaluated. Within the figurative pyramid ten basic vocational evaluation techniques and procedures were logically ordered in the sequence that they would be employed in a systematic program of vocational evaluation. Through the sequential application of the ten techniques and procedures there would be a logical elimination of certain occupations from consideration. As each technique or procedure was applied, the client would move upward on the figurative pyramid toward a meaningful vocational goal (i.e., an ideal occupation) through a logical narrowing of vocational choice. A client would be terminated from vocational evaluation with a mutually agreed upon ideal occupation and a set of appropriate vocational alternatives and priorities.

The Model for Vocational Evaluation, as presented, was purely structural in nature. For this reason, it was isomorphic with the structural qualities of the vocational evaluation process as observed in reality. Since this is a structural model, it should be applicable to any population, regardless of whether that population is disabled or disadvantaged. Furthermore, it was felt that the Model for Vocational Evaluation is a relatively stable entity, since structural changes in the vocational evaluation process and in the Model will occur only as a result of marked and significant changes in function.

CONCLUSIONS

Although the results of this study warrant certain conclusions, some precautions should first be mentioned. Since this was purely a descriptive and global investigation of the vocational evaluation process based upon a limited sample, caution should be exercised in making concrete interpretations from its results. The results of this study should not be interpreted as standards to be adopted by all vocational evaluation programs. Rather, these results and the model derived from them, should be viewed as tentative guidelines against which vocational evaluation practitioners can either establish new programs or alter existing ones and study the results of their efforts. With these precautions in mind, the following conclusions are justified in terms of the purpose of this study:

1. Vocational evaluation programs throughout the nation, regardless of whether rehabilitation or manpower affiliated, are essentially similar in scope and nature and employ the same general categories of techniques and procedures.

2. Vocational evaluation is an individual-oriented service which must encompass the entire world of work if it is to be meaningful and appropriate for each individual client.

3. The goal of vocational evaluation is to determine the most feasible or ideal occupation for each client and to establish meaningful vocational alternatives and priorities for that client.

4. The basic differences that exist among vocational evaluation programs are the direct result of variations in the population served, the facility orientation, or the historical perspective through which the specific vocational evaluation program had evolved.

5. A structural model for vocational evaluation which is *isomorphic* with observed reality can be developed to account for the physical characteristics of the vocational evaluation process and its related techniques and procedures.

6. In order for a vocational evaluation model to possess *complete isomorphism* and to account for the functional or operating changes that occur within the vocational evaluation process, a functional model would have to be developed for each vocational evaluation client.

7. The structural model for vocational evaluation, as presented,

should be applicable to any population, regardless of whether that population is disabled or disadvantaged.

Since this study was a broad and diverse investigation of the vocational evaluation process and its related methodology, several implications can be drawn which could have a significant effect upon training, service, and research in vocational evaluation. The primary significance of this study was that it established a firm, but tentative, foundation for the vocational evaluation process and focused upon the identification of issues or variables that were commonly encountered in vocational evaluation programs. In order to conduct meaningful training, service, or research in vocational evaluation, these issues or variables must be recognized and confronted within the structure of the vocational evaluation process.

The results of this investigation offer certain suggestions to individuals involved in the development and improvement of training programs for vocational evaluators. At the present time, training programs for vocational evaluators are relatively few in number, but it is anticipated that several new training programs will be established within the near future in order to meet the pressing demand for trained personnel. These training programs attempt to train a new breed of *professional*—the vocational evaluator. Such training is currently being accomplished primarily by *borrowing* methodology from the fields of psychology, rehabilitation counseling, medicine, industrial arts, occupational therapy, special education, and related areas. A large, unfilled gap remains at the center of most training programs for vocational evaluators—that related to a shared understanding of the vocational evaluation process and the systematic or sequential application of its techniques and procedures.

Although the results of this investigation did not provide a cohesive body of knowledge that could be disseminated to vocational evaluation students, these results did offer a foundation upon which this body of knowledge could be developed. Furthermore, if students understand the structure and nature of the vocational evaluation process, they will be beeter equipped to incorporate knowledge gained from related disciplines into a meaningful and functional framework. By focusing upon the Model for Vocational Evaluation, training programs can achieve a greater degree of commonality than was previously possible.

The results of this study provide implications which could improve the entire vocational evaluation service structure by attending to the sequential application of the variables encompassed within the Vocational Evaluation Model. These findings could also heighten communication among vocational evaluation practitioners by reference to a similar structure for the vocational evaluation process. For example, the results of vocational evaluation from one agency could be readily understood by the staff of aonther agency since these results would be related to a similar vocational evaluation structure.

Through the establishment of vocational evaluation programs based upon the Model for Vocational Evaluation, both the client and the counselor would have a greater opportunity to understand the vocational evaluation process (its purpose, nature, length, and scope) and to implement its recommendations. Furthermore, service programs based upon the Model for Vocational Evaluation would be applicable to any population. In view of recent federal legislation, this latter implication is important since, in the near future, most vocational evaluation programs will be expected to offer meaningful services to large numbers of the individuals who are confronted with a social or cultural handicap.

With respect to research, the results of this study, and especially the model derived from these results, provides the basis for the formulation of several meaningful hypotheses which could be tested empirically. For example, it could be hypothesized that vocational evaluation programs which are based upon the model are more effective than traditional vocational assessment programs for the culturally disadvantaged or for other populations. Although this hypothesis could be tested empirically, it would be necessary to establish a criteria for effectiveness and to operationally define the population under consideration.

Based upon the Model for Vocational Evaluation it is also possible to formulate and test several other specific hypotheses. For example, one could develop the hypothesis that the provision of occupational exploration procedures as a fourth step in vocational evaluation results in a greater degree of success than when these same procedures are used either earlier or later in the vocational evaluation process or when they are omitted from the process. Of course, the same types of occupational exploration procedures would have to be available and used appropriately with all subjects and the criteria of success would have to be operationally defined. From the Model for Vocational Evaluation, similar hypotheses could be formulated and tested for all variables encompassed within the structure.

In addition to establishing a basis for the generation of meaningful hypotheses, the Model for Vocational Evaluation also provides a direction for the development of a global system of vocational evaluation. As the model indicates, the development of such a system must initially give consideration to the establishment of criteria for vocational evaluation which is relevant to the entire world of work. Based upon these criteria, appropriate existing techniques and procedures could be gathered which measure a client's ability to participate in certain segments of the occupational criteria. These techniques and procedures could be coded to enhance the efficiency of their use. Additional techniques and procedures could be developed and coded to measure the remaining segments of the occupational criteria. By so doing, a meaningful, global, model based system of vocational evaluation could be developed.

Although the availability of such a system would not eliminate clinical judgment in vocational evaluation, it could systematize the process of vocational evaluation to the extent that clinical judgment is firmly based upon standardized and meaningful criteria and techniques. Through a continuous program of system-based research, the occupational criteria and its related techniques and procedures could be validated. The establishment of a model-based system of vocational evaluation would strengthen the entire vocational evaluation profession and provide a much needed systematic methodology for training programs in vocational evaluation. Finally, the evaluation criteria and its related techniques and procedures would provide a realistic approach to vocational evaluation which is extremely necessary when working with the socially and culturally disadvantaged.

REFERENCES

Dictionary of Occupational Titles, 3rd ed., Vols. I and II. U. S. Department of Labor, Bureau of Employment Security. Washington, U. S. Government Printing Office, 1965.

Jewish Employment and Vocational Service: *Work Samples: Signposts on the Road to Occupational Choice.* (Manpower Administration Contract No. 82-40-67-40), Final report. Philadelphia, Jewish Employment and Vocational Service, 1968.

Moed, M.G.: Procedures and practices in pre-vocational evaluation: A review of current programs. Proceedings of the Iowa Conference on Prevocational Activities, State University of Iowa, 1960.

Nadolsky, J. M.: Vocational evaluation theory in perspective. *Rehabilitation Literature, 32:*226-231, 1971b.

Neff, W. S.: Problems of work evaluation. *Personnel and Guidance Journal, 44:*682-688, 1966.

XVI

THE REHABILITATION FACILITY'S ROLE IN EVALUATING THE WELFARE RECIPIENT

JOHN G. CULL AND RICHARD E. HARDY

༺༺༺༺༺༺༺༺༺༺༺༺༺༺༺༺༺༺༺༺༺༺༺༺༺༺༺༺༺༺༺༺༺༺༺

Welfare Reform Legislation and Facilities' Evaluation
Need For Understanding the Welfare Recipient
Impact of Poverty on the Individual
Implications for Evaluation in Facilities
Summary
References

༺༺༺༺༺༺༺༺༺༺༺༺༺༺༺༺༺༺༺༺༺༺༺༺༺༺༺༺༺༺༺༺༺༺༺

WELFARE REFORM LEGISLATION AND FACILITIES' EVALUATION

IT IS GENERALLY accepted that with the advent of Welfare Reform legislation, the rehabilitation facilities in both urban and rural areas will assume a greater role in the evaluation of rehabilitation clients for the rehabilitation process. This increase in the level of expectation for workshops and rehabilitation facilities will be a particularly challenging demand. This trend is an extension of the trend established by Public Law 89-333 as discussed by Hardy and Cull (1969). For too long, the disabled welfare recipients have been denied many of the rehabilitation services traditionally available to the members of other disability categories. There have been many reasons and some justification for denial of such services to this disability group. Lack of counselor time to help motivate these clients and the shortage of training facilities are just two examples of why this disability group has not been served adequately. The time is overdue for private rehabilitation facilities to begin innovative techniques that will be effective in the delivery of services to the disabled welfare recipient.

Workshops must develop a goal oriented philosophy and provide a framework and an appropriate staffing pattern to perform the required duties in serving the disabled welfare recipient if much good is to be accomplished in the delivery of services to this group (Cull and Colvin, 1972).

NEED FOR UNDERSTANDING THE WELFARE RECIPIENT

According to the Eighth Institute of Rehabilitation Services (Hutchinson, 1971), in a recent survey of rehabilitation counselors relative to problem areas in the rehabilitation of this segment of our population, the outstanding cluster of problems centered around a lack of understanding of the background and motivation of the welfare recipient client. Therefore, we feel this is an indication of a prime role in which the private rehabilitation facilities can function; that is, the evaluation and interpretation of behavior, motivations, and potential of the welfare recipient to the rehabilitation counselor charged with the responsibility of working with these individuals. Facility personnel need to be able to interpret to the rehabilitation counselor the general cultural stockpile of the disadvantaged—his family togetherness, his reluctance to relocate, his acceptance of poverty as a way of life, his distrust of outsiders, and the various communication barriers which exist. Also, the facility personnel should be prepared to try to overcome some of the ignorance, apathy, and resistance to the problems of the disadvantaged by the general public and the ultimate employers of this group of people.

The vocational rehabilitation process was developed for the middle class consumer. It was not developed for the public welfare recipient type of client. The rehabilitation process works very smoothly and efficiently if there is an underlying motivation for vocational success and if the client is able to forego short-range goals for long-range planning. The value system of poor persons is different from that of middle class persons, but it should be remembered that these values do not differ in all respects. Persons living in poverty seem to have a strong orientation in the present and short-term perspectives rather than long-term planning and goals. In addition, there is a definite feeling of fatalism and a belief in chance, impulsiveness, and a general inability to delay immediate gratification or make definite plans for the future. Also, there is a thinking process that could be termed much more concrete in character than abstract. There are general feelings of inferiority and acceptance of authoritarianism.

The pattern or culture of poverty is at times viewed as a causative factor in poverty and at other times as a result. In other words, general feelings and emotions resulting from impoverished conditions either can perpetuate the poverty or these same psychological feelings can be viewed as those consequences of the actual environmental conditions. The important question revolves around whether the environment causes the internal psychological make-up, or whether the internal psychological make-up helps create the environmental state in which the individual lives. There are affirmative and negative answers to both questions and there is considerable overlap in any type of explanation which might attempt to give answers.

Poverty is a relative condition since it varies enormously from country to country and region to region. The subculture of poverty, however, in terms of the traits it seems to bring with it transcends regional, racial, social class, and national differences. Of course, there are definite variations among countries and over periods of time. It is a well known fact that poverty in the nineteenth century was a much more tolerable state than poverty in the twentieth century.

It is important for those professionals in the rehabilitation facility working with the disabled disadvantaged to show that they have confidence in these clients' abilities to improve themselves not only from the point of view of a poverty condition, but also from the point of view of whatever handicap the individual may have. In a recent study by Rosenthal and Jacobson (1968), results indicated that teachers who were led to believe that certain lower class students could show unusual gains during the year actually brought about these gains in these children (the students for whom they held positive expectations).

IMPACT OF POVERTY ON THE INDIVIDUAL

Poverty very definitely constitutes one of the most persistent and critical problems of modern life. The factors associated with poverty and destitution influence the individual's feelings of self-worth, self-regard, and general self-concept. When the self-concept is altered, the individual's behavior is altered. In other words, what a man thinks of himself determines to a great extent how he will behave in any given situation. Self-concept greatly influences the behavior an individual exhibits to others. Pockets of poverty then offer their own patterns, their own subcultures, and ways of behavior are determined by persons living within these pockets of poverty. In order for an individual to maintain the level of self-esteem he wishes to hold, he must be accepted by those persons who are important to him. The persons he knows within these pockets of poverty determine his life goals, meanings, and social roles to a considerable degree. The individual identifies himself and gives status to his being according to the value system of those around him, especially those important *others* who also predetermine his present and future behavioral roles. This fact is important in understanding why many persons who live within these pockets of poverty in both our rural areas and our urban areas do not avail themselves of various programs and opportunities and, in general, the services of the rehabilitation counselor. These individuals have found their present identity and any threat to their way of life represents a threat to their person. Proposed changes bring about great feelings of anxiety; and while persons in poverty are unhappy about their fate, they do not have the strength to change what they have become. They do not have the immediate motivation to change the life pattern with which they are comfortable and that pattern of behavior through which they have found identity.

Few individuals are strong enough to make an identity change on their own, and changes within these pockets of destitution often must come through a total community development process. Persons can change as a group once change has begun easier than they can change as separate individuals. Change then must come about within individuals in groups and cannot be achieved just by moving people to new geographic areas or mounting new programs which are aimed at the individual and which put basic and primary responsibility on the individual.

In order for individuals or groups to change, they must be somewhat dissatisfied with their present state and their present self-image. People in poverty as well as people in the middle class and higher classes vary in their satisfaction with their self-image, and this is why some are more susceptible to change than others. It is important for the professionals in the rehabilitation field to ask for opinions of persons living in poverty in order that they can evaluate the present conditions of these individuals' lives and see whether or not the individuals wish to change in their communities and in their individual physical environment. Many poverty stricken individuals have no idea that they can bring about change in their lives and most have given little thought to the possibility of improving living conditions. Rehabilitation workers must be cognizant of the fact that the most effective way to change people is to treat them in accordance with the status in life which they would like to achieve. If an individual is to change behavioral patterns, he must be treated in a different manner from that to which he is accustomed.

The rehabilitation worker or facility employee concerned with the culturally disadvantaged and disabled disadvantaged should keep in mind that the economic system does not provide a sufficient number of employment opportunities in terms of jobs which are actually available to and appropriate for the poor. There is a chronic depression among many poor persons which results from inadequate occupational, educational, social and economic opportunity. This chronic depression is accentuated in our rural areas. This depression leads to a considerable lack of sufficient motivation for adjustment and achievement within the highly competitive society of the United States today. Various facts of life of the hard core jobless are interrelated and multiple.

There is high level of physical and mental deficiency, a low education level, and poverty abounds. There is a general feeling of alienation, a lack of training and employment opportunities, and severe racial and cultural problems.

Persons who live in the culture of poverty adapt to the conditions of that culture. The conditions and general culture of poverty perpetuates itself to its effects on children from generation to generation. It is believed that by the time children are six or seven they have taken on attitudes and values of their subculture and they are not able, psychologically, to cope with the changing conditions and take advantage of various training and job opportunities which may occur later in life. If a break alone is offered to these individuals, it would soon be apparent that they were not favorably disposed toward the generosity. Measures to overcome their basic cultural, social, and economic experiences must be included as a part of any social action program or rehabilitative program before positive change can be expected.

Moynihan (1968) has indicated that intensive family and personal rehabilitation must make up a major part of the war on impoverished conditions. He has said that increased opportunity for decent and well-paying jobs is simply not enough. Moynihan maintains that for an unspecified number of American poor depravation over a long period of time has caused such serious personality difficulties (personality structure problems) that many of these persons are psychologically unable to avail themselves of the various training and job opportunities which might be open to them.

One very important characteristic of poverty families is that they are in constant crisis. It seems that no sooner is one crisis worked out than another takes its place. There is always the financial situation; there is always sickness; there is always the situation of the possibility of divorce due to increased stress; there is always crime and a lack of a safe living environment for the weaker members of the family structure; there is always the child in trouble; and the possibility of the loss of employment. These constant crises have the effect of draining all the energy from the family and its members. Such emotionality takes a high toll in terms of the overall ability of a family unit or an individual within the family.

IMPLICATIONS FOR EVALUATION IN FACILITIES

Now, based upon this pattern, the rehabilitation facilities within our communities will be challenged with evaluating the vocational potential and the rehabilitation feasibility for this segment of our population. Old approaches will no longer work. The facilities which do not tool up and modify their basic approaches to evaluating clients and providing services will be left behind during the mid-seventies when the clamor for welfare reform will reach its peak. Not only must we work with the individual as we have in the past, but we must now work with his family in a more intimate fashion. We must work with other community organizations which are organized for meeting some of the clients' needs. Additionally, we must work with the client in different program approaches than we have recognized in the past.

In working with the disadvantaged, it is clearly indicated that different counseling approaches will need to be developed. A different system of delivery of services will need to be developed. Both rehabilitation facilities and rehabilitation counselors both will have to develop a different relationship; whereas in a few facilities, the relationship between these two has been much deeper than that of a vendor-vendee relationship, this depth of relationship will have to become almost universal. According to Cull and Hardy (1969), the counselor and facility personnel should look to the facility specialist in the state agency to function as an interpretative liaison in developing this integrated relationship. The facility and the counselor will have to demonstrate a readiness in dealing with the client and his family as a unit and significant *other* individuals within the client's environment. They will have to work together to learn how to uncover community resources to work with family members, to deal with the basic problems of transportation, housing, food supplement, etc. Concepts such as self-actualization, client self-direction, etc., should not be ignored, but emphasis in the rehabilitation process must be upon meeting current emergencies. With this approach, self-direction and other long-range goals may eventually become a meaningful reality to the client; however, these should not be interjected as early in the rehabilitation process as they have been in the past. This is a obvious conclusion when one considers the level of our clients in the past in relationship to Maslow's hierarchy (Maslow, 1954). According to Maslow's hierarchy, most of our clients in the past have fulfilled the specified needs at the most basic two levels and are involved in fulfilling love and esteem needs. This new group of clients with which we will be dealing is concerned more with physiological needs and safety needs. Therefore, their concerns are much more immediate and much more urgent.

Basic security in coping with the environment and with immediate concerns and problems are paramount values of the disadvantaged. Planning ahead is often a futile exercise and holds little personal value or reward. For example: the possibility of discontinuance of a basic income supplement through a Social Security pension or welfare is apt to be viewed negatively in light of previous limited job success and long periods of unemployment frustration. Such clients have little assurance that rehabilitation will make them better off than they are now.

An important problem affecting the rehabilitation process is that the client may feel these rehabilitation professionals really do not understand him or his needs; furthermore, he may feel that the team members working in the rehabilitation process may try to convey the attitude of understanding, but from the client's viewpoint, these individuals really do not and cannot understand. For example: the client will agree that personal motivation is necessary for people to get ahead in the world; however, the client is apt to disagree seriously if the rehabilitation worker questions the client's motivation. The need for immediate assistance, medical care, transportation, money, and so on, are seen as the most important first steps. Many people needing the services of vocational rehabilitation feel they previously have been given unfulfilled promises by the professional personnel in the various fields of social service. There are psychological needs requiring immediate reward or service. Long-term planning and vague expectations and promises fail to motivate most disabled disadvantaged people.

Furthermore, a client has a general pessimism which is hard for the highly goal-oriented professionals in the field of rehabilitation to understand. The client has seen few of his people make it. Those who have escaped from poverty seldom remain in his social group, and hence, are not present to serve as models with whom the client might identify. Thus, the things which the client considers to be important are not apt to be congruent with what the facility personnel or the rehabilitation counselor consider to be of importance.

In light of these considerations, perhaps now it can be understood why a client may drop a training program which could eventually lead to a two-or-three-dollar an hour job for an immediate opportunity to accept a job paying $1.50 per hour. Such behavior is understandable even though it appears to us to be a dead-end and self-defeating action.

The client desperately needs to be considered important and may really want to feel that he is being accepted by professionals in the rehabilitation field; yet many clients may have had previous experience with public agencies when they felt that their own personal integrity was questioned and their experience with the agency was a personally degrading one. Thus, they are now apt to view the rehabilitation agency with suspicion and the agency must be proven not guilty. Demonstrating and conveying instant acceptance of the client as a worthwhile individual is a first major step towards establishing a working relationship.

The rehabilitation facility has a prime opportunity to serve in a very basic capacity—that of being the focal point of community action and rehabilitation services. The rehabilitation facility should serve not only as a focal point, but as an energizer of services. There is a common concept that there is a paucity or a lacking of services within our communities organized to meet the needs of this segment of our population. This is not true. Upon investigation, one will find a plethora of services; however, they tend to be somewhat disjointed and directed more toward specific groups of people. Quite often their approach is less broad than we would desire. Therefore, the rehabilitation facility should assume the role of being the uniting force between these diverse service agencies for the benefit of these disadvantaged disabled clients. The rehabilitation facility should develop a very active information and referral program in order to be able to know who is providing services to what groups, where the clientele are located, and what their needs are. In order to serve the welfare recipient, we have to find him. If the rehabilitation facility or the rehabilitation counselor is not able to locate and identify concentrations of welfare recipient clients, we cannot serve as an effective ingredient in the rehabilitation process.

Therefore, it would behoove the facility to take time to learn each agency's function and solicit its cooperation. In order for the facility to achieve the bright promise which lies ahead in fulfilling its role in the rehabilitation of this segment of our population. It should become the guiding force in welding the community together and directing it toward this goal. We feel the rehabilitation facility should become active in developing a community involvement board which serves as a clearing house for problems and is a resource for the solution of these problems. Most of the organizations and agencies listed in community service agency directories should have membership on this action group. They should meet regularly and should identify pockets of disabled disadvantaged individuals, identify the cluster of problems which are evident and plan programs through joint facilities to attack these programs. In addition to this particular approach, the facility should become aware of the many and varied programs supported in part by federal funds that are designed to meet the needs of disadvantaged people. Some of these are established to alleviate the disadvantages peculiar to specific groups of individuals or particular types of citizens. The facility personnel should support and encourage the development of such programs that support handicap people. These programs may be short-term or may develop into lasting programs of considerable impact in practicality. Vocational Rehabilitation personnel should be aware of the opportunities afforded clients by such programs when they are within geographical reach of the client.

When they are not, the facility again should become the focal point of action within the community and develop these programs. When the facilitative services are absent, it is our firm conviction the workshop should mobilize its services to meet these needs. When transportation becomes a major problem in the rehabilitation of an individual or a pocket of individuals, the rehabilitation facility should develop a transportation program to clear the blockage in the rehabilitation process.

Since communicating with the public welfare recipient is a prime obstacle to successful vocational rehabilitation, we feel the facility should initiate the employment of indigenous workers to communicate with these clients. The indigenous worker who is carefully selected to work with his people can do much more in the way of communicating to these citizens in bringing about the necessary changes that are indicated in order for the client to be employed than can a professional worker in many cases.

Since there is a shortage of available manpower within our professional areas, we need to turn to innovative approaches in staffing patterns. One innovative approach is the use of volunteer workers. We have a large reservoir of untapped manpower within the retired ranks of our communities. We feel the rehabilitation facilities within the country have missed the boat by not mobilizing these people for rehabilitation purposes. We have seen evidence that retired people from all walks of life are interested in volunteering their services to rehabilitation facilities. We have seen demonstrated; these individuals are eager to accept responsibility for the transportation of clients to the rehabilitation facilities, to clinics, to various other facilities. We have seen clients who are eager to accept responsibility in functioning as remedial educators for clients who are in need of remedial education; we have seen retired individuals who will volunteer to take work out to clients who are involved in homebound programs. It is our opinion that the rehabilitation facility should make maximum utilization of voluntary service.

At the present time, there are very poor approaches to the vocational evaluation of clients. There is no broad based universal approach to vocational evaluation. There are few structured evaluation tools with wide applicability and there are none that we know of which are applicable to this particular segment of our population. Therefore, we propose that facility personnel jointly devise a basic evaluation tool which would have universal applicability. One of the most pressing challenges in the mid seventies will be for the workshop to evaluate the type of client we have been talking of. Currently, the greatest variability in vocational evaluations across the country is in personnel rather than instruments. With the personnel shortages, we feel there is a real need for the development of an evaluation device; and this evaluation device should be developed prior to the demands which will be descending upon us as a result of welfare reform legislation.

Another recommendation of the Eighth Institute of Rehabilitation Service (Hutchinson, 1970) report is the development of a kit to describe rehabilitation services and services within various facilities. Many of the disabled disadvantaged clients have little understanding of the terms rehabilitation facility, day care center, work evaluation, workshop, rehabilitation center, etc. It will facilitate communication if the rehabilitation personnel and the rehabilitation facility have materials consisting of photographs, film strips, and tapes which explain the purpose, the environment, and methods employed by the various service programs. This kit would be especially valuable if it depicts a successful client the referral is familiar with. The referral could see that his neighbor has benefited from rehabilitation services at a facility. Many clients are reluctant to leave home and travel even short distances to participate in a program unfamiliar to them. We feel this approach will be especially valuable in counseling our clients in the more remote areas to accept services in population centers after they have completed evaluation and work adjustment training services at one of the more rural rehabilitation facilities.

We also feel the information kit will be of value when used in conjunction with the mobile team concept. In serving some of our more rural areas, a mobile unit can be equipped to provide vocational evaluation and work adjustment services. The Georgia

Division of Vocational Rehabilitation has developed such a system and is using it quite successfully.

SUMMARY

In summary we are advocating that in order to rehabilitate the disabled disadvantaged, the rehabilitation facility and the rehabilitation personnel should take a much more active role in community life and community affairs. To do so will mean there is a much improved chance of meeting the demanding challenges of the mid-seventies in rehabilitating the welfare recipient. Specifically, we are suggesting that rehabilitation facilities should change their staffing patterns to be more effective in serving this segment of our population. They should staff up to provide more group work and be prepared to spend more time in evaluation, work adjustment training, personal adjustment training, and vocational training. Not only are we providing these services, we also are modifying attitudes and basic approaches to life; that is, we are trying to modify the life style of our clients. We must change our approach of working with the individual and address our attention more toward the family and the individual in the context of his peers and his environment. The rehabilitation facility should become the focal point of social action in the community. It should develop a very active information and referral service and should become the uniting force between the diverse service agencies of the community. The rehabilitation facility should develop and become active in a Community Action Board.

As a result of manpower shortages within professional areas of rehabilitation, there are several approaches which should be made to more effectively utilize existing manpower resources. One of the more basic approaches is to employ the indigeneous worker. This is a move which will be particularly beneficial with the disabled disadvantaged client. A second approach is the facility should mobilize to utilize the untapped reservoir of manpower in the older retired capable individual in our communities. By doing this, this will assist us in better understanding the clients since the professional individuals working with these clients will have more time to spend with them thereby assisting in developing new more adequate methods of communicating with the disabled disadvantaged.

REFERENCES

Cull, J. G. and Colvin, C. R.: Dilemma diagnosed (developmental aspects of rehabilitation facility administration). *Journal of Rehabilitation,* pp. 28-30, May, June, 1972.

Cull, J. G. and Hardy, R. E.: The facility specialist's role, *Journal of Rehabilitation,* May-June, 1971.

Hardy, R. E. and Cull, J. G.: Standards in evaluation, *Vocational Evaluation and Work Adjustment Bulletin, 2*(1), January-March, 1969.

Hutchinson, J. D. (Ed.): *Vocational Rehabilitation of the Disabled Disadvantaged In A Rural Setting,* Eighth Institute on Rehabilitation Services, U. S. Department of Health, Education and Welfare, Rehabilitation Service Administration, May 1970.

Maslow, A. H.: *Motivation and Personality.* New York, Harper & Row Publishers, 1954.

Moynihan, D. P.: *Maximum Feasible Misunderstanding.* New York, Free Press, 1968.

Rosenthal, R. and Jacobson, L. F.: Teacher expectations for the disadvantaged. *Scientific American, 218*:19-23, 1968.

〉〉 INDEX

A

Achievement tests, 33, 301
AGCT, 301
Air Force Classification Test Battery, 7
Alabama School of Trades, 68, 97
Alexander, F., 46, 59
Allen, C. Thomas, ix, xix, 124 ,135
American Association of Work Evalua-
tors, 10
*American Journal of Occupational
Therapy,* 255
American Personnel and Guidance As-
sociation, 95
American Psychological Association, 95
Anderson, Alan, 84, 97
Anderson, H. C., 42, 61
Anderson, Joel L., 68, 86, 97, 103
Angell, Donald, 104
Antebi, R. N,. 269, 273
Aptitudes, 216
Aptitude Tests, 301
Army General Classification Test (*see*
AGCT)
Arthur, Gary, 99, 100, 103
Aspy, D., 43, 59
Auburn University, 86, 89

B

Baker, Richard J., 86, 97
Baldwin, A. L., 59
Barad, Cary B., 81, 86, 98, 112, 116, 122
Barnard, W. M., 47, 59
Barton, Everett H., Jr., 93
Baymurr, F. B., 49, 59
Beebe, G. N., 49, 59
Behavior Identification Form, 134
Bender-Gestalt Drawings, 233
Bender-Gestalt Test, 301

Bennett, George, 70, 84, 99
Bennett Hard-Tool Dexterity Test, 301
Bennett Test of Mechanical Compre-
hension, 301, 326
Benton, Richard G., 98
Berenson, B. C., 43, 44, 50, 59
Bergen, A. E., 50, 59
Betz, B. J., 59
Biographical Data, 314
Blakeman, J. D., 56, 59
Blood, M. R., 270, 274
Bolton, B. F., 270, 274
Books, 244
Borg, G., 266, 269, 273
Brabham, Robert E., 86, 99
Brammer, C. M., 46, 59
Brandon, Thomas L., 67, 102
Bratfisch, O., 266, 269, 273
Breese, F. H., 59
Bregman, Morton, 7, 27, 69, 79, 98
Brill, N. Q., 49, 59
Broger, G., 51, 59
Bulletin, 94
Burk, Richard D., 77, 93, 98
Burke, M., 270, 274
Buros, O. K., 194
Button, William H., 59, 86, 87, 98

C

Caldwell, T. J., 86, 99
California Picture Interest Inventory,
301
Campbell, D., 262
Campbell, John L., 68, 98
CARF, 78, 81
Carkhuff, R. R., 43, 44, 46, 49, 50, 51,
55, 59, 60, 61, 62
Carnes, G. D., 112, 122

351

Casework interview, 33
Cattell, A. K. S., 190, 194
Cattell, R., 190, 191, 194
Centre Industries, 167, 168, 176
CEP, 69, 76, 297, 298
Chan Dynasty, 140
Chicago JVS, 130
Christensen, C. M., 44, 60
Church, Ralph, 89, 90, 98
Clark, David D., ix, xx, 265, 273
Clark, J. P., 270, 274
Classification of Vocational Evaluation in Educational Settings, 282
Clemons, Roger W., 86, 98
Clerical, 152
Client information synthesis, 260
Coffee, D., 86, 98
Cohen, B. S., 193, 194
Colvin, Craig R., ix, xx, 195, 197, 199, 241, 338, 350
Commission on Accreditation of Rehabilitation Facilities (*see* CARF)
Concentrated Employment Programs (*see* CEP)
Concreteness, 47
Confucius, 140
Content, 53
Content message, 52
Cook, S.
Coping with stress, 269
Cornell University's Rehabilitation Research Institute, 87
Couch, Robert H., ix, xix, 65, 68, 73, 75, 78, 86, 91, 92, 93, 96, 97, 99, 103
Council of State Administrators of Vocational Rehabilitation, 78
Counseling and guidance, 244
Counselor interviewing 33
Cowden J. E. 60
Crawford, Small Parts Dexterity Test, 301
Criterion problems, 106, 107, 109
Crites, J. O., 50, 60
Crow, Stanley H., x, xix, 29
Cull, John G., x, xviii, xx, 74, 78, 100, 197, 199, 241, 337, 338, 343, 350
Culture Fair Intelligence Test, 181, 190

D

Darden Rehabilitation Center, 89
DAT, 301
Data gathering, 33
Davis, Jessee, 68, 74, 99
Dawis, R., 296
Denholm, D. H., 86, 101
Dependency cycle, 37
Deutsch, M., 262
Dexterity Testing, 33
Dexterity Tests, 301
Dickinson, W. A., 47, 60
Dictionary of Occupational Titles (D.O.T), 144, 156, 196ff, 208, 212, 228, 240, 241, 316, 336
Differential Aptitude Test (*see* DAT)
Disability, 249
Disadvantaged, 313
Doll, R. E., 266, 270, 273
Doppett, Jerome E., 70, 84, 99
Dornic, S., 266, 269, 273
Drafting, 152
Drawing, 153
Duluth System, 288
Dunn, Dennis, 68, 99
Dunn, D. J., 60

E

Eber, H. B., 191, 194
Economic Opportunity Act of 1964, 74
Edward Personal Preference Schedule, 301
Egerman, Karl, 15, 27, 99, 110, 122
Electronics assembly, 153
Empathy, 47
Employability factors, 20
Esyenck, H. J., 44, 49, 50, 60
Evaluation, 35, 244
   dynamics, 31
   elements of, 33
   interview, 314
   report, 237
Evaluative interpretation, 33, 34
Event sampling, 257
Experience, 269

F

Facilities, 32
Family Assistance Plan (*see* FAP)

Fantaci, Anthony, 90, 91, 99
FAP, 75
Federal Register, 254
Feeling, 53
Feeling message, 52
Festinger, L., 256, 262
Fiedler, F. E., 60
Fiske, Donald, 11, 27
Flanders, N. A., 43, 60
Fogli, L., 270, 274
Frank, J. D., 49, 60
Friedman, Simon B., 84, 99
Froberg, J., 169, 274
Fry, R., 135

G

Garlick, B. J., 117, 123
GATB, 85, 181, 182, 248, 301
Gates-MacGinitie Reading Test, 301
Gay, E. G., 270, 274
GED, 214, 228
Gellman, William, 11, 27, 60, 68, 69, 71, 83, 84, 88, 96, 99, 100, 117, 122, 130, 135
General Aptitude Test Battery (*see* GATB)
General Educational Development (*see* GED)
Genskow, J., 135
Genuineness, 47
Ghiselli, E. E., 165
Gilbert, J. L., 110, 122
Glanz, Edward C., 73, 100
Goals, 256
Goldman, Leo, 70, 84, 100
Gonyea, C. G., 267, 274
Goodstein, L. D., 50, 60
Gordon, J., 281, 282, 296
Graves Design Judgment Test, 326
Gunderson, E. K., 266, 270, 273
Gunzburg, H. C., 296

H

Hadwin, T. C., 84, 100
Handelsman, Robert D., 87, 100
Handling, 227
Hardy, Richard E., xi, xviii, xx, 74, 78, 86, 100, 241, 337, 343, 350

Harper, L. A., 60
Harris, W. M., 165
Haygood, Gordon, 90, 100
Hefferin, E. A., 108, 122
Heine, R. W., 60
Herzberg, F., 122
Hicks, John D., 95, 100
Hill-Burton Program, 142
Hiten, H., 48, 60, 86, 100
Hobbs, N., 46, 47, 60
Hoffman, Paul R., xii, xix, 5, 27, 41, 61, 68, 71, 82, 83, 96, 99, 100, 135, 165
Hogan, Gail, 87, 98
Holtzman, W. H., 31, 39
House-Tree Person Projective Technique (*see* HTP)
Hovater, A. K., 86, 101
HTP, 301
Hublin, C. L., 270, 274
Human Resources Development, 69
Hume, Bruce C., xii, xx, 86, 100, 167
Hunt, Joseph, 90
Hutchinson, J. D., 338, 348, 350
Hypothesis formulation, 33, 34

I

ICD, 8, 27, 69, 85, 88, 141, 146, 165
Industry Designation, 200
Institute for the Crippled and Disabled (*see* ICD)
Institute for Vocational Rehabilitation, 254
Institute of Rehabilitation Services, 338
Intelligence, 269
Intelligence Tests, 301
Interdistrict System, 287
Interest, 226
Interest inventories, 33
Interest Tests, 301
IQ, 234
Issues in Evaluation in Educational Settings, 292
Izutsu, Si, 166

J

Jacobson, L. F., 350
Jahoda, M., 262
Jantzen, A., 42, 61

Jaques, M. E., 61
J.E.V.S., 13, 27, 76, 85ff, 90, 133, 146, 147, 165, 298, 305, 330, 336
JEVS Work Sample System, 319
Jewelry Manufacturing, 153
Jewish Education and Vocational Services (*see* J.E.V.S.)
Job analysis, 16
Job analysis approach, 329
Job Analysis Formula, 156
Job Corps, 297, 298
Job Corps Centers, 76
Job Sample Tests, 146
Job tryout approach, 310, 329
Job tryouts, 19, 33, 314
Jones, Richard D., xii, xix, 61, 101
Jorgensen, G. Q., 61
Jourard, S., 46, 47, 61
Journal of Rehabilitation, 94

K

Kalhorn, J. I., 59
Katz, A. H., 108, 122
Katz, D., 256, 262
Kimberly, J. R., 59, 98
Kimberly, Robert, 98
Kimberly, R. P., 59
Klopfer, W. G., 259
Knight, Mel, 86, 102
Krantz, Gordon C., xii, xx, 11, 27, 83, 92, 101, 275
Kuder *outdoor,* 265
Kuder Preference Record, 301

L

Ladd, G. T., 95, 101
Leathergoods, 153
Lennard, G. T., 47, 59
Lettering, 153
Levitt, E. E., 44, 49, 50, 61
Lewin, Kurt, 11, 27
Little, N., 135
Little, Neal D., 75, 101
Lobow, B. K., 59
Loftquist, L., 296
Long, J., 193, 194
Longfellow, Richard E., 71
Lopidakins, J. E., 61

Lovell, Malcolm R., 68, 70, 74, 101
Lubow, Bart K., 98

M

Machine Shop, 154
Mail Clerk, 154
Maintenance, 244
Manipulative skills, 269
Mann, Joe, 99, 100, 103
Manpower Administration, 70, 74, 297
Manpower Development Training Act (*see* MDTA)
Manual dexterity, 269
Martin, J. C., 47, 61
Maslow, A. H., 344, 350
Materials Development Center (*see* MDC)
Mausner, B., 122
Mayo, C. C., 270, 274
McDonald Vocational Capacity Scale, 301
McFarlane, Fred, xiii, xix
McGowan, J. F., 61, 243
McLaughlin, K. F., 165
MDC, 10, 87, 124, 126ff, 194
MDC/VGRS Assembly Work Sample, 133
MDTA, 76, 146
Medical examination, 133
Medical Facilities Survey and Construction Act (Hill-Burton), 74, 142
Medley, D. M., 256, 259, 262
Memory for Design Test, 301
Merritt, T. E., 165
Methods Time Measurement (MTM), 133
Miller, M., 117, 123
Miller, M. J., 165
Minneapolis System, 285
Minnesota Clerical Test, 301
Minnesota Multiphasic Personality Inventory (*See* MMPI)
Minnesota Rate of Manipulation Test, 301
Mitzel, H. E., 256, 259, 262
MMPI, 301
MODAPS, 86, 167, 170, 171, 176
Model for vocational evaluation, 316

Modular Arranged Predetermined Time Standards (*see* MODAPTS)
Moed, M. G., 298, 336
Mowrer, O. H., 60
Moynihan, D. P., 342, 350
Murray, Henry A., 27
Mustakas, C. E., 61

N

Nadolsky, Julian, xx, 12, 27, 70, 72, 73, 79, 83, 84, 101, 107, 115, 119, 122, 191, 194, 297, 336
NATB, 70
National Rehabilitation Association (*see* NRA)
Neff, Walter, 9, 16, 27, 40, 56, 61, 70, 96, 101, 165, 298, 336
Neighborhood Youth Corps, 297
Nelson Reading Test, 181, 233
New Careers, 90
Newman, Edward, 74, 75, 79, 91, 101
Nonreading Aptitude Test Battery (*see* NATB)
NRA, 10, 80, 90

O

Obermann, C. E., 39, 102
Observed behavior versus inferred attitudes, 258
Occupational aptitude patterns, 181
Occupational Group Arrangement (*see* OGA)
Occupational information, 314
O'Connor Finger Dexterity Test, 301
OGA, 200, 202, 203
Olshansky, S., 30, 39
Operant conditioning, 117
Optical mechanics, 154
Orthorater, 191
Oswald, Jesse H., 86, 102
O'Toole, Richard, 98
Outcome criterion, 113
Overs, Robert P., xiii, xx, 84, 102, 165, 255

P

Pacht, A. R., 60
Pacinelli, Ralph, 90, 98ff, 136

Pantograph engraving, 154
Parker, Murl W., 86, 102
Patterson, C. H., 49, 59
Payne, Arthur, 95, 102
Peabody Picture Vocabulary Test, 301
Personal adjustment training, 249
Personal skills, 269
Personality Tests, 301
Personnel and Guidance Journal, 16
Phelan, J. G., 269, 274
Philadelphia Jewish Employment and Vocational Service Work Sample System, 70
Philosophy of work evaluation, 40
Physical and Occupational Therapy Examinations, 33
Physical restoration services, 244
Physicians, 73
Piaget, G., 47, 50, 59, 61
Picture Interest Inventory, 182, 183
Pierce, R., 50, 59
Policy and Performance Council of the Rehabilitation Services Administration, 78
Pontvillez School in Belgium, 7, 69
Porter, T. L., 61, 243
Poser, E. G., 51, 61
Position sampling, 258
Predetermined Time Standards, 169
Prevocational evaluation, 5, 6, 242, 250, 251
Prevocational planning and counseling, 248
Prevocational training, 245
Procter, W. M., 95, 102
Projective Technique, 301
Pruitt, Walter, 71, 75, 84, 86, 98, 100, 102, 103, 118, 122, 136
Psychological evaluation, 270
Psychological Test Interpretation, 190
Psychological Testing, 33, 300, 329
Psychological Testing in Work Evaluation, 265
Psychological Tests, 314
Psychologist, 149, 236
Psychometric testing, 17
Public Law
    1920 P. L. 66-236, 73

1943 P. L. 78-113, 73
1954 P. L. 83-565, 125
1965 P. L. 89-333, 23, 125, 244, 337
1968 P. L. 90-391, 244
Purdue Pegboard, 182, 301
Pymond, R. F., 62

Q

Qualifications profile, 209, 213
Questionnaires, 33

R

R and D Funds, 293
Ramsey, G. W., 61
Redkey, Henry, 9, 27, 130, 136, 165
Rehabilitation counselor, 23
Rehabilitation facilitiy, 337
Rehabilitation Literature, 9
Rehabilitation Research and Training Centers for Vocational Rehabilitation, 89
Rehabilitation Services Administration (see RSA)
Related classification, 209
Reliability, 259
Research and Training Center in Vocational Rehabilitation at Johnstown, Penn., 15
Respect, 47
Revised Beta Examination, 181, 301
Richardson, L. H., 50, 61
Robbinsdale System, 289
Roberts, C. L., 41, 61, 110, 122
Rogers, C. R., 46, 47, 61, 62
Role of Prevocational Evaluation in Determining Eligibility, 244
Rorschach, 301
Rosenberg, Bernard, xii, xx, 41, 47, 62, 69, 70, 71, 82, 83, 84, 88, 96, 102, 139, 166, 243, 254
Rosenfield, M., 270, 274
Rosenthal, R., 350
Ross, Donald R., 67, 93, 102
Rotter Incomplete Sentences Blank, 301
RSA, 25, 80, 81

S

Sakata, R., 166
Saltiel, S., 270, 274

Samler, J., 121, 122
Sankowsky, Ray, 80, 86, 91, 93, 96, 99, 100, 102, 103, 110, 116, 123
Sawyer, Horace, W., 86, 97
Sax, Arnold, B., xiii, xix, 85, 87, 99, 101, 124, 134
SCERC, 131
Schafer, R., 46, 62
Schwartz, R., 262
Scope, 256
Scoring criteria, 159
Scott, J. D., 269, 274
SDI, 129
Sechrest, L., 262
Seeman, J., 62
Selected Characteristics of Occupations (Physical Demands, Working Conditions, Training Time), 228
Selective Dissemination of Information (*see* SDI)
Self-direction, 31
Selltiz, C., 262
SERVE, 284, 292
Services of SERVE, 291
Sewing machine operating, 155
Shannon, P. D., 62
Shostrom, E. L., 46, 59
Significant other, 43
Singer Corporation, 147
Singer/Graflex Vocational Evaluation System, 86, 133, 147
Sinick, D., 166
Sink, Jack M., 68, 91, 96, 103
Situational approach, 18, 329
Situational assessments, 33
Situational workshop tasks, 314
Sixteen Personality Factor Test, 182, 183, 191
Smith, David W., 72, 91, 103
Smith, L. A., 86, 101
Smolkin, Charles, xiv, xx, 86, 103, 177, 190, 193, 194
Smolkin Narrative Report Writing Format, 180, 192
Snortuni, J. R., 62
Snyderman, B., 122
Social and Rehabilitation Services (see SRS)

Soldier Rehabilitation Act, 73
Soloff, A., 270, 274
Soloman, S., 50, 59
Spangler, D. P., 166
Specific employability factors, 20
Specific Vocational Preparation (*see* SVP)
Spencer, William, 30, 39
Spergel, R., 62, 85, 87, 96, 114, 222
Stenographic Aptitude Test, 326
Stout, John K., xiv, xix, 78, 85, 93, 104, 105, 123
Stout State University, 41, 62, 82, 86, 89
St. Paul System, 284
Stuckey, T. E., 117, 123
Studies In Continuing Education for Rehabilitation Counselors (*see* SCERC)
Strunk, O., Jr., 46, 62
Strupp, H. H., 46, 62
Summers, G. F., 270, 274
Supplement to the Dictionary of Occupational Titles, 228
SVP, 216, 228
Systematic Human Relations Training Model, 51

T

TAT, 301
Taylor-Johnson Temperament Analysis, 301
Temperament, 226
Teng, S. Y., 166
Testing, achievement, 33, 301
Testing, Orientation and Work Evaluation in Rehabilitation (*see* TOWER)
Thematic Apperception Test (*see* TAT)
Thomas, C. W., 166
Thomas, K. R., 119, 123
Thomasat, 133, 144
Time Sampling, 257
TOWER, 8, 9, 27, 69, 70, 71, 85, 88, 133, 142, 144, 151, 152, 192, 281, 304, 319, 330
Tower Work Sample Approach, 151
Training, 244
Training materials, 244
Transportation, 244

Travers, R., 262
Truax, C. B., 43, 46, 49, 50, 51, 62
Tyler, L. E., 46, 62

U

United States Air Force, 7
United States Government
  Health, Education and Welfare, Department of, 142
  Labor, Department of, 247, 297
  Vocational Rehabilitation, Office of, 166
United States Training and Employment Service, 68
Usdane, W. W., 85, 96, 166

V

Van der Veen, F., 62
Veterans Administration Hospitals, 145
VEWAA, 65, 71, 72, 75, 78, 80, 82, 90ff, 110, 111, 179
VGRS, 27, 144, 166
Vineland Social Maturity Scale, 301
Vinson, Betty, 89
Virginia Commonwealth University, 41, 42, 62
Vocational adjustment, 244
Vocational evaluation, xvii, 5, 6, 12, 119
  disadvantaged, of the, 281
  model, 327, 331, 334, 335
  process, 147, 148
  profession of, 109, 111
  rural educational settings, in, 292
  school settings, in, 276
  special education and, 280
  vocational education and, 280
Vocational Evaluation and Work Adjustment Association (*see* VEWAA)
Vocational evaluation benefits to client and professional team, 148, 149
Vocational Guidance and Rehabilitation Service (Cleveland) (*see* VGRS)
Vocational Guidance Association, 95
Vocational Rehabilitation Act, 244
Vocational Rehabilitation Administration, 28
Vocational Rehabilitation Act Amandments of 1943, 73

Vocational Rehabilitation Act Amendments of 1954 (Public Law 565), 74
Vocational Rehabilitation Amendment of 1968, 75
Vocational rehabilitation counselor, 149
Vocational Service Flow of the Severely Disabled and Marginal Rehabilitation Client, 277
Volsky, T. C., 47, 62

W

WAIS, 301
Walker, R. A., 78, 79, 82, 84, 93, 96, 123
Waters, L. K., 266, 274
Watson, R. I., 106, 123
Webb, E. J., 262
Wechsler, 234
Wechsler Adult Intelligence Scale (*see* WAIS)
Wechsler Intelligence Scale for Children (*see* WISC)
Wegg, Lillian, S., 166
Weiss, D. J., 270, 274, 296
Welding, 155
Welfare Reform Legislation and Facilities Evaluation, 337
Wellerson, Thelma, 243, 254
West Virginia Rehabilitation Research and Training Institute, 87
White, Barbara, 130, 136
Whitehorn, J. C., 59
Whitten, E. B., 89
Wide Range Achievement Test (*see* WRAT)

Williamsport Technical Institute, 143
WIN, 25, 69, 76, 297, 298
WISC, 301
Wolfe, Richard E., xiv, xx, 242
Work adjustment, 5
Work evaluation, xvii, 5, 16, 20ff, 26
Work Evaluation Report, 177
Work evaluators, 13, 23
Work Habit Tests, 146
Work Incentive Now Program (*see* WIN)
Work Samples, 17, 18, 33, 141, 143, 304, 314, 329
  development of, 155
  evaluation categories of, 152
  format, 158
  personality variables, 191
  tasks, 160
Worker requirements, 210
Worker Trait Arrangement (*see* WTA)
Worker trait group, 147
Workshop assembly, 155
World War I
World War II
WRAT, 21, 181, 233, 301
Wright, Herbert F., 252, 262
Writing Work Evaluation Reports, 262
WTA, 200, 203, 207
Wurtz, Robert E., 87, 100

Z

Zdep, S. M., 270, 274
Zimmerman, J., 117, 123
Zytowski, D. G., 119, 123